African Environmental Crisis

This book explores how and why the idea of the African environmental crisis developed and persisted through colonial and post-colonial periods, and why it has been so influential in development discourse. From the beginnings of imperial administration, the idea of the desiccation of African environments grew in popularity, but this crisis discourse was dominated by the imposition of imperial scientific knowledge, neglecting indigenous knowledge and experience.

African Environmental Crisis provides a synthesis of more than one-and-a-half century's research on peasant agriculture and pastoral rangeland development in terms of soil erosion control, animal husbandry, grazing schemes, large-scale agricultural schemes, social and administrative science research, and vector-disease and pest controls. Drawing on comparative socio-ecological perspectives of African peoples across the East African colonies and post-independent states, this book refutes the hypothesis that African peoples were responsible for environmental degradation. Instead, Gufu Oba argues that flawed imperial assumptions and short-term research projects generated an inaccurate view of the environment in Africa.

This book's discussion of the history of science for development provides researchers across environmental studies, agronomy, African history and development studies with a lens through which to understand the underlying assumptions behind development projects in Africa.

Gufu Oba is professor at the Faculty of Landscape and Society (LANDSAM) in the Norwegian University of Life Sciences. His work is interdisciplinary; combining natural sciences, pastoralism and environmental history. His previous books include; *Nomads in the shadows of empires* (2013), *Climate change adaptation in Africa* (2014) and *Herder warfare in East Africa* (2017).

Routledge Studies in African Development

Peacebuilding in Contemporary Africa
In Search of Alternative Strategies
Edited by Kenneth Omeje

The Challenge of Governance in South Sudan
Corruption, Peacebuilding, and Foreign Intervention
Edited by Steven C. Roach and Derrick K. Hudson

African Peacekeeping Training Centres
Socialisation as a Tool for Peace?
Anne Flaspöler

Corporate Governance in Tanzania
Ethics and Accountability at the Crossroads
Peter C. Mhando

Economic Dualism in Zimbabwe
From Colonial Rhodesia to Post-Independence
Daniel B. Ndlela

Rethinking Ownership of Development in Africa
T.D. Harper-Shipman

African Environmental Crisis
A History of Science for Development
Gufu Oba

Development in Nigeria
Promise on Hold?
Edlyne Eze Anugwom

African Environmental Crisis
A History of Science for Development

Gufu Oba

LONDON AND NEW YORK

First published 2020 by Routledge

2 Park Square, Milton Park, Abingdon, Oxon OX14 4RN
605 Third Avenue, New York, NY 10017

Routledge is an imprint of the Taylor & Francis Group, an informal business

First issued in paperback 2021

Copyright © 2020 Gufu Oba

The right of Gufu Oba to be identified as author of this work has been asserted by him in accordance with sections 77 and 78 of the Copyright, Designs and Patents Act 1988.

All rights reserved. No part of this book may be reprinted or reproduced or utilised in any form or by any electronic, mechanical, or other means, now known or hereafter invented, including photocopying and recording, or in any information storage or retrieval system, without permission in writing from the publishers.

Notice:
Product or corporate names may be trademarks or registered trademarks, and are used only for identification and explanation without intent to infringe.

Publisher's Note

The publisher has gone to great lengths to ensure the quality of this reprint but points out that some imperfections in the original copies may be apparent.

British Library Cataloguing-in-Publication Data
A catalogue record for this book is available from the British Library

Library of Congress Cataloging-in-Publication Data
Names: Oba, Gufu, author.
Title: African environmental crisis : a history of science for development / Gufu Oba.
Other titles: Routledge studies in African development.
Description: New York : Routledge, 2020. | Series: Routledge studies in African development | Includes bibliographical references and index. |
Identifiers: LCCN 2019056931 (print) | LCCN 2019056932 (ebook) | ISBN 9780367432614 (hardback) | ISBN 9781003002161 (ebook)
Subjects: LCSH: Economic development–Environmental aspects–Africa. | Science–Africa–History. | Land use, Rural–Africa–History. | Africa–Environmental conditions–Research–History.
Classification: LCC GE160.A35 O34 2020 (print) | LCC GE160.A35 (ebook) | DDC 333.72096–dc23
LC record available at https://lccn.loc.gov/2019056931
LC ebook record available at https://lccn.loc.gov/2019056932

ISBN: 978-0-367-43261-4 (hbk)
ISBN: 978-1-03-217308-5 (pbk)
DOI: 10.4324/9781003002161

Typeset in Goudy
by Wearset Ltd, Boldon, Tyne and Wear

I dedicate this book to Liban, Halakhe, Jiiru, Mya and Adam Eebbaa

Contents

List of figures ix
List of tables xi
Preface xii

1 The African environmental crisis: is it a myth? An introduction — 1

PART I
Empire, science, society and development — 23

2 European exploration of East Africa: textual analysis of travel narratives, 1831–1900 — 25

3 Imperial scientific infrastructure: science for development, 1848–1960s — 45

4 African environmental crisis narratives: schemes, technology and development, 1904–1960 — 70

PART II
Ecological and social research — 97

5 Experimental science and development: a re-evaluation of the environmental crisis hypothesis, 1939–1960 — 99

6 Social science research: behavioral responses to development, 1919–1950 — 122

7 Administrative science for development dialogue: three Kenyan case studies, 1943–1954 — 140

PART III
Vectors, pests and environmental change   161

8   Tsetse fly control in East Africa: environmental and social impacts, 1880–1959   163

9   Locust invasion and control in East Africa: economic and environmental impacts, 1890–1960s   187

10   A synthesis: conclusions and epilog   213

Index   234

Figures

1.1	Colonial East Africa	3
1.2	Schematic representation of 'events history' of research and development in East Africa, 1848–1990s	7
2.1	The natural and physical geographical features of East and Central Africa	28
3.1	Distributions of research stations in East Africa	50
5.1	Scenarios of hypothetical intensities of land use and corresponding proxy environmental indicators	101
5.2	(A) Percentage run-off and (B) soil erosion in tons per acre per year, from treatment plots	104
5.3	Relationship between storm intensity and discharge in an experimental watershed	105
5.4	Effects of phosphate fertilizer on two grain crops (maize and millet) and two legume crops (groundnuts and soya beans) over four years	107
5.5	Responses of maize grain in cwt/acre to fertilizer applications	108
5.6	(A) Data showing relationships between rainfalls and grazing capacity and (B) carrying capacity and time	109
5.7	Rotational grazing experiments stocked at 4 acres per steer, 7 acres per steer and 13 acres per steer compared to continuous grazing	114
7.1	Eastern part of Lake Victoria	142
7.2	Sketch of Kimalot area in conflict with the European Tea estates	145
8.1	Lake Victoria Basin in East Africa	164
8.2	Annual costs of aerial sprays of DDT for tsetse fly control	178
8.3	Number of cattle reported sick and those diagnosed positive for trypanosome parasites in their blood	179
8.4	Cattle census in Ankole, Uganda, 1942–1965	180
9.1	Desert locusts' migration routes from the outbreak areas in Indo-Pakistan and Arabia to the regions of East Africa	189

x *Figures*

9.2 Outbreak area of red locusts in the marshes of Lake Rukwa in Tanganyika   192
10.1 Conceptual model for the socio-economic and ecological model (SEEM) for integration of ecological and anthropogenic indicators for land-use assessments   228

Tables

4.1 Grazing schemes in the East African territories, 1936–1959   85
5.1 Rates of soil loss, soil moisture and soil fertility based on research studies conducted in Kenya and Tanganyika, 1950s–1960s   103
5.2 Impacts of rotational grazing, fire, bush clearing and reseeding on rangeland rehabilitation, 1948–1960s   111

Preface

In this book, the author analyzes the African environmental crisis hypothesis by re-appraising the contributions of imperial science for development. The work is analytical and practical, offering a historical lens covering nearly one-and-a-half centuries, through which to examine development research in Africa in general and in East Africa in particular. It combines the intellectual traditions and methods of analysis used in the fields of environmental history, ecology and social science. By placing the study in a spatial context (i.e., regional) and organizing the analysis chronologically, the work compares the application of imperial science for development across the former three East African colonies and post-independent states (Kenya, Tanganyika (Tanzania) and Uganda).

The book is composed of ten chapters, organized in three parts, including an introduction (Chapter 1) and a synthesis (Chapter 10). Part I (comprising Chapters 2, 3 and 4) presents a review of imperial science. Chapter 2 highlights pre-colonial African societies and environments during the late nineteenth and early twentieth centuries. The chapter uses texts written by European explorers and missionaries to evaluate the hypothesis of environmental desiccation (first raised during the mid-nineteenth century). Chapter 3 interrogates event ecological history to discuss scientific research infrastructure. It examines how the growth of imperial scientific ideas in East Africa was influenced by historical and political events in the metropole and the colonies. Chapter 4 explores the global and local origins of the African environmental crisis in relation to changing colonial agricultural and rangeland development policies. The chapter further examines the extent to which the establishment of large-scale development schemes altered indigenous land use and aggravated environmental problems.

Part II comprises Chapters 5, 6 and 7. This part examines the contributions of ecological science, social science research and administrative science in development planning. Chapter 5 analyzes agronomic and range science experiments from published works to test the African environmental crisis hypothesis (termed the 'equilibrium hypothesis') over the alternative 'disequilibrium hypothesis.' The experimental works involve different forms of land-use intensification and use measurable environmental proxy indicators to evaluate the extent to which the findings were used to verify the environmental crisis hypothesis. Chapter 6 focuses on the application of social science and questions whether the way that African peasants and herders responded to development programs was predetermined by their economies, local ecologies and cultural values. By conducting comparative analyses of African communities across East Africa, it concludes that—contrary to official colonial claims—African societies showed flexibility in their responses to, and acceptance of development programs. The work in Chapter 7 uses 'administrative science' as a practical approach to interrogate development initiatives. It presents three land-related case studies to highlight dialogue among hierarchies of officials and local people. Further, it presents studies on how the government's land alienation practices were overturned in a court petition, and discusses agricultural settlements, soil conservation and clearing of bush to settle people and control tsetse flies.

Part III of the book (comprising Chapters 8 and 9) investigates the history of insect disease vectors and agricultural pest controls and environmental changes, thereby demystifying the human causes of African environmental crisis. Chapter 8 examines the environmental history of tsetse fly and *trypanosomiasis* control in East Africa. Initial attempts to control the tsetse fly involved the destruction of natural vegetation and the elimination of wildlife by means of mass killing. The vector showed persistence against all known forms of control for over 50 years, during which time it displaced populations and caused pandemics of sleeping sickness that killed hundreds of Africans. Chapter 9 describes the history of invasions of locust plagues in East Africa, the Horn of Africa and neighboring regions. It describes economic damage to agricultural production and analyzes how researchers combined manipulations of the environment with a variety of control methods to destroy locust swarms. It presents evidence of the damage caused to the environments by pesticides that were applied to kill the locusts. The partial success of locust control during 50 years of monitoring was possible only with the participation of international scientists, and logistical and funding contributions from international agencies.

Chapter 10 synthesizes the work, draws conclusions from the key findings, and presents an epilog to reflect on the changing trends in research and development during post-independence periods. Additionally, it highlights emerging scientific issues that are likely to influence the future direction of development programs.

The Faculty of Landscape and Society (LANDSAM) at the Norwegian University of Life Sciences funded the research for this work. I appreciate the services provided by the library, especially inter-library loans. Liv Ellingsen has always been keen about the project and has supported it in many ways. The Kenya National Archives in Nairobi and the archivists—who over the years have become my great friends—are acknowledged for their diligence in locating suitable colonial archival materials.

My editor, Dr Jill Fresen, paid attention to the use of language and increased the clarity of the work. I received useful comments on earlier drafts of some of the chapters from Professor Tor Arve Benjaminsen and Dr Fatuma Guyo. Comments by three anonymous referees have been considered in revising the manuscript. The commissioning editor, Helena Hurd of Routledge Development Studies Series, for the invitation to produce this volume, and Rosie Anderson, the editorial assistant, are thanked for facilitation of the processes. Dennis Milewa drew all the maps, while the author produced other figures presented in this work. John Wiley & Sons, Ltd. is thanked for granting copyright transfer of my article 'Framework for participatory assessments and implementation of global environmental conventions at the community level,' originally published in *Land Degradation and Development* 19: 65–76 (2008).

My children, who are now young men and women, have been a source of joy in our family. It was their great help at home while I was away that enabled me to complete this work in good time. It is, however, to my grandchildren: Liban, Halakhe, Jiiru, Mya and Adam Eebbaa, that I dedicate the book so that their future will be one full of knowledge, insight and meaningful perspectives on their heritage.

Gufu Oba
Ås, Norway
November 2019

1 The African environmental crisis—is it a myth?

An introduction

The motivation for writing this book was a need to understand the roles played by imperial science in the process of development in the former British colonies in East Africa over a period of nearly one-and-half centuries. Given that the origin of imperial science itself is from outside Africa—with different ecological, social and historical bearings—the imposition of foreign scientific knowledge and its impacts must not only be evaluated, but also understood in terms of how development processes were influenced by popular hypotheses, in particular the African environmental crisis. This hypothesis surmises that the African environmental crisis was induced mainly by indigenous systems of resource use—and that the purpose of imperial science was to rectify the situation. The intention was to provide alternative methods of resource use by introducing new technologies and scientific knowledge to expand economic production, while at the same time promoting environmental conservation. However, in the development process, while local African communities were the subject of research initiatives, they were not participants in the identification of environmental and developmental problems.[1]

If local communities took no part in problem identification, on what basis was imperial science used to link those societies to the presumed African environmental crisis? In order to answer this question, we need to conduct a historical analysis. For example, Kate Showers[2] has argued that historical assessment methods should have the capacity to produce qualitative data that describes 'processes of change, sequences of events and identification of relationships.' Accordingly, imperial science research and development findings that failed to identify events but that scapegoated African land uses for environmental degradation will be contested.[3] In sum, imperial science created a myth about adverse environmental changes—not only did they blame indigenous systems of land use, they also failed to acknowledge indigenous knowledge and the huge environmental damage caused by development programs or application of a faulty science.[4]

We will go even further by posing the same questions asked by Brian Goldstone and Juan Obarrio[5] in their edited essays *African Futures*, on dimensions of African crisis. 'How might we provincialize, cut down to size, the very concept of crisis? What functions does the term perform? Can we begin to imagine Africa beyond the pervasive sign of "crisis"?' In unpacking the proposition and the questions, we examine if the opinions were persuaded by evidence provided by imperial science, or by the social and political prejudices of imperialism towards resource use by African societies.[6]

This book endeavors to synthesize imperial science and development literature spanning three historical periods: pre-colonial, colonial and post-independence (1848–1990). We discuss the origin, causes and processes of the presumed environmental crisis. We use the protectorates of Kenya, Uganda and the British Trust Territory of Tanganyika (a German colony until 1916) and their post-independence counterparts (Figure 1.1) as a template to provide common intellectual perspectives of the African environmental crisis.[7] We examine the scientific and social theories that might have contributed to misinterpretations of the African environmental crisis hypothesis. We do so in the context of roles played by peasant agriculture, pastoralism and soil conservation, large-scale agricultural and grazing schemes, control of disease vectors such as tsetse flies (that cause human sleeping sickness and *trypanosomiasis* in cattle), and locust plagues; each of which influenced the way the hypothesis was applied to development initiatives in East Africa.

The discussions fall under the following sections. The first section defines key terms—environmental crisis, imperial science and development—to understand how they are applied in the present work. The second section introduces the framework of environmental history to highlight processes of environmental and socio-economic changes. The third section highlights the relations between empires, science, colonized societies and development. We describe environmental causalities that linked the populations to the African environmental crisis hypothesis. In the context of the pre-colonial period, the work examines the late nineteenth-century European textual narratives on the conditions of the African environment. Additionally, the work examines the imperial research infrastructure and the mismatch between science and development. It scrutinizes the origin of the environmental crisis proposition. The fourth section examines how the experimental and social science research might be used to verify the environmental crisis hypothesis. It scrutinizes factors that influence African peoples' responses to development and the roles played by administrative science in development dialogue among officials and with the African peasants and herders. The fifth section scrutinizes the roles played by disease vectors and agricultural pests in environmental change.

Defining terms

Our use of the term 'African environmental crisis hypothesis' is purposeful. Therefore, rather than giving the dictionary meaning of the term, we

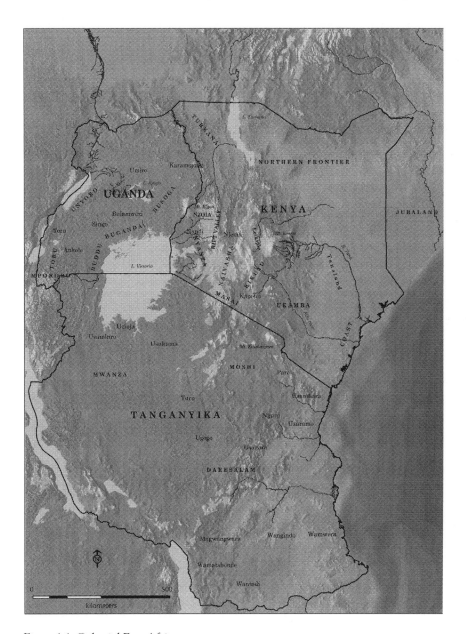

Figure 1.1 Colonial East Africa.

prefer defining it in the context it is used. It simply infers the destruction of natural environment by indigenous systems of land use—such as crop overcultivation and livestock overgrazing. The hypothesis might have had its origin in the thinking of western science before it was applied for planning development in Africa. It has persisted from colonial periods and continued to the decade of post-independence. In Africa, from the beginnings of imperial administrations in the late nineteenth century and the early twentieth century, the environmental crisis hypothesis had gained popularity among colonial officials. Earlier, some European explorers and missionaries had proposed a similar hypothesis—that there was a gradual desiccation of African environments. The popularity of the African environmental crisis narrative had increased during the depression decades of the 1930s.[8] The narrative by this time had become imminent in scientific debates in the USA.[9] The colonial governments perceived that representative environmental conditions described by the scientific debates in the USA also existed in Africa.[10] This hypothesis surmises that the African environmental crisis was caused mainly by soil erosion, loss of soil fertility, periodic fires, deforestation, poor methods of crop cultivation and overgrazing of rangelands.[11] Imperial science was therefore assumed to be an appropriate tool to remedying environmental crisis.

The notion of imperial science required the pooling of knowledge and sharing of research information through international collaboration, in order to build crucial regional and local research networks.[12] As Richard Grove[13] states in his work *Green Imperialism*, '[c]olonial expansion ... promoted the rapid diffusion of new scientific ideas between colonies and between metropole and colony'—through masses of scientists committed to pioneering research on basic and applied sciences.

Basic science is a discipline for acquiring new knowledge; it is usually conducted in research stations or laboratories under controlled environmental conditions.[14] Conversely, applied science (including the social sciences) functions at management levels and scales (see separate section). Opinions are divided as to the applicability of basic science for development initiatives over large areas. Sir Andrew Cohen[15] was among those who pronounced basic science research to be 'useless' in solving development problems under field conditions in Africa. He suggested that basic science research (i.e., station-based research) failed to provide an accurate picture of socio-economic problems at geographical scales. In addition, because basic science research is conducted in restricted and controlled environments, it requires pre-testing in the field, which then entails management decisions. Consequently, basic scientific research with limited field application has little value in unravelling real-life social, environmental and economic problems.[16] In disagreement with this view, Lord E. B. Worthington[17] suggested that there are no fundamental discrepancies between basic and applied sciences. Basic science might be regarded as rendering 'practical applications,' in terms of the management levels at which such applications operate.[18] The main difference lies in the scales at which the two types of research are applied: basic science functions at restricted and controlled scales, while applied science (including social science—treated in more detail elsewhere) functions at large geographical scales.[19] We have referred to this as 'big science' in the present work (more on this in Chapter 10).

Similarly, there are varied opinions on what development entails. The African continent—as the last frontier of European colonialism—was used as a site to experiment with development.[20] In Africa, the term 'development' was introduced by the empires, even if the concept may be thought to be a modern approach.[21] The concept of 'development' differed in the way colonial and post-independent states defined it, and the way African communities perceived what development should be. Development is often used to imply modernization—in other words, transformation of the indigenous production into a capitalist system, shifting production from subsistence to a more efficient monetarized production. The change imbues institutional and structural changes in the society. It shifts production from small to large scale (the so-called economy of scale). Thus, development is expected to be forward-looking through transformation of social and economic systems. Among its many goals, development inspires opportunities for local communities by transforming their socio-economic needs coupled with better protection of the environments on which they depend.[22] Because of these variations in expectations, the concept of development is 'imprecise, normative and teleological.'[23] This has had influence on how science was applied to implement development by varieties of actors. We examine the inter-relations of the concepts using environmental history framework.

Environmental history framework

Environmental history lends itself to the study of global political and ecological causalities of the phenomenon of environmental change.[24] According to Jane Carruthers,[25] it describes 'how people use, manage or interrelate with natural resources and the natural environment, in social circumstances at given times and places.' Donald Hughes[26] also discusses environmental history from this perspective, describing the relationships between nature and society as 'reciprocal.'[27] In terms of ecology, environmental change can be metaphorically described as the 'ecological footprint' that communicates the impacts on the environment, whenever such impacts may occur.[28] Bradley Walters and Andrew Vayda[29] refer to such environmental footprints as 'event ecology' and point out that environmental change can be used to analyze complex interdisciplinary environmental and human ecology relationships. The event ecology approach answers the why question in order to reconstruct past environmental changes and their historical impact.

Similarly, Kate Showers[30]—in describing 'historical impact assessment' as past environmental 'footprints'—uses a five-step enquiry process to orient environmental historical analysis that catalogs environmental changes over time. The first step describes the key questions that identify the evidence by locating the problems geographically and suggesting solutions. The second step applies existing knowledge to conduct assessments by interpreting historical records and collecting views of scientists and officials, as well as local communities, on environmental problems. The third step is to organize the available information chronologically, from which an environmental historian creates a meta-analysis to appraise the environmental change. The fourth step relies on the availability of technical information (such as maps, aerial photographs, surveys, instrumental climate data and archives) to understand relations with the environment over time. The fifth step describes the effects of institutional power by considering relationships between state officials and local communities, to try and understand why and how societies respond to development project interventions.

Accordingly, environmental history supposes that science and development might have linkages at five levels: historical, local, national, regional and global. At the historical level, environmental history is indispensable in scrutinizing the roles played by development programs in environmental changes, particularly by considering 'cyclic' environmental events.[31] At the local level, it deals with how societies respond to their immediate environments and the extent to which changes in local environments influence social adaptations. At the national level, the relations are between the governance and development, working at the interface between scientific research and societal responses to policy recommendations. At the regional level, the linkages are between politics and research coordination and research networks at the global level.

Unfortunately, imperial science research lacked foresight and failed to offer understanding of any trends in environmental change. What we have instead are snapshots of events that often repeated themselves from time to time, but without any clear progression. Historians by organizing research and development as chronological events (i.e., events history) would have better insights—by presenting the trajectory of shifting opinions in scientific thinking.[32] By organizing our material chronologically, we have recreated such possible trends (Figure 1.2).

We next examine the extent to which the ideology of empires and its application of science for development contributed to the debate on the African environmental crisis.

Empire, science, society and development

The notion of 'empire and ecology' describes the powers of empires over nature—not necessarily only in Europe, but also in overseas colonies.[33] Ecology,[34] as an interactive process of nature and culture, represents the ways in which nature is imagined and managed by societies.[35] Therefore, by historicizing ecological trends, environmental causalities linked to African peasants and herders may be discussed,[36] in order to make decisions on how and when the environment may be described as being in a 'crisis.'[37]

African environmental crisis: is it a myth? 7

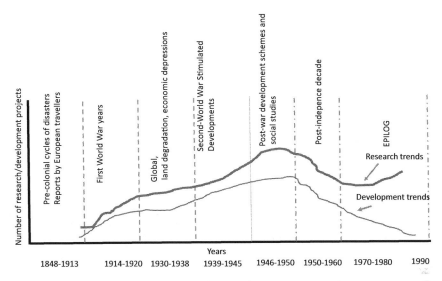

Figure 1.2 Schematic representation of 'events history' of research and development in East Africa, 1848–1990s.

The colonial empires approached the hypothesis of the African environmental crisis in two ways. First, since the goals of imperial science were Eurocentric,[38] research initiatives ignored the indigenous knowledge of African communities.[39] Second, as Luise White[40] argues, colonial science 'was not a European mirror image of an African intellectual faddishness,' but a creation of European knowledge that provided 'credibility' to colonial rule as a creative system. The purpose was not to appreciate existing viewpoints of African societies, but rather to promote the views and goals of the colonial authorities. This approach reflects the argument of Mark Harrison[41] that 'scientific ideas were seldom transplanted fully into colonial soil'; rather, imperial science was adapted and transplanted in the colonies. One might agree with this viewpoint only partially, the problem being that imperial science ignored the complexity of the African environment which was driven by forces such as rainfall variability, and the diversity of physical and biological environments, in combination with diverse cultural landuse systems.[42]

One might therefore ask, why did the perceived environmental predicament in Africa become a working hypothesis for colonial empires managing local agrarian production systems? The answer to the question is fundamental to understanding the history of development in East Africa in the context of the environmental crisis hypothesis. Paul Richards[43] sums up his view on this point as follows: '[e]cological crisis in Africa ... is as much a crisis arising from the nature of environmental science, its organization and the social interests that it represents.' Accordingly, Richards much later

8 *African environmental crisis: is it a myth?*

proposed two notions that fundamentally predisposed the direction of research and development in Africa during the colonial century. His first proposition was that the main trigger of the perceived environmental crisis was the cultural behavior of African communities in terms of indigenous systems of agriculture and animal husbandry (more on this in Chapter 6). As a result, African farmers and herders became not only the subjects of colonial empires, but also objects of development experimentation.[44] We show that there is no evidence that environmental causalities linked to African peasants and herders approached the proportion of a 'crisis.' Instead, the pre-colonial African environment was considered 'pristine' as opposed to an image of 'apocalypse.'[45]

The pre-colonial European textual narratives

Our sources of knowledge for this period are European travel journals. The European pioneers described the environments in terms of images of 'best-kept' European landscapes, for example, parklands and beautiful scenery. Depending on the season of the year, the pre-colonial African environments were presented as 'pristine,' and the human-environmental relationship was described as 'Arcadian'—referring to harmony between nature and people.[46] The local societies had sufficient food and through networks of exchange between neighboring agricultural communities (via trade caravans), they had created an integrated economic and ecological system throughout the region. Some of these communities had developed sophisticated irrigation and farming systems that served as 'food baskets' for entire regions before the arrival of the nineteenth-century European travelers.[47]

Notably, a decade or two later (from the 1890s), the opinion of Arcadian nature had changed. This period coincided with long cycles of environmental disasters—a collapsed pastoral production system, tribal warfare, slavery, diseases, locust plagues, droughts and famine, and the expansion of tsetse flies—these disasters turned the environment into 'wild' nature (as opposed to Arcadian). The combined effects of these calamities were a decline in human demography and the breakdown of political systems.[48] From the 1900s onwards there was a significant change in European perceptions of African environments towards an image of 'apocalypse'—the so-called 'African environmental crisis,' for which African societies were blamed.[49] The solution envisaged was building imperial scientific infrastructure to promote development and environmental conservation (Chapter 3).

Imperial scientific research infrastructure and development

At the core of colonial development initiatives was the transfer of technological expertise to the colonies in the hope that extraction of raw materials would become more efficient. In that scenario, development involved economic growth—it was 'not merely an increase in national production,' but also increases in 'material goods,' while at the same time 'development' was claimed to expand social services to the colonized populations.[50] However, there is a catch here. Despite attempts to link science and development, in terms of the scientific research infrastructure, there was no obvious direct relationship, contrary to claims made by various stakeholders.[51] It is from this perspective that one may justifiably question whether science drove development, or if the two subjects had no significant relationship.

Lynton Caldwell[52] presents six reasons for the mismatch between science and development, which we paraphrase here. First, development in the colonies—despite imperial desires—had little regard for scientific methods. Second, the optimism of science did not translate into successful development processes. Third, the reality was that there were no developmental institutions—even where such institutions were identified, they lacked the capacity to implement development programs. Fourth, development opportunism displayed in the colonies was driven more by political processes than by research questions. Fifth, discrepancies existed between scientific ideas and development processes. The sixth reason is that cultural, regional and inter-regional communication barriers undermined development processes.

Would the lack of link between science and development processes, and the scale of research initiatives account for the shifting narratives of 'environmental apocalypse'?[53] The question is justified in the light of the shifting nature of scientific ideas during the twentieth century. For example, by the 1920s, the British Empire referred to its colonies as 'discoveries,' with the empire shining light on underdevelopment in Africa. Later in the 1930s, development was understood as being 'experimental,' and in the 1950s it represented 'expert knowledge,' as applied to agricultural and grazing schemes. Yet, the latter period—although considered at the time as the 'golden age of the developmentalist era'—was later described as 'monstrous,' because of the extent of damage caused to the environment.[54]

Claude Alvares[55] describes another aspect of mismatch between science and development emphasizing its 'international dimensions, intimately secured and supported by international capital, conceived and executed in the interests of the designers of the project.' Development assistance provided by international capital reflects what Keith Nurse and Daniel Wight[56] refer to as the 'parachute model.' This model of development comprises packages of technical assistance 'parachuted in' and run by technical experts and project managers with a predetermined global agenda. We may use an example here.

In the pastoral lands, experimentation neglected to include development planning based on the premises of ecological and social sciences.[57] From the early twentieth century, researchers misjudged the situation; they assumed that the African peasants and pastoralists would accept development schemes because that would improve their economies and provide access to free services, which would in turn motivate them to increase production.

Rather than designing projects to implement gradual changes over time, projects had a short shelf-life, expecting quick economic returns that, in most cases, never materialized.

Additionally, although the post-independence period offered technical solutions, international development programs during that time failed to learn from past mistakes.[58] The expectations of different actors influenced project outcomes, and not in small part.[59] In particular, the expectations of administrative officials did not match those of African societies.[60] Regarding research activities, colonial administrators were more concerned with practical solutions and less about 'people working in laboratories' whose findings did not immediately relate to field conditions.[61] For development-oriented science, therefore, the main challenge was how to address the needs of different groups of actors: imperial scientists who were seeking long-term solutions to solve problems; colonial officials who were seeking practical actions; and African societies who were more anxious about their immediate survival needs.[62]

One would, therefore, be able to recognize the false assumptions of imperial science that might have been the cause of the misinterpretations of development outcomes.[63] The first false assumption was that the scientific theories and methods developed in Europe could be exported to the African colonies without modification. The second false assumption was that indigenous African knowledge systems—that for centuries had been responsible for management of the variable environments—could be ignored. Such false assumptions are clearly reflected in the failed agricultural and pastoral development programs that were attempted during those periods.[64] This is the consequence of African environmental crisis hypothesis and its application.

The origin of African environmental crisis hypothesis

The hypothesis of Africa's environmental crisis emerged from various global and scientific theories (Chapter 4). The perceived apocalyptic environmental discourse that motivated the application of imperial science[65] had its origins in a global doctrine borrowed from experiences in the midwest rangelands of the United States.[66] After the cattle boom of the 1880s, severe rangeland degradation and soil erosion had reached the level of an environmental disaster by the 1930s—the phenomenon referred to as 'dust bowl.' The overarching drivers of the crisis were droughts running over several years and ploughing up the prairie grasslands with heavy machinery, exposing the soil to wind erosion.[67] Donald Worster[68] suggests that the changes presented 'irresistible' questions as to whether the grazing or environmental drivers were the causal factors—an aspect that required close scrutiny by environmental historians. The global 'dust bowl' phenomenon was anticipated in Africa and agricultural policies were developed with the intention of halting the problem.[69]

In addition, about the time of the 'dust bowl' phenomenon, agronomic research had produced influential theories associated with ecological changes. Fredrick Clements from the University of Nebraska developed an ecological theory that predicted how vegetation might respond to grazing pressure by livestock, with the trajectory of change being predicted along a singular pathway until it reaches a climax.[70] According to this succession-climax theory, vegetation is most productive and vegetation communities are stable within climate limitations at the climax stage. Arthur Sampson[71] then expanded on Clements' theory, advocating the regulation of grazing pressure in order to manage the stages of vegetation succession at optimal rangeland production levels, thus enabling better livestock performance. Accordingly, range managers would maintain succession at the desired sub-climax levels by adjusting stocking rates.[72] During the colonial period in Africa, 'succession' theory (hereafter referred to as equilibrium) was used as the dominant model to interpret degradation of rangelands when the vegetation shifted from the trajectory of a hypothetical 'climax,' at which point it was claimed that the vegetation communities had become degraded.[73] However, the equilibrium model ignores natural variability, which causes grazing lands to behave in disequilibrium in drier environments, in contrast to the temperate environments where the theory was first developed.[74]

In Africa, the presumed causal factors of the crisis are multiple. In addition to ecological factors, a common claim has been increasing population growth that was said to have contributed to environmental degradation. Yet we know that in the late nineteenth century, the African population had collapsed due to epidemics, famine, warfare and slavery; and population growth did not recover sufficiently until the late 1930s, when it again declined due to famine.[75] Additionally, there is no evidence that the pre-colonial African environments were degraded—or that soil erosion and gully formations had occurred on the scale described during the colonial period. Indeed, Kate Showers[76] reports that 'gully erosion was unknown in [the Kingdom of Lesotho] by the 1830s,' but gullies were reported from the 1890s onwards. Even then, reports of gully erosion emerged despite evidence of healthy livestock and agricultural production. In other cases, colonial reports associated soil erosion with the smelting of iron by African societies—a distant argument that Paul Lane[77] dismisses as merely 'shifting blame from one set of actors to another.' Given the energy efficiency of indigenous metal smelting works, it is unlikely that large forest areas were cleared for the purpose (which, in turn, could have contributed to soil erosion).

The underlying assumptions of the environmental crisis hypothesis was that the main drivers of environmental degradation were sociological factors, as opposed to ecological ones alone. This opinion was influenced by a controversial development theory first published by Melville Herskovits in 1936, called the 'cattle complex.' Herskovits proposed that pastoralists have a behavioral attachment to their livestock. According to his theory, African herders—by accumulating large herds on the rangelands—inadvertently induced environmental degradation.[78] The 'cattle complex' theory was most pronounced from the 1930s when global discourses of environmental degradation were described in relation to 'dust bowl' incidents in the American Central Plains;[79] and also from the 1940s through to the 1960s when desertification became a major environmental issue in Africa.[80] It was in this context that Elspeth Huxley warned, stating: 'if man continues to follow the same destructive course that he has done in the United States and is already doing today in Africa, there can be little doubt but that the soil fertility will decline rapidly and irrevocably.'[81] That warning became a major point of reference for ongoing research and development in Africa[82]—in particular where development drew on sociological theories of development.

Expanding on the ideas of Melville Herskovits, Garrett Hardin[83] developed his theory of the 'tragedy of the commons' which significantly influenced the privatization of communal grazing lands. The theory argued that communal resources in general, and common pastures, encouraged individuals to add more stock to their herds,[84] leading to overgrazing and degradation. The argument was that the rangelands in Africa carried more stock than their acceptable 'carrying capacities'—which, it was claimed, were fixed for individual rangelands. In tackling the problem, colonial officials advocated forceful destocking of pastoralist herds and the establishment of large-scale soil conservation programs.[85]

Unfortunately, imperial science failed to appreciate that the productivities of African rangelands fluctuate between periods of high and low rainfall. In the former, greater volumes of forage are produced, resulting in surpluses; while in dry years, the carrying capacities of the same rangelands would decline drastically. Consequently, the controlling factor is not grazer populations, but climate variability—providing evidence that rangeland production in arid and semi-arid African environments has always been dynamic, unstable and fluctuating.[86] We argue that the historical literature that inferred widespread problems of degradation due to large pastoral herds[87] suffered this misreading of the ecology of the African rangelands. Accordingly, long-held predictions of the imminent collapse of traditional pastoral production due to deteriorating environments never materialized; and any disasters that did occur can be ascribed to different causes.[88] Although ecological consequences were not a deliberate goal of the economic and environmental engineering schemes, development planning in this respect proved to be inadequate.[89] Thus, researchers would have made better progress if they had considered what Mariam Chertow and Daniel Esty[90] call 'thinking ecologically.' Rather than improving indigenous systems of land use, development aggravated the environmental situation[91]—described as the African environmental crisis. We next examine experimental and social science research for testing the African environmental crisis hypothesis.

Experimental and social science research

We used published agronomic and range science research to verify if the results reported supported the crisis hypothesis. We begin with the domain of agronomic and range science research as applied ecological ideas of development (Chapter 5). The agronomic and range science research were premised on the equilibrium model (i.e., environmental crisis) but their outcomes exhibited the alternative disequilibrium model, showing a lack of support for the environmental crisis. The results were misapplied in planning development. The other weakness of the agronomic research was that experiments were rarely conducted at the scales of indigenous land use and therefore could not be used to make inferences about the impacts on the environment at that scale.[92]

All range science experiments disclosed the superiority of the indigenous systems of rangeland use over the alternative systems recommended by technical officials—thus supporting the alternative disequilibrium model. In the absence of long-term research data, laying blame on the land-use systems of African people for causing widespread soil erosion is unconvincing.[93] Further, in absence of long-term experiments, evidence in support of environmental crisis could not be obtained. The long-term experiments should be able to disentangle natural variability from development-induced changes. Suitable long-term research—that is, collecting and analyzing decadal data—would be necessary to appraise environmental changes and disaggregate influence of climate variability from management impacts.[94] The challenge lies in different priorities among managers and researchers; while researchers tend to be unprepared to provide immediate solutions or recommendations before their research 'matures,' by that time, the development manager would have moved on with other projects.[95] This had influenced how Africans responded to development.

Social science research

Social science investigates cultural knowledge, perceptions and decisions concerning the management of nature by societies (Chapter 6). John Mackenzie[96] describes the history of social science according to three premises. The first is that social science is based on social and cultural constructions and has political implications. The second is that social science can be applied to local contexts in order to gain a better understanding of societal behavior towards development changes. The third is that failure to understand the dynamics of social science contributed to failure in comprehending African peoples' responses to development.[97] Nonetheless, by conducting a synchronic analysis of specific communities in their responses to development, and making comparisons across the regions in East Africa, it could have been possible to re-appraise how different societies responded to development advocated by colonial and post-independent states.[98]

14 *African environmental crisis: is it a myth?*

The implications of these premises are critical, considering that the African continent is culturally rich with diverse cultural systems that are best studied by means of interdisciplinary science research methods (i.e., integrating ecological and social sciences).[99] Bearing in mind that the African environments are disturbance prone, the extraction of resources in regions with such high natural variability will be bound to change socio-ecological systems on the scale of 'human lifetimes,'[100] (as opposed to weeks or months). Perhaps the colonial ideas of static African societies were the reason for their use of force to bring about rapid changes. It was only later (1950s) that investigations of social behavior and local institutions occurred, by involving anthropologists to consider the social aspects of development planning.[101]

Administrative method

Administrative science is another type of applied social science research—this is often based on practical solutions that follow administrative organizational decisions instead of scientific deductions (Chapter 7). The purpose of this so-called 'government method' (or 'administrative science')[102] is the practical application of development projects as experimental work, based on technical and administrative knowledge. It sets priorities for implementing government policies and was applied through dialogue among technical departments and the colonial administration, involving scientific researchers peripherally for advice. The subjects of such dialogue were demonstrating so-called 'participation in development.' In fact, using ordinances, African peasants were forced to implement soil conservation and tsetse fly controls and regulate livestock stockings on the settlement schemes. Archival sources show that while the methodology used narratives of officials on matters related to land use, Africans were rarely offered any forum in which to present their views, other than defending their cases in Crown courts. Administrative science, combined with ecological science, had been applied widely for the control of disease vectors and agricultural pests—involving large-scale environmental manipulation.

Vectors, pests and environmental change

Tsetse fly control in East Africa

Development in the East African colonies was adversely affected by disease vectors such as tsetse flies (*Glossina* species)[103] that, from the beginning of the colonial period, had posed a great threat to public health and to pastoral and agricultural production (Chapter 8). Tsetse flies and the trypanosome protozoan that cause disease in people and livestock present one of the most stubborn ecological and epidemiological problems ever encountered by imperial science.[104] The tsetse flies by the late nineteenth century had infested an estimated ten million km² of Africa, along a fly belt that straddles the rain forest into the dry savanna, south of the Sahara and north of the Kalahari deserts.[105] An estimated seven million km² of rangelands and agricultural lands were affected, covering 75 percent of Uganda, two-thirds of Tanganyika and 20 percent of Kenya.[106] The *Glossina* species[107] exploited varieties of ideal habitats,[108] including bushlands and the vegetation of river valleys.[109] The tsetse flies take their blood meals from vertebrate hosts in a process through which the life cycle of the trypanosome protozoan circulates between infected insects, people, cattle and wild game. To date, there are no known permanent medical solutions to stop infection by the trypanosome parasites that cause *trypanosomiasis* (sleeping sickness).[110]

The control of, and research into, tsetse flies and *trypanosomiasis* attempted varieties of methods, including the destruction of the habitats through bush clearing, destruction of the wild game and the application of environmentally persistent pesticides. Another attempted control method was the removal of people and livestock—however, this process allowed the tsetse to expand their frontiers.[111] In the process, millions of hectares of natural vegetation were cleared, although the outcomes of such interventions were not discussed in the context of the African environmental crisis. The problem would also apply to African locust plagues as the most destructive agents of the environment and economies of the East African colonies.

Locust invasion and control

The East African region had been periodically visited by plagues of desert locusts (*Schistocerca gregaria* Forsk) and red locusts (*Nomadaries septermfasciata* Serville) that ruined agricultural and pastoral economies in East and the Horn of Africa (Chapter 9). The desert locust is among the most widespread pests, with breeding grounds extending from the deserts on the Indo-Pakistan borders, the Arabian Peninsula, the Red Sea coast, to Somaliland and some regions of East Africa. The red locust breeds in the floodplains of Uganda, as well as southern Tanzania in the region of Lake Rukwa from where they pose a great danger to the economies in East Africa.[112]

Locusts are voracious feeders, consuming huge amounts of vegetation and crops on their flight paths or in their development stages, causing economic losses in millions of British pounds. Huge financial resources had been committed over a period of half a century to control the plagues. Efforts to control the desert locust and the red locust[113] had motivated international collaboration. Control methods involved mobilizing African labor to attack the pest during its various phases of development. Both ground and aerial methods were used to spray the swarms. Aerial spraying was popular for controlling mobile swarms in flight between the outbreak areas and the target regions in East Africa. Although effective, the methods did not eliminate different generations of swarms; thus, locust control was always a state of emergency, allowing little time to conduct controlled

16 *African environmental crisis: is it a myth?*

experiments. The destruction of agricultural economies caused by locusts occurred at a time when researchers and colonial officials were blaming local land-use methods for environmental crisis.

These and other related discussions will be expounded in the coming case study chapters (under the three themes: empire, science, society and development; experimental and social science research; and vectors, pests and environmental change). In the final chapter of the book (Chapter 10), we synthesize the key findings of the work and in an epilog, map out the progress of scientific research for development during the later periods of post-independence.

Notes

1 Livingstone, D.N., *Putting science in its place: Geographies of scientific knowledge* (Chicago: University of Chicago Press. 2003), 107, 111, 140.
2 Showers, Kate B., 'Soil erosion in the Kingdom of Lesotho and development of historical environmental impact assessment,' *Ecological Applications* 6.2 (1996): 653–664.
3 Mackenzie, A. and Fiona, D., 'Contested ground: Colonial narratives and the Kenyan environment, 1920–1845,' *Journal of Southern African Studies* 26.4 (2000): 697–718.
4 DeAngelis, D.L. and Huston, Michael, A., 'Further considerations on the debate over herbivore optimization theory,' *Ecological Applications* 3.1 (1993): 30–31, 30.
5 Goldstone, B. and Obarrio, J. (eds), *African futures: Essays on crisis, emergence, and possibility* (Chicago: University of Chicago Press, 2016), 5.
6 Mizuno, N. and Okazawa, R., 'Colonial experience and post-colonial underdevelopment in Africa,' *Public Choice* 141.3/4 (2009): 405–419; De Vos, A., *Africa, the devastated continent? Man's impact on the ecology of Africa* (Hague: D.W. Junk Publishers, 1975).
7 Hailey, M. (Lord), *An African survey revised 1956: A study of problems arising in Africa south of Sahara* (London: Oxford University Press, 1957), 36.
8 Anderson, D., 'Depression, dust bowl, demography, and drought: The colonial state and soil conservation in East Africa during the 1930s,' *African Affairs* 83 (1984): 321–343.
9 Worster, D., *Dust bowl: The southern plains in the 1930s* (Oxford: Oxford University Press, 2004).
10 Stebbing, E.P., 'The encroaching Sahara: The threat to the West African colonies,' *The Geographical Journal* 85.6 (1935): 506–519.
11 Huxley, E., 'The menace of soil erosion,' *Journal of the Royal African Society* 36.144 (1937): 357–370, 368.
12 Howard, A.M., 'Nodes, networks, landscapes, and regions: Reading of social history of tropical Africa 1700–1920,' in Howard, A.M. and Shain, R.M. (eds.), *The spatial factor in African history: The relationship the social, material and conceptual* (Leiden: Brill, 2005).
13 Grove, R.H., *Green imperialism: Colonial expansion: Tropical island Edens and the origins of environmentalism, 1600–1860* (Cambridge: Cambridge University Press, 1995).

14 Sinclair, A.R.E., 'Science and the practice of wildlife management,' *Journal of Wildlife Management* 55.4 (1991): 767–773.
15 Cohen, A., (Sir), 'Conference on the medical, agricultural and veterinary aspects of food production in East Africa, opening address by His excellence the Governor of Uganda,' *East African Agricultural Journal* XX.1 (1954): 3–11.
16 Keay, R.W.J., 'The natural sciences in Africa,' *African Affairs* 64 (1965): 50–54, 53.
17 Worthington, E.B., *Science in Africa: A review of scientific research relating to tropical and southern Africa* (Oxford: Oxford University Press, 1938), 17.
18 Beeby, A., *Applying Ecology* (New York: Chapman & Hall, 1993), 372; Phillips, J., 'Ecological investigation in south, central and East Africa: Outline of a progressive scheme,' *Journal of Ecology* 19.2 (1931): 474–482.
19 Odhiambo, T.R., 'East Africa: Science for development,' *Science* 158.3803 (1967): 876–881; Kumar, D., 'Emergence of "Scientocracy": Snippets from colonial India,' *Economic and Political Weekly* 39.35 (2004): 3893–3898.
20 Tilley, H., *Africa as a living laboratory: Empire, development, and the problem of scientific knowledge, 1890–1950* (Chicago: University of Chicago Press, 2011), 123.
21 Van Beusekom, M.M., *Negotiating development: African farmers and colonial experts at the office Du Niger, 1920–1960* (Portsmouth: Heinemann, 2002), xi.
22 Weiss, B., 'Getting a head when we're behind: Time, potential, and value in urban Tanzania,' in Goldstone, B. and Obbario, J. (eds), *African futures: Essays on crisis, emergence, and possibility* (Chicago: University of Chicago Press, 2016).
23 Caldwell, L.K., 'An ecological approach to international development: Problems of policy and administration,' in Borgstrom, G., Farvar, M.T. and Milton, J.P. (eds.), *The careless technology: Ecology and international development* (Tom Stacey, 1973), 927.
24 Cumple, C.L., 'Forward,' in Baleè, W. (ed.), *Advances in historical ecology* (New York: Columbia University Press, 1998).
25 Carruthers, J., 'Environmental history in South Africa: An overview,' in Dovers, S., Edgelcombe, R. and Guest B. (eds.), *South Africa's environmental history: Cases and comparisons* (Athens: Ohio University Press, 2002), 4.
26 Hughes, J.D., 'Three dimensions of environmental history,' *Environment and History* 14 (2008): 319–330.
27 Howard, 'Nodes, networks, landscapes, and regions,' 25–26.
28 McManus, P. and Houghton, G., 'Planning with ecological footprints: A synthetic critique of theory and practice,' *Environmental and Urbanization* 18.1 (2006): 113–127, 114.
29 Walters, B.B. and Vayda, A.P., 'Event ecology, causal historical analysis, and human-environmental research,' *Annals of the Associations of the American Geographers* 99.3 (2009): 534–553.
30 Showers, 'Soil erosion in the Kingdom of Lesotho,' 659–662; Showers, K.B. and Malahleha, G.M., 'Oral evidence in historical environmental impact assessment: Soil conservation in Lesotho in the 1930s and 1940s,' *Journal of Southern African Studies* 18.2 (1992): 276–296.
31 Londsdale, J. 'African pasts in Africa's future,' *Canadian Journal of African Studies* 23.1 (1979): 126–146; Waller, Richard D., 'Tsetse fly in western Narok, Kenya,' *Journal of African History* 31.1 (1990): 81–101, 100; White, L., 'Tsetse visions: Narratives of blood and bugs in colonial Northern Rhodesia, 1931–9,' *Journal of African History* 36.2 (1995): 219–245.

32 Beinart, W. and Coates, P., *Environment and history: The taming of nature in the USA and South Africa* (London: Routledge, 1995).
33 Williams, M., 'Ecology, imperialism and deforestation,' in Griffiths, T. and Robin, L. (eds.), *Ecology and empire: Environmental history of settler societies* (Edinburgh: Keele University Press, 1997), 170; Kreike, E., *Re-creating Eden: Land use, environment, and society in southern Angola and northern Namibia* (Portsmouth, NH: Heinemann, 2004).
34 Here we are using science and ecology synonymously, though their exact scope does vary.
35 Robin, L., 'Ecology: A science of empire?' in Griffiths, T. and Robin, L. (eds.), *Ecology and empire: Environmental history of settler societies* (Edinburgh: Keele University Press, 1997), 63.
36 Malin, J.C., 'Ecology and history,' *Scientific Monthly* 70.5 (1950): 295–298.
37 Beinart, W. and McGregor, J., *Social history and African environments* (Oxford: James Currey, 2003).
38 Brockway, L.H., *Science and colonial expansion: The role of the British Royal Botanic Gardens* (London: Academic Press, 1979); Bennett, B.M. and Hodge, J.M., *Science and empire: Knowledge and networks of science across the British empire, 1800–1970* (New York: Palgrave MacMillan, 2011).
39 White, 'Tsetse visions,' 232; Håkanson, N.T., Widgren, M. and Börjeson, L., 'Introduction: Historical and regional perspectives on landscape transformations in northern Tanzania, 1850–2000,' *International Journal of African Historical Studies* 41.3 (2008): 369–382.
40 White, 'Tsetse visions.'
41 Harrison, M. 'Science and the British empire,' *Isis* 96.1 (2005): 56 63, 58.
42 See for example, McDowell, P.F., Webb, Thomas III and Bartlein Patrick, 'Long-term environmental change,' in Powell, T.M. and Steele, J. H. (eds.), *Ecological time series* (New York: Chapman & Hall, 1995), 329.
43 Richards, P., 'Ecological change and the politics of African land use,' *African Studies Review* 26.2 (1983): 1–72.
44 Bouneuil, C., 'Development as an experiment: Science and state building in late colonial and post-colonial Africa, 1930–1970,' *Osiris* 15 (2000): 258–281, 281.
45 Kreike, *Environmental infrastructure in African history*.
46 Oba, G., *Climate change adaptations in Africa: An historical ecology* (London: Routledge, 2014).
47 Widgren, M. and Sutton, J.E.G., *Islands of intensive agriculture in East Africa* (Oxford: James Currey, 2004); Adams, W.M. and Anderson, D.M., 'Irrigation before development: Indigenous and induced change in agricultural water management in East Africa,' *African Affairs* 87.349 (1988): 519–535.
48 Kreike, *Environmental infrastructure in African history*; Ford, John, *The role of the trypanosomiases in African ecology: A study of the tsetse fly problem* (Oxford: Clarendon Press, 1971).
49 Gove, A.T., 'Desertification in the African environment,' *African Affairs* 73.291 (1974): 137–151, 145/6.
50 Havinden, M. and Meredith, D., *Colonialism and development* (London: Routledge, 1993), 5; Schiebinger, L., 'Forum introduction: The European colonial science complex,' *Isis* 96.1 (2005): 52–55, 52.
51 Mackenzie, J.M., 'Comments by general editor,' in Dubow S. (ed.), *Science and society in southern Africa* (Manchester: Manchester University Press, 2000);

Claude, A., *Science, development and violence: The revolt against modernity* (Delhi: Oxford University Press, 1992), 1, 66, 68.
52 Caldwell, 'An ecological approach to international development,' 936.
53 DeAngelis, D.L. and Michael, A.H., 'Further considerations on the debate over herbivore optimization theory,' *Ecological Applications* 3.1 (1993): 30–31, 30.
54 Bonneuil, C., 'Development as experiment: Science and state building in late colonial and postcolonial Africa, 1930–1970,' *Osiris* 15 (2000): 258–281, 280.
55 Alvares, *Science, development and violence*, 94.
56 Nurse, K. and Wight, D., 'Development assistance and research capacity strengthening: The commissioning of health research in East Africa,' *Journal of East African Studies* 5.2 (2011): 233–251.
57 Frankel, S.H., 'Foreword,' in Baldwin, K.D.S. (ed.), *The Niger Agricultural project: An experiment in African development* (London: Basil Blackwell, 1957).
58 Warren, A., 'Changing understandings of African pastoralism and the nature of environmental paradigms,' *Transactions of the British Geographers* 20.2 (1995): 193–203, 198–199.
59 Shine, T. and Dunford., B., 'What value for pastoral livelihoods? An economic valuation of development alternatives for ephemeral wetlands in eastern Mauritania,' *Pastoralism* 6.1 (2016): 9.
60 Sluyter, A., *Black ranching frontiers: African cattle herders of the Atlantic world, 1500–1900* (New Haven: Yale University Press, 2012), x.
61 Worthington, E.B., 'Organization of research in Africa,' *Scientific Monthly* 74.1 (1952): 39–44.
62 Saleem, M.A.M., 'Experience gained in the research-to-development continuum: Livestock research for sustainable livelihoods in the East African mountains,' *Mountain Research & Development* 21.2 (2001): 118–122.
63 Tilley, *Africa as a living laboratory*, 10–12.
64 Lewis, J.K., 'Range management viewed in the ecosystem framework,' in Van Dyne, G., *The ecosystem concept in natural resource management* (New York: Academic Press, 1969), 100–109.
65 Grove, *Green imperialism*, 15.
66 Knowlton, C., *Cattle kingdom: The hidden history of the cowboy west* (Boston: An Eamon Dolan Book, 2017); Strander, J., *The blue and the green: A cultural ecological history of Arizona ranching community* (Nevada: University of Nevada Press, 2016), 29–34.
67 Worster, *Dust bowl*.
68 Worster, D., 'The vulnerable Earth: Toward a planetary history,' in Worster, D. (ed.), *The ends of the earth: Perspectives on modern environmental history* (Cambridge: Cambridge University Press, 1988).
69 Beinart, W., *The rise of conservation in South Africa: Settlers, livestock, and environment 1770–1950* (Oxford: Oxford University Press, 2003).
70 Clements, F.E., *Plant succession: An analysis of the development of vegetation* (Carnegie Institute of Washington Publication, 1916).
71 Sampson, A.W., *Rangeland management: Principles and practice* (New York: Wiley, 1952).
72 Sayre, N.F., *The politics of scale: A history of rangeland science* (Chicago: Chicago University Press, 2017), 74–75, 78.
73 Cronon, W., *Changes in the land: Indians, colonists, and the ecology of New England* (New York: Hill and Wang, 2003), xv, 10.

20 African environmental crisis: is it a myth?

74 Contemporary ecological theories have discarded the succession-climax theory in the arid and semi-arid grazing lands.

75 Champion, A.M., 'Soil erosion in Africa,' *The Geographical Journal* 82.2 (1933): 130–139.

76 Showers, 'Soil erosion in the kingdom of Lesotho.'

77 Lane, P., 'Environmental narratives and the history of soil erosion in Kondoa District, Tanzania: An archaeological perspective,' *International Journal of African Historical Studies* 42.3 (2009): 457–483, 477.

78 Herskovits, M.J., 'The cattle complex in East Africa,' *American Anthropologist* 28.1 (1926): 230–272, 28, Parts 1–4; Windstrand, C.G., 'The rationale of nomad economy,' *Ambio* 4.4 (1975): 146–153.

79 Worster, *Dust bowl*.

80 Gonzalez, P., 'Desertification and a shift of forest species in the West African Sahel,' *Climate Research* 17.2 (2001): 217–228.

81 Huxley, E., 'The menace of soil erosion,' *Journal of the Royal African Society* 36.144 (1937), 357–370.

82 Anderson, D., *Eroding the commons: The politics of ecology in Baringo, Kenya, 1890–1963* (Oxford: James Currey, 2002).

83 Hardin, G., 'The tragedy of the commons,' *Science*, 162.3859 (1968): 1243–1248.

84 Mwangi, E. and Ostrom, E., 'Top-down solutions: Looking up from East Africa's rangelands,' *Environment: Science and Policy for Sustainable Development* 51.1 (2009): 34–45, 36.

85 Shutt, A.K, 'The settlers' cattle complex: The etiquette of culling cattle in colonial Zimbabwe, 1938,' *Journal of African History* 48.2 (2002): 263–287, 270.

86 See Behnke, R. 'Natural resource management in pastoral Africa,' in Stiles D. (ed.), *Social aspects of sustainable dryland management* (New York: John Wiley & Sons, 1995), 145.

87 Maddox, G.H., *Sub-Saharan Africa: An environmental history* (Santa Barbara, California: ABC-CL10, 2006).

88 Warren, 'Changing understandings of African pastoralism,' 196.

89 Talbot, L.M., 'Ecological aspects of aid programs in East Africa, with particular reference to rangelands,' *Bulletins from Ecological Research Committee* 13 (1971): 21–51, 21–24.

90 Chertow, Mariam R. and Esty, Daniel C., *Thinking ecologically: The next generation of environmental policy* (New Haven: Yale University Press, 1997).

91 Radding, C., *Landscapes of power and identity: Comparative histories in the Sonoran Desert and the forests of Amazonia from colony to republic* (Durham, NC: Duke University Press, 2005), 3–4.

92 Tilman, D., 'Ecological experimentation: Strengths and conceptual problems,' in Likens, G..E., *Long-term studies in ecology* (Springer, New York, NY, 1989), 136–157, 155; Pereira, H.C., 'Practical aspects of field experimentation in Africa,' *East African Agricultural and Forestry Journal* XXVI.1 (1960): 35–41, 36.

93 Bahre, C.J., *A legacy of change: Historic human impact on vegetation of Arizona borderlands* (Tucson: University of Arizona Press, 1981).

94 Franklin, F., 'Importance and justification of long-term studies in ecology,' in Likens G.E. (ed.), *Long-term studies in ecology approaches and alternatives* (New York: Springer, 1989), 3.

95 McAninch, J.B. and Strayer, D.L., 'What are the tradeoffs between the immediacy of management needs and the longer process of scientific discovery?' in Likens,

G.E. (ed.), *Long-term studies in ecology approaches and alternatives* (New York: Springer, 1989).
96 Mackenzie, 'Comments by general editor.'
97 Dubowl, S., 'Introduction,' in Dubow, Saul (ed.), *Science and society in southern Africa* (Manchester: Manchester University Press, 2000), 1.
98 Herskovits, M.J., 'Anthropology and Africa: A wider perspective,' *Africa* 29.3 (1959): 225–238.
99 Gilbert, E., 'Coastal East Africa and the western Indian Ocean: Long-distance trade, empire, migration and regional unity 1750–1970,' *History Teacher* 36.1 (2002): 7–34.
100 Pickett, S.T.A., Burch, W.R. and Grove, J.M., 'Interdisciplinary research: Maintaining the constructive impulse in a culture of criticism,' *Ecosystems* 2.4 (1999): 302–307, 303.
101 Bennett, J.W., Lawry, S.W. and Ridell, J.C., *Land tenure and livestock development in sub-Saharan Africa: AID Evaluation special study No. 39*, U.S. Agency for International Development (May 1986), 2.
102 Worthington, E.B., 'Organization of research in Africa,' *Scientific Monthly* 74.1 (1952): 39–44.
103 Tilley, H., 'Ecologies of complexity: Tropical environments, African trypanosomiasis, and the science of disease control in British colonial Africa, 1900–1940,' *Osiris* 19 (2004): 21–38.
104 Shantz, H.L., 'Agricultural regions of Africa: Part II. Vegetation and potential productivity of the land,' *Economic Geography* 16.4 (1940): 341–389.
105 Rogers, D.J. and Randolph, S.E., 'Distribution and abundance of Tsetse flies (*Glossina* species),' *Journal of Animal Ecology* 55.3 (1986): 1007–1025.
106 Bates, M.L., 'Tanganyika: The development of a trust territory,' *International Organization* 9.1 (1955): 32–51.
107 Five of the tsetse fly species known to be widely distributed across East Africa are: *Glossina morsitans*, *G. pallidipes*, *G. palpalis*, *G. swynnertoni* and *G. brevipalpis*.
108 Whiteside, E.F., 'The control of cattle trypanosomiasis with drugs in Kenya: Methods and costs,' *East African Agricultural and Forestry Journal* XXVIII.2 (1962): 67–73.
109 Sharpe, A., 'The geography and economic development of British central Africa,' *The Geographical Journal* 39.1 (1912): 1–17.
110 The medical analysis of the diseases is beyond the scope of the current chapter. See Malvy, D. and Chappuis, F., 'Sleeping sickness,' *Clinical Microbiology and Infection* 17 (2011): 986–995.
111 Ford, J. and Clifford, H.R., 'Changes in the distribution of cattle and of Bovine Trypanosomiasis associated with the spread of Tsetse-flies (*Glossina*) in southwest Uganda,' *Journal of Applied Ecology* 5.2 (1968): 301–337.
112 Hailey, *An African Survey*, 898.
113 Lecoq, M., 'Desert locust management: From ecology to anthropology,' *Journal of Orthoptera Research* 14 (2005): 179–186.

Part I
Empire, science, society and development

2 European exploration of East Africa

Textual analysis of travel narratives, 1831–1900

Major historical and political changes took place in East Africa in the nineteenth and early twentieth centuries, when European explorers and missionaries began to travel to the interior of Africa. Up to this period, Africa was known as the 'dark continent,' a metaphor of how little the European nations of the time knew about the region.[1] The European travel narratives written between 1831 and 1900 imply that the aim of expeditions was to produce knowledge by describing the processes of cultural contacts, collecting plant and zoological materials for European institutions, producing scientific reports and cartographic works.[2] Scientific geography in particular has its origins in the texts[3] of explorers and missionaries' reports.[4]

From these textual narratives, as interpreted by the readers of the reports in the metropole, some important propositions can be made. Some argue that the travelers—missionaries and explorers—were not trained scientists and that their reports therefore cannot be regarded as reliable sources for reconstructing the pre-colonial environmental history of East Africa. Indeed, later Africanist scholars claim that observations in the corpus of ethnographic sources were 'superficial' and tainted with racial bias against the African peoples.[5] Some European 'armchair experts' also doubted the scientific value of the travelers' reports where it was evident that they had relied on African indigenous knowledge.

Others, nonetheless, suggest that the geographical methods used by the explorers and missionaries were scientifically and sufficiently robust to reconstruct the environmental history of nineteenth-century East Africa[6] and that these historical narratives might serve as a benchmark for assessing the environmental and social changes that ensued.[7] By comparing the texts of different travelers and their observations of cultural and environmental changes, and environmental collapse in the late nineteenth century, a different picture of the East African environment emerges.

The goal of this chapter is to analyze these opposing propositions using European travelers' texts in the following six sections: (1) East Africa as a political and social frontier; (2) application of spatial and scientific geography; (3) the environmental desiccation hypothesis; (4) European environmental narratives; (5) comparative narratives of environmental change; and (6) ecological and demographic collapse in the late nineteenth century.

East Africa as a political and social frontier

Politically, East Africa consisted of diverse cultural communities that included centralized African states and close-knit kinship systems.[8] Throughout the region, the different socio-cultural and ecological systems were linked in complex social networks. The combination of crop cultivation and keeping livestock ensured that food was available for most of the time.[9] Livestock was involved in every transaction.[10] The size of the human settlements varied between the societies that practiced agro-pastoralism and those based on pure pastoral systems.[11]

Socially, East Africa displayed another characteristic of a frontier—the relationships between societies were very fluid. It was common for communities to cross ethnic boundaries during periods of crisis, when the populations that suffered the most sought new ethnic identities by merging with their neighbors. The early European travelers described areas with large human populations and cultivated lands as well as others with sparse populations, where the main economic pursuit was livestock husbandry. There was continuity between farming and animal husbandry, with the emphasis shifting as environmental conditions changed. Settlement patterns and crop fields were clearly demarcated. Agricultural practices included permanent plots as well as shifting cultivation. William Allan[12] warns that the distinction between shifting cultivation and cultivation of permanent plots may be blurred, with the former simply describing the rotational use of the same landscape.

Talal Asad[13] contends that the knowledge of such dynamic social-environmental systems falls in the realm of 'functional anthropology,' which places societies in the context of their economics and social functions. The travelers' descriptions of the patterns of settlements and croplands of nineteenth-century East Africa suggest that social factors played a role in the spatial relations of farmlands and homesteads.[14] The region was therefore also a social-environmental frontier where African societies existed as independent tribal communities prior to the colonial partitioning of East Africa. Their cultural experiences may have shaped the use of their environments and thus their economies. Pastoralism was the common land use in drier environments, while in the sub-humid zones, people practiced mixed farming and kept livestock.[15] The indigenous farming and pastoral economies were nested in the rhythms of nature, with land use following seasonal patterns. The ways in which societies were organized and their dealings with neighbors helped to define their local knowledge systems in relation to the social and political changes around them.[16] It is also significant that communities were able to select appropriate land resources such as soils for planting crops and understood the natural ecosystems for the management of livestock. Both political decisions and proximity to critical natural resources influenced their settlement patterns. Social groups had communal ownership of territories.

Additionally, the interior of East Africa consisted of social networks in which complementary subsistence economies occupied specific ecological niches. The agro-pastoral and pastoral production systems relied on each other's resources, which they accessed through exchange systems.[17] Ecological historians therefore cannot understand past land uses without studying these systems during different historical periods. By examining the close relations between societies and their environments, it is possible to gain a full appreciation of the environmental and social history of the region and the significant roles played by different cultures.[18] The cultural groups helped to solve social and environmental problems and served as custodians of indigenous knowledge.[19] The system of resource tenure allowed simultaneous use of semi-private farmlands and communal grazing lands. Settlements were also the locus of socio-political activities. The early European travelers asked for directions, visited the local chiefs and replenished their food supplies at such settlements. The relations formed there became the basis of European investigations of spatial and scientific geography (Figure 2.1).

Application of spatial and scientific geography

Between 1848 and 1876, regarded as the classic period of European exploration of Africa, expeditions were sponsored by scientific institutions such as the Royal Geographical Society (RGS), Kew Gardens, and European herbaria and zoos to explore the regions of Africa. The RGS, founded in 1830, sent expert individuals to discover new territories. Its reports provide historical snapshots of nineteenth-century East Africa, based on European explorers' narratives on the modes of land use, food production and types of vegetation and soils, the social and political organization of major cultural groups, geographical spaces, trade routes, the abundant wildlife, tribal wars, slave trade, and occasional epidemics.[20]

The explorers investigated the potential of African rivers as waterways for expeditions into the interior and gathered scientific knowledge for exploiting the various types of environments for future European settlements. In the territories they visited, the explorers were interested in methods that European settlers could use to improve crop cultivation, carry out surveys about important minerals and their potential for economic exploitation.[21]

It was Dr David Livingstone's report that 'opened floodgates for European imperialism.'[22] Livingstone's scientific interests included a passion for geology, botany, history and human geography. He was a keen

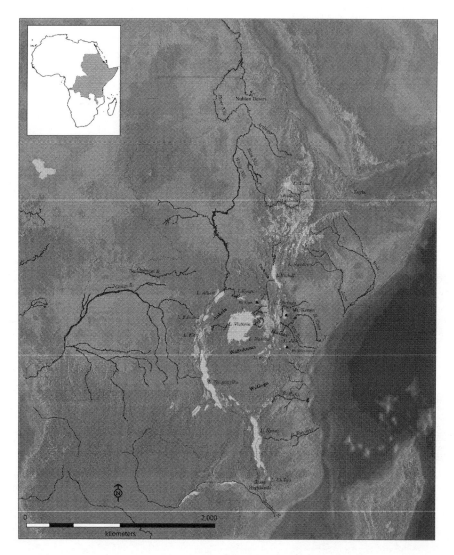

Figure 2.1 The natural and physical geographical features of East and Central Africa.

observer of the political dynamics and human security issues in the regions he visited. He described how inter-tribal wars devastated some regions, uprooting populations and ruining their economies. In the case of the Ngoni–Zulu wars in central Africa in the mid-nineteenth century, he outlined their effects on the environment, stating: '[t]he resources of the luxuriant land is going to waste due to tribal wars and slave-trading.'[23]

Thanks to his extensive skills as a medical doctor, missionary and scientist, Livingstone's work attracted a wide readership. His contributions to the geographical knowledge of East and central East Africa are noteworthy, particularly owing to his systematic and scientific methods, some of which were later tested by other explorers. European researchers interested in Africa were influenced by his knowledge of ethnography, zoology and botany. For example, during his Zambezi expedition of 1858–1864, he collected botanical specimens specifically to identify indigenous flora suitable for commercial production. His description of diseases and disease vectors motivated scholars in European universities and scientific societies to conduct further investigations.[24]

Methods of scientific research of geography

From the time of its publication in 1831, the *Journal of the Royal Geographical Society of London* (JRGS) provided the platform for disseminating the scientific findings of explorations. In order to control the quality of the scientific information gathered by explorers, the RGS provided them with guidebooks on the methods of collecting social and environmental information.[25] Through the RGS, the travelers 'paraded their contributions to science.' Among the expeditions that raised huge interest in Europe were the Zambezi mission and the discovery of the source of the Nile (Figure 2.1).

Readers of the geographical reports relied on the narratives of the explorers, particularly their textual descriptions. However, some skeptics suggest that these travels through the remote regions of East Africa were relatively short, preventing travelers from developing a 'lasting impression.' Furthermore, if the travelers traversed the same routes during dry and wet seasons, they might have interpreted the same environments differently.[26] Additionally, opinions differ about the narratives that broadly describe the African social systems and their economies and environments. One group holds that the explorers were not trained scientists and that the opinions they presented cannot be generalized. Others believe that many of the explorers were people of learning exposed to the scientific literature of the time and the sharing of scientific information through institutions such as the RGS. Considering that the explorers supported by RGS were learned, their reports would therefore be valuable sources of knowledge.

Those who questioned the texts of the European explorers suggested that the inclusion of indigenous knowledge in their reports compromised their information. Where the explorers admitted that they had relied on indigenous knowledge sources, this might have created doubts and suspicion in the minds of European armchair experts. The alternative view was that the travelers and explorers needed local travel guides, who provided the information. It has been argued further that without the use of local guides and interpreters, the European travelers' exploits would have been fruitless.[27] It was common practice to mention the individual Africans who provided information. Indeed, the explorers negotiated their passage through regions and traded with local communities. In the process, the explorers and local guides shared information about geographical features of interest and their meaning in local dialects.

John Hanning Speke[28] wrote detailed accounts of how he relied on the African communities in the territories through which he traveled, locating water sources with their help and exploring their knowledge about the source of the White Nile. The credibility of explorers' reports depended on the interpretations by local informants, who also helped them to navigate physical spaces.[29] David Livingstone's thinking was even more progressive for using indigenous knowledge to verify his own observations.[30] Joseph Thomson,[31] for his part, relied on African informants for guidance and information about the tribal territories his routes crossed, while the travel records of Von Höhnel,[32] Sámuel Teleki's travel companion, clearly state that Teleki's two Swahili assistants, knew all his requirements, 'exactly, and really surprised' him with their knowledge.

Local communities provided the geographic information needed for cartographic mapping and demographics.[33] The European travelers used maps to mark the locations from which botanical and zoological materials were collected. Further, their cartographic mapping allowed the explorers to present various landscapes of interest, naming and plotting their routes, with spatial measurements of distances and the elevations of important geographical features.[34] Their copious notebooks containing daily records, drawings of plants, specimens of animals and cultural artifacts and descriptions of the types of economies along their routes and the conditions of vegetation and their accessibility have become a treasure trove for environmental historians.[35]

Where the botanical materials that they collected had the potential for commercial production, the explorers reported on traditional methods for processing the crops as well as the farmers' knowledge about the crops. This was particularly relevant during the Zambezi exploration. During the expedition, Livingstone had developed a 'friendly relationship with Sekeleta,' the monarch, to obtain support for his plans to introduce legitimate trade as opposed to the slave trade that had devastated the region.[36] The Zambezi mission, in particular, was eager to identify places where cotton was grown by the local African populations, hoping that it would promote commercial opening up of the region. Collecting botanical specimens for European herbaria required providing geographical place names, descriptions of the topography and the types of soils and often the local uses of the plant specimens. Using such information, analysts at the herbaria could compare sample variations and their distribution.[37]

It is significant that the European travelers attempted to compare their observations of nature with the European environments with which they were most familiar.[38] The reports presented systematic observations of the African societies encountered, often revealing personal opinions and prejudices. Even so, not all reports were negative. We have already mentioned how David Livingstone befriended African leaders to facilitate his exploration of the Zambezi in preparation for potential future European settlements of the Shire Highlands. When missionaries arrived in a remote region, they were among the first Europeans to interact with African societies, particularly providing medical services. Besides doing humanitarian work and 'civilizing missions,' the missionaries, just like other European explorers, made significant contributions to 'scientific geography' by making accurate records of African environments, fixing the geodesic locations of important geographical features such as the courses of rivers and lakes, describing trade routes, and mapping landscapes and important geographical features. Every effort was made to identify regions where local communities planted commercial crops and to study the land potential for crop production.[39] The missionaries reported through their letters to missionary offices in Europe as well as in journals—enriching the knowledge of the socio-ecological systems of pre-colonial East Africa.[40] Of greatest interest was the hypothesis of environmental desiccation postulated by David Livingstone and other explorers.

Environmental desiccation hypothesis

The information collected by missionaries and explorers influenced some theories of environmental changes in Africa. The hypothesis of progressive environmental desiccation began to attract scholarly attention by 1900. The theory was reinforced by the prevalence of extended and frequent droughts.[41] David Livingstone based his postulation of the desiccation of the African environment on oral sources and his field observations of dry streams and shrinking and drying lakes in East and Central Africa. Presuming that the African environment was gradually drying up led to speculation about whether African populations could survive or perhaps even die out. Alfred Sharpe[42] added that East Africa might be undergoing desiccation.

While there was no scientific basis for these predictions, those endorsing the postulations alleged that they were reinforced by African people's reliance on rainmakers. The rainmakers supposedly possessed supernatural powers to make rains to fall. The European argument was that if the environment were not drying up, the rainmakers would not be needed. It was a popular theory and believed to be true, although it was unsubstantiated by journal accounts.

The first source of the desiccation theory is the environmental and climatic data collected by missionaries at their stations and on their travels. The second source is found in their reports of indigenous knowledge of environmental and climate change. For example, David Livingstone relied on the terminology of landscapes used by African people, such as 'dry river valleys,' which he interpreted to mean that waters had flowed through them earlier and had since ceased. Nonetheless, no historical chronology was given of when such changes might have occurred. Conversely, African societies also associated the drying up of the land with the arrival of white people in their territories—regarding it as a bad omen. The missionaries dismissed the African belief in rainmaking and the connection between the arrival of white people and dry periods as myths. In this context, it is therefore surprising that the information provided by African informants was accepted as accurate about environmental desiccation. The desiccation theory ignored the evidence that the climate of Africa fluctuated between dry and wet episodes, as opposed to describing progressive changes from wetter to drier conditions.[43]

Georgina Endfield and David Nash[44] evaluated the veracity of the theory of desiccation, using original, unpublished sources in the archives of the London Missionary Society. The authors reconstructed the purported environmental changes using the historical chronology in the sources and found no evidence that supported the theory. The authors contend that 'the observational basis of the entire argument for desiccation in Africa may be untenable.'[45] What geographical science lacked in predictive power it therefore gained from observation and spatial analysis. In the next section, we use European textual narratives to reflect on spatial analysis of African environments during the middle and late nineteenth century.

European environmental narratives

The explorers traversed different parts of East Africa—across different geographical spaces, encountering different African communities and often crossing the countries during different seasons of the year.[46] Whereas the explorers provided different analyses in their narratives, perhaps reflecting the purposes of their journeys, we find comparable highlights about the environments they traversed. Different readings of the narratives, unless supported by adequate knowledge of the environments in question, could lead to diverse conclusions about environmental change. Some examples will suffice.

Richard Burton,[47] while crossing the Horn of Africa from the coast of the Red Sea and traversing a hyper-arid environment inland from Zayla, described the environment as barren (Figure 2.1). His visit was during a dry season after the trees had dropped their leaves and the annual grasses had withered away. The boulder-strewn landscape appeared desolate and lacked aesthetic value to the observer. In the second example, Major H. Austin,[48] during his journey across the present-day Turkana region of Kenya, described the country as very stony and uninhabited at the time. These two examples infer that the territories that these travelers explored were arid; however, their dryness had little to do with human activities or recent climate change.

Our next set of examples comes from explorers reporting their observations during dry and wet seasons. Count Sámuel Teleki,[49] on his journey through the Maasai plains in the area of Lake Jibe (north-east of Mount Kilimanjaro), describes the vegetation and the topography surrounding the lake as follows: 'charming ... with *acacia*-woods lining its shores and the rugged heights of the Ugweno mountains forming a back ground; but very dreary was the view on the east of the monotonous bush-clad steppes stretching away.' In the same region, Joseph Thomson[50] traveled from the coast into the interior of East Africa, first during a dry season and again after the rains, describing the variations of the environment and its spatial-temporal characteristics. He found the dry season objectionable, while the region appealed to his aesthetic senses after the rains. In his report of the dry season, he refers to the landscape as 'dreary' topography, except for the presence of large *Acacia* trees and *Euphorbia* alternating with open grassland, which 'at this period formed yellow fields of burnt up grass, making us wonder where the [cattle] herds ... get sufficient sustenance to keep them alive.' A few days later, he entered an area that had recently received rain. The vegetation made a positive impact on his judgment:

> Curiously enough there is more variety of flowers in these wastes than in the richer lowlands. In the tropics, where everything is favorable to a luxuriant [vegetation] growth, nature usually spends her energies in producing an infinite variety in [plant] form and green ... foliage.

These readings of landscapes during differed seasons were quite revealing about European visions of pre-colonial African environments.

Our previous discussion showed how David Livingstone presented lakes drying up, seasonal rivers and widespread vegetation dieback as evidence in support of the desiccation theory. However, the reports we consulted contain few examples that might be used as proof of environmental desiccation. The purported evidence lacks descriptions of cause and effect factors. The closest is the observation by Count Teleki when his caravan visited Lake Stefanie (Figure 2.1). He remarks:

> Close to the northern edge of the lake were numerous dead trees, and from the tortuous windings of a brook flowing into it at the north-eastern corner—stretched up the bleached skeletons of many others, but [what happened to them]... was somewhat of a puzzle.[51]

Count Teleki did not attempt to interpret the causes of the mass tree deaths. Two plausible explanations present themselves. The first suggests that the water of the lake had dried, causing mass mortality of the vegetation. This is a common ecological phenomenon. The second explanation is that if the lake water were salty, seepage into the soil around the lake would kill the plants that were not salt tolerant. This might provide a chronological history of environmental change—if analyzed with the site showing expansion and contraction of the lake waters, which would reflect alternating dry and wet cycles and mass mortality and regeneration of vegetation. By studying changes in water levels and shifts in the composition of woody and herbaceous vegetation, a history of vegetation change could be reconstructed.[52]

Earlier, however, Count Teleki[53] gave a graphic description of the landscape and topography of the plains on his way to Mount Kenya:

> [the] scene spread out before us was of character, it was wanting in charm, for the fresh green woods of the valley ... were untenanted by any living creature.... On the wide plain the hot sun seemed to have withered up every trace of vegetation.

The text depicts the traveler's impression of the environment during a dry season. A reader might note that the judgment of the environment was based on Teleki's failure to observe any wildlife, which he would have hunted. His claim that there were no living creatures was an exaggeration. Although the dried-up vegetation would indicate the absence of rainfall, it did not imply environmental desiccation.

While journeying through the central Rift Valley of the Maasai steppe, Teleki[54] gives two other accounts of the changing landscapes. First, he describes the grasslands, and, second, the cultivated landscapes of the Mount Kenya region. The text of the first narrative states:

> The beginning of the next march was across a district.... Undulating ground ... fairly sprinkled with *acacias*, but with little grass.... As we advanced the district became more and more undulating, the trees rarer ... while the grass became more and more luxuriant.

The landscapes varied, shifting between wooded landscapes to grasslands. In each case, the travelers seem to be inspired by what they see. In the second report, the travelers use metaphors that point to European landscapes. Count Teleki[55] states: 'we had passed through Districts [in the Kikuyu country] so carefully and systematically cultivated [landscapes] that we might have been in Europe.' The text is a clear indication of the advanced nature of African cultivation systems before the region came under British colonial rule. The greater part of the narratives does not support the environmental desiccation theory popularized in Europe. The journals contain detailed descriptions of the potential of the environments traversed. We provide a general viewpoint.

Using the journal reports, we can compare the accounts of several of the travelers (both missionaries and explorers) and make deductions about environmental conditions at the time of reporting. As much as possible, the explorers traveled along the roads and routes that the African people used. Johan Tyrrell,[56] for example, explains how the observations were made: 'Travellers using narrow winding tracts traveling on foot recorded significantly more detail than others.' Some of the narratives could therefore have referred to the same regions, crossed by several of the travelers at different times. While the political situation in some cases had changed, consistent presentations of the African environments can be recognized. In these reports, the physical and biological features of the environment were described in detail, including the colors of the foliage of vegetation and growth patterns across landscapes.

Comparative textual narratives of environmental change

The reports provide a comparative European view of African environments, settlements and types of agriculture, indicating the fertility of the soil, among others. Explorers started from different points, moving from the coast of East Africa into the interior. The regions they traversed varied from tropical forests to deserts and savanna grasslands, and from marshes, swamps, river valleys and thickly vegetated bushlands to desert borders, to mention but a few.[57] We may use a few more examples here.

James MacQueen[58] describes the vegetation of the area in the metaphors of European landscapes: 'the vegetation around had completely changed, and the trees and foliage here were like those of Europe, and continued ranges of hills began to cover the country in all direction.' The European landscape represents an image of a perfectly managed land. Others described varied landscapes paying more attention to the geographical features in their reports, from which one would be able to deduce if the described features might be designated as undesirable or not. Bushy landscapes that impaired the passage of the travelers were described in negative terms and open, grassy areas in favorable terms.

Some of the environments were compared with paintings by famous European painters. William Walter Augustine Fitzgerald,[59] while journeying from the coast into the interior, commented: 'For half-an-hour's tramp the country was again park like in appearance, with short grass and clumps of bush.' The 'park like' evokes images of European landscapes. It represents the aesthetic aspect of nature to the European imagination and thoughts. Further into the interior, the observation of Joseph Thomson[60] is even more revealing. 'The scenery around Pambete is picturesque in the extreme. Seen from a distance, the place has the appearance of a pretty landscape modelled in relief and set in a niche cut out of the surrounding mountain.' Here, we have an interpretation of the landscape through the eyes of a painter doing a painting. Sometimes, the explorers asked readers to imagine what they were observing, signifying that there was no better way of appreciating what was reported. We return to the report of Joseph Thomson.[61] He states, 'Let the reader figure to himself a forest of the densest nature, formed of colossal trees, with deep green shady foliage, among which that prince of African trees the *mparamusi* or yellow-wood ... rises prominently in stately grace.' By inviting his readers to 'imagine,' the author helps them to create an impression of nature, in which the central feature is an indigenous tree species that he has christened a 'prince' of the tropical environment. The narratives of African cultural landscapes were even more imaginative.

Narratives of cultural landscapes

Geographical explorers provided geodesic locations of landscape features that had earlier been reported by other travelers. For example, James A. Grant[62] reports on Stanley's verification of Speke's discoveries to locate geographical features using the coordinates provided by Speke. Because the report mentions specific land features, its accuracy can be confirmed by comparing it with what was reported earlier by Speke. We can retrieve a greater deal of information from the reports on cultural landscapes, including details of land with farming potential.

We will use an example here from the report of Dr. Livingstone[63] who describes the farming systems of communities. In the country bordering the Ruvuma River, in present-day Tanzania, he reports: 'We now came along through a country comparatively free of wood.' Other descriptions of landscapes showed evidence of human activities such as smelting of metals and crop cultivation. He continues: 'The rest of the country, where not cultivated, is covered with grass the seed stalks about knee deep.' Along the routes were also 'enclaves of cultivation' where the communities cultivated crops.[64] On the Zambezi expedition, Livingstone[65] described the land's agricultural potential. He writes: 'The soil formed by the disintegration of igneous rocks is amazingly fertile, and the people are all fond of agriculture. I have seen maize of nearly the same size of grain as that sold by the Americans.' In another case, he describes an ingenious method for maintaining soil fertility:

> All the people are engaged at present in making mounds six or eight feet square, ... from two to three feet height. The sods in places not before hoed are separated from the soil beneath and collected into flattened heaps, the grass uppermost; when dried, fire is applied and slow combustion goes on; most of the products of the burning being retained in the ground, much of the soil incinerated. The final preparation if effected by the men digging up the subsoil round the mound, passing each hoe full into the left hand, where it pulverizes, and then thrown onto the heap. It is thus virgin soil on top of the ashes and burned ground of the original heap, very clear of weeds. At present many mounds have beans and maize about four inches deep.... These are watered by hand and calabash, and kept growing till the rains set in, when early crop is secured.

In his reconstruction of the history of pre-colonial farming systems in the region of Lake Nyasa (present-day Lake Malawi), Juhani Koponen[66] describes how the Matengo people developed a sophisticated indigenous farming system called the 'pit system.'

> A whole hillside appeared to have been dug full of pits. On closer inspection this was ... but a skillful combination of horizontal contour ridges with diagonal up and down ridges composed of a mixture of

grass and earth. Nothing was planted in the pit area, but weeds and grass from the ridges were thrown into it to form a compost. In the following year the process was reversed: what had been a pit now became a ridge. This prevented erosion even on the steepest slopes and could be continued for years before a fallow was needed.

The texts remark on the fertility of the soils and farming methods. Some of the travelers' notes are discussed here. About soil fertility on the east coast, Joseph Thomson[67] observes: 'The soil is extremely fertile, and well cultivated; it yields all the varied products of the East Coast and supports a large population of well-to-do natives of mixed Wazaramo and Waswahili.' The different cultivation methods made a significant impression on travelers. The methods used for the rich crops grown by various African communities were described as complex and sustainable. There was evidence of soil-water conservation, rotation of crops and maintenance of soil fertility. Where the soil fertility was low, compost pitting was common, and legumes and grains were cultivated in rotation to maintain soil fertility in ways comparable to contemporary practices.[68]

Rev. Dr Laws[69] describes soil fertility on the western side of Lake Nysa (Lake Malawi), supported by evidence of good crop harvest by local communities. He reports good pasture conditions around settlements, where people kept sheep and goats in large numbers. He also notes that the people of the area lacked fuel, which forced them to dig out the roots of dried maize plants for cooking and lighting. He confirms that trees were scarce in the area. Was this natural or evidence of human overexploitation? Let us consider the evidence. First, Laws indicates that human settlements were large consisting of small villages. Second, the villages were densely clustered on hillslopes and had granaries where food was stored. The two facts indicate that people had been living in the area for the long term. Farming appeared to be a well-established economic enterprise. However, the evidence that the villages were settled on hillslopes suggests other possible interpretations. Did the higher ground offer security, or did people live there for health reasons, to avoid mosquitoes in the lower lands during the wet seasons? One would suppose that the hills were better wooded than the grassy plain where crops were cultivated. If trees were scarce, as Laws stated, what happened to the vegetation on the hillsides? We can only speculate about what possibly happened. Apart from Dr Laws, other travelers did not remark on the scarcity of trees and/or a lack of fuel.

What we read from other reports is that the East African region was highly varied in vegetation cover—from open grasslands to dense forest, each described in relation to patterns of human settlements. From the diversity of crops grown, one would deduce the fertility of the soil, on which the European observers often remarked. We also notice from many of the reports that communities managed different types of livestock—varying between sheep, goats and cattle.[70]

Except where occurrences of warfare were reported, the human settlements were generally described as nucleated or scattered. In places that were heavily vegetated by woody cover, villages were found in open clearings, which were also sites of crop cultivation. Usually, large herds of cattle were observed in open grassy plains but not in the thickly wooded areas.[71] The reports, illustrated by photographs or sketch drawings, depict agreeable environmental conditions.[72]

The oral history of the African communities told about the environment as it had been. In her book *Imaging Serengeti*, Bender Shetler[73] describes the pre-colonial environment of the Serengeti ecosystem, remarking that the Serengeti was landscapes of memory, which among others featured the social and political imaging of societies that had long been removed. Similarly, Yusufu Lawi[74] reports how from oral history one can build a picture of what sustained the pre-colonial environment of Africa. He shows how human decisions and actions transformed natural landscapes and made them more appealing to human habitation.

Other reports presented evidence of political conflicts and showed the general distribution of the population. In his letter from the Albert Nyanza, the southern side of the Victoria Nyanza covering Tanganyika (modern-day Tanzania), Henry Morton Stanley[75] describes the vegetation changes using three significant indicators. First, the landscape he crossed was a grassy valley with scattered *Acacia* trees. The second indicator was that the season of the year was dry. Third, he describes an environment where tribal warfare had affected settlement patterns. On the evidence of abandoned settlements, he conjectures that the area was thickly populated before disruption by the war. The evidence of tribal warfare is sufficient explanation for the abandonment.

The missionary and traveler, W.P. Johnson,[76] reports his experience in the same region east of Lake Nyasa from where Morton Stanley had reported earlier. He indicates that settlements were located on hilltops for defensive purposes. From an ecological perspective, the environment was described as 'very rich in its wide grassy glades.' The burnt-out and abandoned settlements were evidence of tribal warfare. Invading groups such as the Ngoni who originated from southern Africa appear to have had the greatest impact on southern and southwestern and East Africa in the mid-nineteenth century.[77] Alfred Sharpe[78] reported passing through land occupied by the Ngoni and mentions that the regions that bordered them had been depopulated. In these areas, regular burning of the grass left the area open for crop cultivation. The travelers arrived during a rainy season when rain was 'incessant.' The travelers were struck by the 'rolling downs, covered with grasses.' This symbolized the English countryside with which the travelers were familiar. The presence of cattle implied that the environment was free from the tsetse fly.

In the Ankole plateau in central Africa, travelers reported open 'grassy downs' with large herds of long-horned Hima cattle. Toward the Bunyoro, the villagers were cultivators. The climate was described as healthy and the soil fertile for crop growing. The land was generally covered by forests.[79] This region was crisscrossed by European travelers, who described a land with large populations of wildlife. Its beauty and fertility were the subject of much discussion among the explorers.[80] Grass burning was common. In the main, burning was intentional and carried out during the dry season to 'cure' old grass growth and control pests such as ticks and the tsetse fly. Most grass species in East Africa are stimulated by periodic fires. In depopulated areas, the reverse occurs: the bush cover increases and the tsetse returns.[81] This was the case during the last two decades of the nineteenth century when East Africa experienced major political and economic shocks that sent the pastoral and agro-pastoral economies to the edge of collapse.

Ecological and demographic collapse in the late nineteenth century

In the late nineteenth and early twentieth centuries, East Africa experienced social, political and economic upheavals. Disasters came in waves and in diverse types. It began with the spread of epidemics of *trypanosomiasis*—sleeping sickness—in and around the lake regions of central and eastern Africa. Then came smallpox, a devastating disease spread by caravans and the slave trade, and warriors who raided their neighbors.[82] Cholera also had spread to the interior along the slave and trade routes between 1836 and 1870. The history of cholera in East Africa has been described by Dr. James Christie,[83] tracing the routes through which the disease spread from the coast to the interior. Although the data on fatalities are unavailable or scanty, the deaths by the epidemics were recalled locally as the worst ever experienced.[84]

The litany of disasters broke the backbone of the African pastoral and agricultural societies.[85] By the end of that period, the previously most fertile land with a large human population would be described as 'desolate' following processes that broke human and environmental harmony. The collapse of human and livestock populations implies that few people were left to cultivate the land. The concomitant encroachment of bushlands—ideal habitats for tsetse fly—literally drove the few surviving humans from many millions of acres of land.[86]

In the footsteps of these disasters followed an outbreak of bovine pleuropneumonia. The Maasai named the period *emutai*—the end of, or termination of cattle pastoralism—in 1883.[87] Joseph Thomson[88] described the scenes of devastation in his book *Through Masai land*. As if that crisis were not enough, the last decade of the nineteenth century saw the rinderpest epizootic sweep across the Horn, eastern and southern Africa.[89] The rinderpest virus (*Tortoboris*) is spread through the air and is highly contagious.[90] The rinderpest destroyed herds of cattle, the main source of livelihood of the pastoralists, and brought hunger and famine. The biological catastrophe which so comprehensively struck East Africa stuck in the African mind—the period is known by various names depending on the local dialects. In Oromo it is known as *ciinna*, which refers to the end of time.[91] The ramifications of the disasters are not only expressed in linguistic terms, but they also reflect survivors' memories of a collapsed social, economic and political system.[92]

The demographic collapse caused the vegetation of the region to shift from open grass savanna to bushy thickets, expanding the home range of the tsetse fly, which remained a threat for decades (see Chapter 8). The effect on pastoralists and the agricultural communities was devastating.[93] The period also saw outbreaks of locust plagues[94] that destroyed the croplands, further aggravating famine conditions (Chapter 9). The multiple sequences of events had caused irreparable damage to the economies of East Africa by the time the region was divided up into colonial spheres of influence.[95]

In Chapter 3, we describe the main characteristics of scientific research infrastructure and its chronological establishment that anchored imperial science in the three East African colonies of Kenya, Tanganyika and Uganda.

Notes

1 Jarosz, L., 'Constructing the Dark Continent: Metaphor as geographic representation of Africa,' *Geografiska Annaler: Series B, Human Geography* 74.2 (1992): 105–115.
2 Naylor, S. and Ryan, J.R., *New spaces of exploration: Geographies of discovery in the twentieth century* (London: I.B. Tauris, 2010), 2.
3 Bridges, R., 'Explorers' texts and the problem of reactions by non-literate peoples: Some nineteenth century East African examples,' *Studies in Travel Writing* 2.1 (1998): 65–84.
4 Howard, A.M. and Shain, R.M., 'Introduction: African history and social space in Africa,' in Howard, A.M. and Shain, R.M. (eds.), The *spatial factor in African history: The relationship of the social, material and perceptual* (Leiden: Brill, 2005), 4.
5 Kopenen, J., *People and production in late precolonial Tanzania: History and structures* (Stockholm: Scandinavian Institute of African Studies, 1988), 25.
6 Barnett, C., 'Impure and worldly geography: The Africanist discourse of the Royal Geographical Society, 1831–73,' *Transactions of the Institute of British Geographers* 23.2 (1998): 239–251.
7 Kreike, E., 'The nature-culture trap of the late 20th century: Global paradigms of the environmental change in Africa and beyond,' *Global Environment* 1.1 (2008): 114–145.
8 Newbury, D., 'Precolonial Burundi and Rwanda: Local loyalties regional royalties,' *International Journal of African Historical Studies* 34.2 (2001): 255–314.
9 Ibid.
10 Ambler, C.H., 'Population movements, social formation and exchange: Central Kenya in the nineteenth century,' *International Journal of African Historical Studies* 18.2 (1985): 201–222.
11 Swynnerton, R.J.M., 'Agricultural advances in East Africa,' *African Affairs* 61.244 (1962): 201–215.
12 Allan, W., *The African husbandman*; New introduction by H. Tilley (Münster: LIT Verlag, 2004), 5–6.

13 Talal, A., *Anthropology and the colonial encounter* (London: Ithaca Press, 1973).
14 Concklin, H.C., 'The study of shifting cultivation,' *Current Anthropology* 2.1 (1961): 27–61.
15 Hjort, A., 'Traditional land use in marginal drylands,' *Ecological Bulletins* 24 (1976): 43–53.
16 Cooper, F. and Packard, R.M. (eds.), *International development and the social sciences: Essays on the history and politics of knowledge* (University of California Press, 1997), 4.
17 Londsdale, J. and Berman, B., 'Coping with the contradictions: The development of the colonial state in Kenya, 1895–1914,' *Journal of African History* 20.4 (1979): 487–505, 494.
18 Stauder, J., *The blue and the green: A cultural ecological history of an Arizona ranching community* (Nevada: University of Nevada Press, 2016).
19 Rivera, N., Calderon-Ayala, J., Calle L., Due, S., Gerald, B., Lanas, M., Lualhati, M., Moreno L., Pérez Ana, E., Sylvain, I., Vieira, D. and Armstrong, M., 'Multidisciplinary and multimedia approaches to action-oriented ecology,' *Bulletin of the Ecological Society of America* 91.3 (2010): 313–316.
20 Kreike, 'The nature-culture trap of the late 20th century.'
21 Breitenbach, E., 'Scottish encounters with Africa in the nineteenth century: Accounts of explorers, travelers and missionaries,' in Adogame, A.U. (ed.), *Africa in Scotland, Scotland in Africa: Historical legacies and contemporary hybridities* (Leiden: Brill, 2014), 36
22 Adogame, A.U. and Lawrence, A., 'Africa-Scotland: Exploring historical and contemporary relations in global contexts,' in Adogame, A.U. (ed.), *Africa in Scotland, Scotland in Africa: Historical legacies and contemporary hybridities* (Leiden: Brill, 2014), 6.
23 Johnston, H.H., 'Livingstone as an explorer,' *The Geographical Journal* 41.5 (1913): 423–446.
24 Sharp, A., Murray, J. and Travers, D., 'Livingstone as an explorer: Discussion,' *The Geographical Journal* 41.5 (1913): 446–448.
25 Middleton, D., 'Guide to the publications of the Royal Geographical Society 1830–1892,' *The Geographical Journal* 144.1 (1978): 99–116.
26 Bridges, R., 'Explorers' texts and the problem of reactions by non-literate peoples: Some nineteenth century East African examples,' *Studies in Travel writing* 2.1 (1998): 65–84.
27 Rotberg, Robert I., *Joseph Thomson and the exploration of Africa* (London: Chatto & Windus, 1971).
28 Barnett, 'Impure and worldly geography.'
29 Dristsas, L.S., *The Zambesi expedition, 1858–64: African nature in the British Scientific metropolis*, PhD Thesis (Edinburgh University, 2005).
30 Dristsas, L., 'From Lake Nyasa to Philadelphia: A geography of the Zambesi expedition, 1858–64,' *British Journal for the History of Science* 38.1 (2005): 35–52.
31 Thomson, J., *To central African lakes and back: The narratives of the Royal Geographical Society's East Central African expedition 1878–80, Vol. I* (New York: Frank Cass & Co., 1968), 65.
32 Von Hönel, L, *Discovery of Lakes Rudolf and Stefane: A narrative of count Sameul Teleki's exploring and hunting expedition in eastern equatorial Africa in 1887 and 1888, Vol. 1* (New York: Frank Cass & Co., 1968), 406.
33 Etherington, N.E., 'A false emptiness: How historians may have been misled by early nineteenth century maps of south-eastern Africa,' *Imago Mundi* 56.1 (2004): 67–86.
34 Naylor and Ryan, *New spaces of exploration*, 6.
35 Waller, H., *The last Journals of David Livingstone, in central Africa from eighteen hundred and sixty-five to his death* (New York: Harper & Brothers, publishers, 1875).

36 Dristsas, 'From Lake Nyasa to Philadelphia.'
37 Figueiredo, E., Soares, M., Sibert, G., Smith, G.F. and Faden, R.B., 'The botany of the Cunene-Zambezi expedition with notes on Hugo Baum (1967–1950),' *Bothalia* 39.2 (2009): 185–211.
38 Breitenbach, 'Scottish encounters with Africa in the nineteenth century,' 23.
39 Ndille, R., 'Missionaries as imperialists: Decolonial subalternity in the missionary enterprise on the coast of Cameroon 1841–1914,' *Sumerianz Journal of Social Science* 1.2 (2018): 51–58.
40 Calhoun, D., 'Colonial collectors: Missionaries botanical and linguistic prospecting in French colonial Africa,' *Canadian Journal of African Studies* 52.2 (2018): 205–228.
41 Grove, R. and, Damodaran, V., 'Imperialism intellectual networks, and environmental change: Origins and evolution of Global Environmental history, 1676–2000, Part 1,' *Economic and Political Weekly* 41.41 (2006): 4345–4354.
42 Sharpe, Alfred, 'The geography and resources of British central Africa,' *The Geographical Journal* 7.4 (1896): 366–387.
43 For ancient historical views, see Oba, G., *Climate change adaptations in Africa: An historical ecology* (London: Routledge, 2014).
44 Endfield, G.H. and Nash, D.J., 'Drought, desiccation and discourse: Missionary correspondence and the nineteenth century climate change in central southern Africa,' *The Geographical Journal* 168.1 (2002): 33–47; Nash, D.J. and Endfield, G.H., '19th century climate chronology for the Kalahari region of central southern Africa derived from missionary correspondence,' *International Journal of Climatology* 22 (2002): 821–841.
45 Endfield and Nash, 'Drought, desiccation and discourse,' 42, 43, 44, 45.
46 Beinart, W., 'Men, science, travel and nature in the eighteenth and nineteenth century Cape,' *Journal of Southern African Studies* 24.4 (1998): 775–799.
47 Burton, R., *First footsteps in East Africa* (London: Routledge & Kegan Paul, 1986).
48 Austin, H.H., 'Journeys to the north of Uganda. II. Lake Rudolf,' *The Geographical Journal* 14.2 (1899): 148–152.
49 Von Hönel, *Discovery of Lakes Rudolf and Stefane, Vol. I*, 90.
50 Thomson, *To central African lakes and back*, 226, 239.
51 Von Hönel, *Discovery of Lakes Rudolf and Stefanie, Vol. I.*, 159.
52 Ryner, M.A., Bonnefille, R., Holmgren, K. and Muzuka, A., 'Vegetation changes in Empakaai Crater, northern Tanzania, at 14,800–9,300 cal Yr BP,' *Review of Palaeobotany and Palynology* 14.3 (2006): 163–174.
53 Von Hönel, L., *Discovery of Lakes Rudolf and Stefane: A narrative of count Samuel Teleki's exploring and hunting expedition in eastern equatorial Africa in 1887 and 1888, Vol. II* (New York: Frank Cass & Co., 1968), 60.
54 Von Hönel, *Discovery of Lakes Rudolf and Stefanie, Vol. I.*, 365.
55 Ibid., 382.
56 Tyrrell, J.G., 'Observations of environment and vegetation by early European travelers in East Africa,' *Geografiska Annaler, Series B, Human Geography* 67.1 (1985): 29–34.
57 Archer, G.F. and Williams, G.C., 'Recent exploration and survey in north of British East Africa,' *The Geographical Journal* 42.5 (1913): 421–430.
58 MacQueen, James, 'Kilimanjaro and the White Nile,' *Journal of the Royal Geographical Society of London* 30 (1860): 128–136.
59 Fitzgerald, W.W.A., *Travels in the coastlands of British East Africa and the islands of Zanzibar and Pemba* (London: Chapman & Hall, 1898), 47.
60 Thomson, *To central African lakes and back*.
61 Ibid., 144.
62 Grant, J.A., 'Stanley's verification of Speke's discoveries,' *Journal of the American Geographical Society of New York* 7 (1875): 311–323.

63 Waller, *The last journals of David Livingstone*, 113.
64 Austen, R.A., 'Patterns of development in nineteenth-century East Africa,' *African Historical Studies* 4.3 (1971): 645–657.
65 Livingstone, D., 'Explorations into the interior of Africa,' *Journal of the Royal Geographical Society of London* 27 (1857): 349–387.
66 Kopenen, *People and production in late precolonial Tanzania*, 228.
67 Thomson, *To central African lakes and back*, 105.
68 Kopenen, J., *People and production in late precolonial Tanzania*, 227, 228.
69 Laws, Dr, 'Journey along part of the western side of lake Nyassa, in 1878,' *Proceedings of the Royal Geographical Society and Monthly Record of Geography* 1.5 (1879): 305–324.
70 Chauncy, Maples, 'Masasi and the Rovma District in East Africa,' *Proceedings of the Royal Geographical Society and Monthly Record of Geography* 2.6 (1880): 337–353.
71 Beringer, Otto L., 'Notes on the country between Lake Nyasa and Victoria Nyanza,' *The Geographical Journal* 21.1 (1903): 25–36.
72 Clendennen, G.W., *David Livingstone on the Zambesi: Letters to John Washington, 1861–1863* (Munger Africana notes, California Institute of Technology, 1976).
73 Bender, Jan Shetler, *Imaging Serengeti: A history of landscape memory in Tanzania from earliest times to the present* (Athens: Ohio University Press, 2007), 31.
74 Lawi, Y.Q., 'Tanzania's Operation Vijiji and local ecological consciousness: The case of Eastern Iraqwland, 1974–1976,' *Journal of African History* 48.1 (2007): 69–93.
75 Stanley, Henry M., 'Letter from H.M. Stanley on his journey from the Albert Nyanza to the southern side of Victoria Nyanza,' *Proceedings of the Royal Geographical Society and Monthly Record of Geography* 11.12 (1889): 720–726.
76 Johnson, W.P., 'Seven years' travels in the region East of Lake Nyassa,' *Proceedings of the Royal Geographical Society and Monthly Record of Geography* 6.9 (1884): 512–536.
77 King, K., 'The Kenya Maasai and the protest phenomenon, 1900–1960,' *Journal of African History* 12.1 (1971): 117–137; Oba, G., *Herder warfare in East Africa: A social and spatial history* (Winwick: White Horse Press, 2017).
78 Sharpe, A., 'A journey through the country lying between the Shire and Loangwa River,' *Proceedings of the Royal Geographical Society and Monthly Record of Geography* 12.3 (1890): 744–751.
79 Bright, R.G.T., 'Survey and exploration in the Ruwenzori and Lake region, central Africa,' *Geographical Journal* 34.2 (1909): 128–153.
80 Vannutelli, L. and Citerni, C., 'A record of exploration in north-east Africa: Second Spendizione B'ottego L'omo,' *The Geographical Journal* 15.1 (1900): 50–52.
81 Ndawula-Senyimba, M.S., 'Some aspects of the ecology of Themeda triandra,' *East African Agricultural and Forestry Journal* 38.1 (1972): 83–93.
82 Kjeshus, Helge, *Ecology control and economic development in East African history: The case of Tanganyika 18550–1950* (London: James Currey, 1996).
83 Christie, James, *Cholera epidemics in East Africa* (New York: Macmillan, 1876); Hartwig, Gerald W., 'Economic consequences of long-distance trade in East Africa: The disease factor,' *African Studies Review* 18.2 (1975): 63–73.
84 Kopenen, *People and production in late precolonial Tanzania*, 663, 665.
85 Giblin, J.L., 'East coast fever in socio-historical context: A case study from Tanzania,' *International Journal of African Historical Studies* 23.3 (1990): 401–421.
86 Phillips, J., *Agriculture and ecology in Africa: A study of actual and potential development south of the Sahara* (London: Faber & Faber, 1959), 60; Vail, Leroy, 'Ecology and history: The example of Eastern Zambia,' *Journal of Southern African Studies* 3.2 (1977): 129–155.

87 Waller, R., '*Emutai*: Crisis and response in Maasailand, 1884–1904,' in Johnson, D.H. and Anderson, D.M. (eds.), *The ecology of survival: Case studies from northeast African history* (Oxford: University of Oxford, 1988), 72–112.
88 Thomson, J., *Through the Masai land: A journey of exploration, among the snow-clad volcanic mountains and strange tribes of eastern equatorial Africa* (London: Sampson Low, 1885).
89 Mack, R., 'The great African cattle plague epidemic of the 1890s,' *Tropical Animal Health and Production* 2 (1970): 210–219.
90 Jacobs, Nancy J., *Environment, power, and justice: A south African history* (Cambridge: Cambridge University Press, 2003), 101.
91 Tiki, W. and Oba, G., '*Ciinna*: The Borana Oromo narration of the 1890s great rinderpest epizootic in north eastern Africa,' *Journal of Eastern African Studies* 3.3 (2009): 479–508.
92 Ford, John, *The role of the trypanosomiases in African ecology: A study of the tsetse fly problem* (London: Clarendon Press, Oxford University Press, 1971), 141/42.
93 Smith, G.E., 'From the Victoria Nyanza to Kilimanjaro,' *The Geographical Journal* 29.3 (1907): 249–269.
94 Phoofolo, Pule, 'Face to face with famine: The BaSatho and the rinderpest 1897–1899,' *Journal of Southern African Studies* 29.2 (2003): 503–527.
95 Håkansson, T., 'Regional political ecology and intensive cultivation in pre-colonial and colonial south Pare, Tanzania,' *International Journal of African Historical Studies* 41.3 (2008): 433–459.

3 Imperial scientific infrastructure
Science for development, 1848–1960s

Imperial scientific infrastructure describes the support knowledge systems, financial, technology and official policy on which science operates,[1] particularly for the purpose of promoting development. Emmanuel Kreike,[2] in his work in Namibia, highlights the ways in which human actions influence the 'architecture' of nature, in the form of relationships between environmental infrastructure and human agencies. He submits that 'environmental infrastructure is not confined to the realm of culture' alone, but includes changes in agricultural landscapes, grazing lands and soil works, all of which are exploited to meet human food requirements. Environmental infrastructure may be modified according to political, economic or ecological events. The infrastructure also influences how application of science was motivated by the 'big politics' of resource exploitation, with the aim of 'environmental control and the governmentality of subject' peoples in the colonies. Nevertheless, the putative political objectives of applying science for solving development problems has changed over time.[3] As a product of the metropole, science examines the periphery colonies through the particular lens of testing European ideas of development,[4] with colonial scientists making predictions (using either deductive or inductive reasoning) to guide the planning and implementation of development initiatives.

Equally important to understand is that the application of imperial science did not expect African societies to make useful contributions to support their own welfare, even though they were the subject of investigation. Early attitudes were that Africans needed European science in order to progress. Robert W. Steel captures these European viewpoints eloquently:

> Africans need our expertise, our technical knowledge and our skill, and they also deserve our understanding and our sympathy as they face problems that are almost certainly incapable of solution, certainly in the foreseeable future, unless they have the fullest help and co-operation, scientific as well as financial, of developed and more affluent nations of the world such as our own.[5]

46 *Empire, science, society and development*

Regarding Steel's observation, opinions might vary between African peoples and colonial officials on two counts. First, we have presented evidence earlier (Chapter 2) that the pre-colonial African communities were self-sufficient in terms of food production. Second, colonial empires ignored the knowledge of African people, while attempting to bring about development under the hubris of science. In addressing these issues this chapter aims at describing events historical ecology of development in East Africa as follows: (1) pioneer research; (2) the First World War years; (3) the economic depressions of the 1930s; (4) the Second World War years; (5) the post-war years; and (6) the post-independence period. We present brief discussions of each of these periods in turn.

Pioneer research, 1848–1913

Science, as a 'service to the empire,' was a vehicle for generating wealth, according to Joseph Banks,[6] whose vision was the integration of science with political ventures in the colonies. By linking the application of science to the 'cumbersome' colonial machinery, Banks recommended the building of research infrastructure in the colonies. As a leading scientist himself, president of the British Royal Society, and with wide networks among European countries, he emphasized the beneficial use of science as a cosmopolitan vehicle to benefit most of humanity. The European colonial visions for development were varied.

For the French, the goal was to conduct exploratory scientific missions to document and make inventories of the flora and fauna in the colonies, often with the aim of supplying specimens to botanical gardens and zoos in France. This approach changed following the First World War, when the interest became what Van Beusekom[7] calls *mise en valeur* (or 'development and improvement'), when the French focused on food production using new scientific methods. French researchers acknowledged the function of colonial science as a 'civilizing mission,' thereby separating colonial sciences needed for developing the colonies and those that targeted exportable products from the colonies to France.[8] The French were aware that 'science was ever changing'—implying that science and development in the colonies were largely 'experimental,' changing from one time period to another, including the ways in which science might be applied to promote food production among African farming societies.

In comparison, the Germans, in their East African colony of Tanganyika, approached research from two perspectives in what Andrew Zimmerman calls 'the binary option': namely to apply research to nature and to the cultures of the peoples in the colony. The view of the German researchers was that local cultures did not transform nature but co-existed with it. To achieve their purpose of working with both nature and the African people, the Germans sent expeditions to conduct scientific surveys of local soils, collect crop seeds, establish research stations, and understand the cultures of the African peoples. German East Africa received funds subsidized by German scientific societies to the tune of £7,500 per year—a huge sum at that time.[9]

Conversely, the long-term goal of the British Empire was to prioritize the extraction of surplus produce in the East African colonies of Kenya and Uganda for the benefit of the metropole.[10] British pioneers established the African Association which renewed interest in discovering and exploring the interior of the African continent.[11] By the late nineteenth century, Sir H. Rawlinson and others had established the African Exploration Fund to facilitate the journeys of early travelers in the continent. The 'Exploration of East Africa' expeditions (1848–1876) were sponsored by the Royal Geographical Society and produced the earliest maps with accurate geodesic references for important geographical features. This was the beginning of the field of 'scientific geography.'[12]

For the British, the relationship between science and empire reflected an evolution—at times, they shifted the balance of resource allocations between science and development.[13] This was until Joseph Chamberlain became Secretary of State for the colonies in 1895 and implemented changes in colonial policies towards development. Even so, funding was irregular, and was available mostly in response to emergency situations.[14] Initial interests were in medical research which spurred training in tropical diseases in British universities. The first task of the British researchers was to understand the causes of and find cures for diseases that threatened European settlements in the colonies. Their second task was to initiate organized agricultural production.[15] By the 1890s, the extent of imperial scientific research had grown, even though the British Foreign Office had not planned any development schemes, despite Joseph Chamberlain's new policy.[16]

For much of eastern and southern Africa, the 1890s was a calamitous period for both humans and beasts.[17] The environments from which human and livestock populations had been divested became overgrown with bushy vegetation, providing an ideal habitat for tsetse flies—the vector of sleeping sickness in people and *trypanosomiasis* in cattle. British medical research projects received funds between 1895 and 1900 to investigate the strain of the *trypanosomiasis* that had devastated African populations and ruined their economies.[18] Due to this emergency situation, the number of researchers visiting the colonies increased.[19] It was also during this early period (around 1900) that the Society for the Preservation of Wild Fauna was founded.[20]

During this early period (1900), in principle, the British planned to modernize the colonies by uplifting the welfare of African societies; however, in practice, this involved the promotion of mercantile economies through scientific research.[21] In Tanganyika, the Germans established biological and agricultural research stations at Amani and Rugwe in 1902.[22] Five years earlier, a research station had been established at Kwai, but this was later abandoned.[23] Through Frank Stuhlmann, the director of the Amani Institute in 1905, the Germans began gathering information on the peasant economy in Tanganyika as part of their agricultural research.[24] In Kenya, the British established the Scott Agricultural Laboratory at Kabete (later renamed Muguga), near Nairobi, in 1907.[25] In German East Africa, research activities focused on soil erosion control.[26] By 1907, neither the British nor the Germans had completed any concrete development plans for the colonies.[27] Research activities were then sporadic until after the First World War.[28]

The First World War years, 1914–1920s

J.C. Smuts,[29]—then Commander of the Allied armies attacking the German East African forces under the command of General Paul von Lettowvortek—concluded his field observations during the war thus: 'the time is not distant when science will overcome [problems of accessibility], and when central and East Africa will have become one of the most productive and valuable parts of the tropics.' Despite Smuts' optimism, the war years were a period of great economic stress in East Africa. European agricultural staff had volunteered to fight in the war, hence forcing the colonies to shelve their agricultural development plans. Paradoxically, African peasants and herders supplied the bulk of grains and beef for the army and the Carrier Corps, thereby increasing the consumption of local goods.[30] In the German colony of Tanganyika, the Amani research station began processing agricultural products, including wines and spirits that were supplied to the German army.[31]

The period coincided with invasions by locust plagues in 1916 that devastated agriculture and grazing lands across northern Africa, the Sahel zone, East Africa and the Middle East. The result was a famine which became an international issue. The International Institute of Agriculture (based in Rome) mobilized the countries affected to attend a conference on control of the desert locust. This conference did not take place until 1920, when it adopted the International Convention by which the signatory states committed themselves to controlling the migratory locusts[32] (more on this in Chapter 9). Other international research collaborations at this time included soil and vegetation mapping, and investigations on tsetse flies.[33] Frank Leonard Engledow, chairman of the Cambridge School of Agriculture, emphasized that development in the British Empire should be based on science.[34] Nonetheless, by 1918 and 1919, development had still not taken a foothold in the colonies.

On matters of funding, there were disagreements between the Colonial Office in East Africa and the Treasury in London in releasing funds for development in the colonies. The decisions made prioritized livestock disease control, to curb disease transmission to European herds. This proposition was not implemented until 1923.[35] It was for this purpose that

Sir Robert Coryndon, the Governor of Uganda, proposed establishing a veterinary office to advise the governments of Uganda, Kenya and Tanganyika on the control of livestock diseases. In Kenya, the focus was on the Maasai land. According to Archibald Church,[36] if their country was to be used for stock breeding, '[t]he Masai reserves would no longer specialize in stagnation and continue to be regarded as "human zoos," but would assume a position of great importance in the economies of East Africa.' Under the administration of Sir Donald Cameron (Governor of the Tanganyika Trust Territory), the Maasai were separated from those in Kenya, while on the Tanganyikan side of the border, the agro-pastoral Maasai were detached from the nomadic Maasai.[37] During this period, research returned to being station-based.

Station based research

A major purpose in establishing research stations in the three colonies (Kenya, Tanganyika and Uganda) was to conduct research under controlled conditions[38] (Figure 3.1). It was the practical work on soil erosion control that gained pre-eminence in terms of funding and political commitment by the colonial governments.[39] Earlier, soil erosion had been investigated by Gillman, a professional engineer who had worked on the German railway lines in Tanganyika, where he learnt a great deal about soil and water conservation. Using his geographical knowledge, he was probably the first to argue for large-scale development.[40]

In Tanganyika, research progress had not been smooth under the British mandate.[41] Archibald Church[42] highlighted the lack of funding which resulted in neglect of the Amani Research Institute—it had been a premier institution whose research findings had contributed significantly to growing scientific knowledge in East Africa. However, the institute fell into a derelict condition after the British takeover and the station was temporarily abandoned in 1922 due to a lack of funding. An estimated annual budget of £20,000 was required to run the research station, but British colonial authorities did not want to commit to supporting the project. Archibald Church[43] attributed this failure to the 'appalling lack of appreciation of the function of scientific research in development.' This was despite efforts made by Lord Milner, and those who succeeded him in the office of the Secretary of State, to raise funds to save Amani. Of the total sum of £100,000 requested, the station was allocated a paltry £2,000 per year. Further, Mpwapwa in Tanganyika, a veterinary research station that had made important contributions to research on animal diseases and pasture management, was closed for lack of funds.[44]

During the post-war years (1926 and 1927), the Amani station was revived under the British mandate for herbaria collections in collaboration with Kew Gardens, and building a depository for East African flora. It was later (1920s) reassigned to investigate the ecology of coffee plantations and

50 Empire, science, society and development

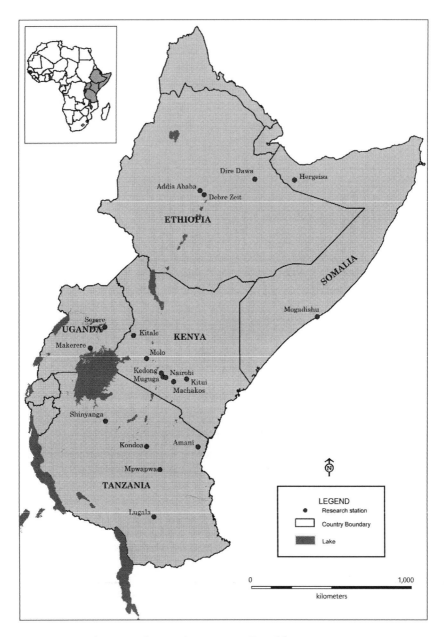

Figure 3.1 Distributions of research stations in East Africa.

various insect pests affecting crops.[45] In 1927, the Imperial Agricultural Research conference organized in London proposed long-term research by technical staff under a single administration to focus on broad-ranging investigations.[46] Additional agricultural institutions—similar to the one that existed at Amani—were expected to respond to various research needs in the British colonies in East Africa. However, due to a lack of technical capacity, the research on commercial agricultural production had to wait and, instead, research networks were established.

Research networks

The late 1920s was a period in the history of science, during which more scientific organizations were established in East Africa. Throughout the colonies, exploratory scientific assignments were undertaken with the goal of establishing agricultural plantations under European supervision.[47] Particularly in the British colony of Kenya, the settler economy had spurred growth in agricultural research by pioneering scientifically innovative agricultural production methods.[48] In 1925 the Committee of Civil Research in Britain established critical standards for solving practical research problems and sharing information between different disciplines working in agricultural laboratories. By 1926 the cooperation was extended to soil mapping.[49] There were two further developments: the first was the implementation of five-to-ten-year research plans, and the second was further advances in social science research (see Chapter 6). By 1929, the Colonial Development Act enabled colonial governments to make more concerted efforts by reviewing economic policies; in particular, they made a conscious effort to increase the production of raw materials for export.[50] Still, by this date, the establishment of research networks across the colonies—to investigate problems of agricultural production and demonstrate improvements—was not fully established. This coupled with the looming economic depression in the 1930s, further undermined progress in scientific research.

The economic depression of the 1930s

The 1930s left deep marks on the psyche of the colonies in Africa. Based on the experiences from the southwestern United States—events referred to as the 'dust bowl'—colonial authorities were concerned that a similar environmental crisis would occur in Africa.[51] This global vision of environmental crisis took center-stage in academic debates, both in the colonies and within empires. It resulted in a vigorous convergence of writings and discussions about the African environmental crisis by professional geographers, anthropologists and ecologists. The global viewpoints on environmental change were prescriptive about the actions required to resolve the problem.[52] At the same time, the period was marked by extended droughts and famine. Influenced by what had happened elsewhere, colonial science, blamed the changes on long-term 'misuse of the land' by African peasants and pastoralists. A further claim (although unproven) was that the depression had created disorders in environmental and social systems[53] (see Chapter 4).

After nearly three decades, the colonial administrations in East Africa attempted to accelerate scientific research but met with one failure after another. To begin with, economic depressions in the 1930s decelerated research work, most notably due to the lack of funds.[54] The most significant aspect of government action was the distribution of free seeds to farmers. This was despite disagreements among officials regarding the claim that African peasants had little to offer in terms of improving farming practices. Accordingly, Lord Stanley[55] of Alderley, the chairman of the joint agricultural committee in London, claimed that consultations with African communities would yield no beneficial information. The official explanation was that African societies were incapable of offering solutions to their own problems, let alone advancing new ones.[56] The officials blamed the African peasants for the decline in agricultural production and, by focusing on soil erosion, they failed to investigate the sources of economic depression.[57]

The most significant contribution of scientific research at this time was the publication of the African Survey Report that assigned priority to increasing both agricultural production and soil erosion control.[58] By 1933, the idea of science had gained significant currency to establish a baseline for biological and social science research in the colonies.[59] Sir Sydney Henn, then in the British House of Commons, proposed a resolution for a parliamentary commission to be sent to East Africa, to report to the secretary of the colonies on how to coordinate and stimulate their economies.[60]

By 1935, the British Government had established the Colonial Agricultural Service, charged with unifying research throughout the colonies.[61] One such area of research interest was soil fertility. The decline in soil fertility associated with indigenous farming systems was attributed to reduced crop production. The outcome was claimed to result in land degradation (for contrasting evidence, see Chapter 5). Yet, the rainfall failure—which was, in fact, the main cause of famine—was not even mentioned. For the colonial officials, the future looked grim, unless drastic changes to indigenous farming systems were undertaken. Consequently, advisers insisted that 'if something is not done, in less than twenty years a certain well-populated district would be reduced to desert.'[62] Mr Nowell, in his contribution during the Royal African conferences held in East Africa, went even further in the rhetoric: '[w]e did not put it at hundred years. We put it at twenty.'[63] From this melodramatic prediction, perhaps with hindsight, one may infer that the whole affair of land degradation was exaggerated. Development programs from the late 1930s onwards recommended 'prepackaged settlement schemes,' referred to as 'tests,' by which any failure would be explained as part of the process of 'testing' new ideas.[64] (see Chapter 4). These implementations had to wait (until 1943), owing to the outbreak of the Second World War in 1939.

The Second World War years, 1939–1945

The Second World War influenced the progress of research in two noteworthy ways: one negative and the second positive. The negative outcome was that research and development activities were scaled down due to contingencies brought about by the war.[65] The positive outcome was that military demands for beef and other animal products reached such volumes that despite the lower prices, the inflow of cash to peasants and pastoralist communities suddenly increased their purchasing capacity for consumer goods. The war years produced urgent requirements for the immediate utilization of research results for development. Taking credit for this outcome, the colonial governments invoked a reconstruction program to try to comprehend the economic potential of the pastoral regions in the colonies.[66] An ongoing challenge during the war years was the lack of finances which accounted for the failure to accelerate scientific research.[67] Endeavors were invigorated by the passing of the Colonial Development and Welfare Act of 1940.[68] In London, the Act was followed by the establishment of scientific committees and councils to advise the Colonial Office. Colonial scientists made short visits to East Africa, to develop research proposals for funding through grants made available via the Act.[69] The overall aspiration of the Act was to end the menace of famine and hunger in the colonies.[70]

Experience had shown that new scientific knowledge was needed to meet complex development imperatives. This was the beginning of the applied scientific research era, when different scientific disciplines came to be integrated. Rather than being conducted by individual scientists, research activities were organized under research teams. Perhaps the motivation for this was the increasing emphasis on large-scale development programs as opposed to singular experimental trials. The motivation might have also been trends in industrial production in the west, where the processes of industrial growth had shifted from simple manufacturing to complex industrial units. Consequently, large research teams were established, led by experienced scientists bringing together varieties of scientific expertise.[71] The government provided services in support of research activities by promoting increased agrarian production, and improving social services such as public health, social welfare and the use of community labor.[72] A significant scientific breakthrough in East Africa from the 1940s was the launch of the *Agricultural and Forestry Journal* that communicated research results from across colonies in Africa (more on this in Chapter 5).

In the 1940s, the Colonial Office appointed research councils to oversee the implementation of research in the colonies. The councils recruited experienced researchers to improve communication between the councils and among the researchers. The research councils provided researchers with autonomy to maintain the professional status they enjoyed in the metropole institutions. In practice, however, research involved close collaboration with colonial administrations.[73] For the colonial officials, the priority was to improve agricultural production by focusing on soil erosion control.[74] Therefore the three colonies adopted a common policy which was envisaged to promote better methods of soil conservation. Indeed, Sir Philip Mitchell, the Governor of Kenya (during 1944) had called for greater efficiency in dealing with the problem. It was during his term that large-scale development programs were introduced, for which a sum of £8.1 million was allocated to the African Land Development Organization (ALDEV).[75] These programs treated development as experimental science.

Development as experimental science

Development programs focused on large-scale schemes, funded in cycles of four-year plans. According to official views, large-scale schemes were of strategic economic importance, and served as a laboratory to test forward-looking policies on agrarian reforms in Africa. Yet, throughout the decade of the 1940s, the colonial government had practiced contradictory development policies; on the one hand, the desired policy was to 'preserve African community during the process of economic growth'[76]; while on the other hand, the large-scale schemes displaced many African communities from their lands. Therefore, the 'moralization' effort—in the sense of colonists preserving African societies and their environments—had inbuilt barriers to progress. We will use an example here. The Colonial Development and Welfare Act of 1945 provided Tanganyika with £90,000 for a five-year anti-soil erosion campaign in the Mbulu District. The funds enabled a large social and landscape engineering project, combining soil erosion controls, population removal, and clearing of natural vegetation in order to control tsetse flies.[77]

After the publication of the African survey,[78] research projects recruited social scientists for the second time, to promote community participation in development. This time around, research advisers made direct contributions to implementing development schemes.[79] The British Government made available an estimated £5 million per year over five to ten years (1940–1945) to support development in the East African colonies, in addition to £500,000 earmarked for social science research. In 1941, the Colonial Office stressed the importance of international cooperation through subcommittees on agriculture, animal health and forestry.[80]

Subsequent to the renewal of the Colonial Development and Welfare Act in 1945, the research grant from 1945 was increased by £1 million per year for the three colonies.[81] The additional funding enabled the expansion of inter-territorial collaboration to meet the needs of rapidly expanding research activities in the colonies.[82] In addition, ALDEV was allocated

£3 million under a ten-year development plan in Kenya and Tanganyika. Much of this funding was allocated to water development schemes and soil conservation in the Machakos District in Kenya. In western, central and southern Tanganyika, the program experimented with new technology in the form of mechanized agriculture.[83] The aim of the agricultural development policy was to concentrate funding on areas that had better infrastructure, in order to optimize anticipated returns on investment.[84]

Nevertheless, two contrasting ideas had emerged; on the one hand, science was considered as an appropriate tool to experiment with new development ideas and there was an emphasis on balancing science and development in order to increase food production. On the other hand was the idea that the application of scientific research would increase livestock numbers with adverse consequences for the environment.[85] Considering this dilemma, Edgar B. Worthington, a British biologist who later became the Secretary General of the Inter-Colonial Scientific Council for Africa South of the Sahara (1950–1955), considered Africa as a 'fruitful field of history for experiments for expert scientific knowledge.'[86] It was Worthington's interpretations that shifted thinking from 'science for development' to 'development as experimental science.'[87]

The post-Second World War years, 1945–1959

The post-war years continued to demonstrate a proliferation of large agricultural schemes, informed by global trends in development. The Commission for Social Science took an interest in funding anthropological research, with selective coverage of African societies.[88] Research activities expanded,[89] with increased influence by foreign experts (i.e., consultants).[90] The experts might have left voluminous records of their work behind in the colonies for posterity, but in their absence, no one understood how the plans were intended to work. More critically, in line with earlier concerns, research approaches that focused on technical matters and ignored social issues resulted in failures. By 1945, researchers had begun using extension personnel to persuade African farmers to utilize new technologies to promote the growth of food crops for the market economy.[91] However, colonial administrators were often 'disappoint[ed] when they [i.e., scientists] could not supply an immediate remedy' for development. They complained that failure to control scientists would lead to their own isolation from practical problems.[92] Here, one might infer differences in power relations between colonial administrators and scientists.[93]

Comparatively, for the colonial officials, science was a medium for achieving development goals, while for the scientists, research was a medium for increasing knowledge, and it did not necessarily matter if that knowledge was translated into development. Therefore, to ensure that researchers did not work in isolation, the Agricultural Research Council for the three East African colonies developed plans to expand research coordination under groups focusing on agriculture, forestry and grazing management. Although members of the council participated in planning research projects, most of the plans remained in experimental stages.[94]

The 'post-war' period had implications for how scientific research was applied to development by administrators who controlled the development agenda, while scientists investigated research problems.[95] Drawing on experiences from Nigeria,[96] the colonial authorities argued for the recruitment of persons with expertise to work on East African soil erosion problems. However, colonial authorities demonstrated ambivalence as a rule, by failing to stay focused, and changing their priorities—allocating more resources to emergencies instead of waiting for long-term research results to be applied in order to achieve development goals. A good example occurred in 1946 when soil erosion control and grazing schemes were temporarily scaled down, while research on controlling tsetse flies and locusts was prioritized.[97]

Under the Colonial Development and Welfare Act of 1945, the three colonies received £6,000,000 to establish more than 300 research stations catering for wide-ranging biological and social science research activities.[98] The Research Department at the Colonial Office created additional research institutions focusing on tsetse flies and *trypanosomiasis* (EAATTRRO), and desert locust control (the Desert Locust Survey).[99] There was positive progress between 1947 and 1950: in 1947, the old Amani research station was taken over by the East African Agricultural and Forestry Organization (EAAFRO)[100] and the East African High Commission was given the role of coordinating inter-territorial research. At this time, the Muguga research station in Kenya gained prominence as a regional research institution,[101] and the East African Veterinary Organization (EAVRO) at the same station became responsible for vaccine research.[102]

In 1947, through the Colonial Development Corporation, various agricultural schemes were established to foster development.[103] Between 1946 and 1955, agricultural development research prioritized crop production on farmers' lands, combined with testing soil conservation technologies.[104] While the essentials of scientific research were perceived to have a direct impact on practical fields such as economics, social sciences and engineering, scientific research for development activities continued to fail, crushing the hopes of the researchers. Kenneth Bradley[105] summed up such disappointments as follows: 'The tropics are cruel, and they do not tolerate mistakes; many a promising enterprise … has had to be abandoned, and many stout hearts have been broken.'

The failures did not halt support for research by the colonial authorities, partly because of the empire's trust in science as an instrument of progress. For the colonial officials, it was the absence of competent scientists that contributed to the failure of scientific research. There were some exceptions. During a visit (the early 1950s) to the Kawanda Research Station near Kampala in Uganda, the station housed a group of agricultural scientists who had worked on commercial agricultural research projects longer than any other institution in East Africa,[106] with the exception of the Amani station in Tanganyika. The high-quality research in some of these institutions had indeed motivated further investment in research. Accordingly, the colonial governments began attracting distinguished scientists to advise on development projects, hoping that research collaboration across the British colonies would increase the success of project outcomes.[107]

During the 1950s, researchers conducted extensive surveys to gather information on demographic statistics, as well as opinion polls.[108] Notwithstanding the rapid expansion of research during the economic stimulus, colonial administrators continued to find disparities between the application of research findings and development progress; thus the lack of synchrony between research and development remained prevalent.[109] Sir Andrew Cohen,[110] in his opening address to the conference on medical, agricultural and veterinary aspects of food production, concluded that

> [r]esearch institutes now stand poised to address themselves with the help ... of the East African governments and peoples, to the great task of pushing back the frontiers of darkness ... the highest and most exciting task known to man

—adding that research would contribute to the 'progress of colonial territories.'

Despite the prevailing optimism, the colonial authorities faced three challenges. The first challenge was the low number of professional researchers, many of whom were preoccupied with routine technical activities not priority subjects in social and economic development. Indeed, among them, those with expertise in development were even fewer. E.B. Worthington[111] reported that scientists working in Africa were 'apt to follow rather than lead.' They were required to solve problems of development on demand, as opposed to developing their own visions of development. The second challenge was the need to survey soil erosion over wide areas outside farms where terracing was used. This was addressed by the use of aerial photographs, based on technology used by the Royal Air Force during the Second World War.[112] Unfortunately, the soil erosion control programs used forced labor by the African farmers to build terraces.[113] The third challenge was the lack of mechanisms for sharing scientific information (with the one exception of the *East African Agricultural and Forestry Journal*) among the three East African colonies, despite the need recognized earlier. This was the question raised during the 1952 governors' conference held in East Africa,[114] when international collaboration was considered as a solution to sharing scientific information.

International collaboration

During the 1950s, various transnational research institutions had shown interest in funding and coordinating pilot projects in the colonies.[115] The

58 *Empire, science, society and development*

British Government cooperated with international agencies such as the Food and Agricultural Organization (FAO) of the United Nations (UN), as well as private institutions such as the Rockefeller Foundation, to fund research on the eradication of diseases across East Africa.[116] They also internationalized research projects on tsetse flies and *trypanosomiasis*, and the control of desert locusts.[117] Such collaborative long-term research projects had earlier been attempted at Amani in Tanganyika and at Muguga in Kenya. The latter research station had demonstrated distinct advances in animal science research and it was for this reason that the Committee of Civil Research had discouraged the duplication of similar activities across East Africa.[118] This approach appeared to contradict the stated intention of sharing scientific information, which created a dilemma for the officials. On the one hand, there was a perception that research at the station level was too specialized to apply to conditions in rural areas.[119] On the other hand, the sharing of research information could break down territorial barriers, thus allowing better coordination across the colonies where comparable research could be applied more widely.[120]

Ronald Keay[121] identified five factors necessary for inter-state research collaboration to succeed: first, the work needs to be conducted by collaborating scientists; second, the research should be headed by senior and outstanding scientists; third, scientists can recognize the merits of science as a collaborative exercise, regardless of the local political situation; fourth, research collaboration creates links between African colonial states; and fifth, international research collaboration strengthens the work of researchers across institutions in individual countries. Keay, particularly in the third factor, appears to suggest that the universality of science can be applied across research groups and across political borders. Inadequacies in international collaboration in the colonies at the time had been partly the result of approaching research activities by relying heavily on expatriate staff. Although the expatriate researchers lent global prominence to the research projects, the success of this type of research depended on the availability of funds to hire them.[122] In other cases, large-scale schemes tended to serve as an 'overseas field station' where research of global importance was conducted, but to which local African peasants were opposed.

Responses of Africans to experimental science

During the 1950s, African societies were still considered 'backward' and not expected to advance based on their own efforts. The persistent policy that '[i]t is the task of the more technically advanced [western] peoples to lead the less advanced peoples forward,'[123] had produced two impediments for colonial development projects. The first impediment was that development initiatives seldom involved Africans themselves, except where schemes demanded African labor. The second impediment was that due to altered systems of traditional land use, the African peasants responded either violently, or by passive resistance. In central Kenya, forced labor in soil conservation projects and land alienation were the main triggers of the Mau Mau rebellion.[124] In Tanganyika, the 1950s witnessed peasant opposition to government schemes such as soil conservation, forest reserves and national parks, which caused displacement of local communities.[125] Local communities in Uganda resisted settler farming outright. Thus, enforced actions on the part of the colonial authorities clearly did not produce the desired results in terms of cooperation by African peasants.[126]

The emphasis at this time was again on large-scale agricultural developments, such as the groundnut schemes that ultimately failed (see Chapter 4). However, the schemes cleared large areas of natural vegetation using heavy machinery,[127] thereby aggravating soil erosion problems. In the Kondoa District in Tanganyika, sites of previous soil erosion control interventions were the focus of renewed research that attempted land rehabilitation,[128] instead of evaluating why the previous projects had failed. The repeat projects suffered the same fate, since fundamental, historical processes of soil erosion and prevention were ignored in the analysis. Similar outcomes occurred across East Africa.

Subsequently, regional research specialization fields were merged under the control of the East African High Commission that supervised the Agriculture and Forestry organization at Muguga, to serve all the three colonies—Kenya, Tanganyika and Uganda.[129] Even under this research direction, the subject of soil erosion continued to be the basis of the hypothesis of Africa's environmental crisis, yet after five decades it had not yielded any better understanding thereof (see Chapters 4 and 5). As the end of the colonial era approached, discussions on the African environmental crisis shifted to the topic of general desiccation of the environment. This was partly due to the dry climate of the late 1950s.[130] It was, however, not possible for the colonies to take a common position against environmental desiccation—perceived or real. The imperial research agenda was forced to shift focus again, following outbreaks of desert locust plagues in the 1950s.[131]

During the late 1950s, research and development focused on agriculture, while rangeland and pastoral research lost the edge it had had in the 1930s and 1940s. This was until Roger Swynnerton, formerly Director of Tsetse Fly Research in Tanganyika, arrived in Kenya in 1954 and prepared a report which, among other things, attempted to present coherence in terms of long-term agricultural development planning. Swynnerton also outlined the achievements under the colonial agricultural research and development corporations in East African countries.[132] The core aspects of the Swynnerton Plan were land improvements, land consolidation and training of extension personnel, as well as the development of pastoral lands. As the colonies approached independence, grievances by African populations against the overbearing colonial administration became part of slogans prompting political and social change.[133]

Research and development in the 1960s

The 1960s formed a dividing line between colonial administration and independence of the East African states—Kenya, Tanganyika and Uganda. It was a decade of optimism and new opportunities.[134] The period showed a continuum, as well as discontinuities, in approaches to research and development that had been evident under colonialism.[135] The countries faced challenges on three fronts. The first was that development was donor dependent in terms of 'project financing, capital expenditure and technical assistance.'[136] Since sources of funding started to diminish with the waning of colonization, it became impossible to coordinate research and development activities. Second, expatriate staff—who made up the bulk of researchers—were leaving, thus handicapping research projects in these East African countries. Lacking trained scientific staff locally, the countries planned to keep the research stations working through international collaboration. The third challenge was accessing international funding for collaborative research.[137]

International research was sponsored by the United Nations and the World Bank to increase research capacities in the newly independent African states.[138] The increased presence of international organizations such as the FAO provided additional funds and injected new scientific research ideas. The new international participation changed the research agenda by focusing on short-term plans. For example, the 1964 conference on organized research called by the United Nations Economic Commission for Africa (established by UNESCO in 1958), was attended by representatives from 28 African countries. The conference laid the groundwork for international organizations to coordinate programs and provided technical personnel to the newly independent African states to help establish scientific infrastructure (see section below).

The regional and local offices of the multilateral agencies facilitated two types of programs: those focusing on global issues, and those focusing on regional or national projects. The latter type of programs had lower levels of monetary capital and the local offices lacked control over the research agendas.[139] When the funding periods ended, the project implementations were terminated, with few prospects for revival. Since the 'multilateral agency model' was based on a 'consultancy' model—that is, short-term visits by experts who departed after their assignment ended, often never to return. Consequently, the official creed of 'modernization' of independent states, coupled with assistance provided by international agencies, perpetuated the planning of development initiatives along the same lines as those that had failed during the colonial era.[140]

Again, development was not based on the findings of scientific research, and thus produced the same outcomes—repeated over and again, with little success. Contrary to the expectations of governments and donors, the development projects had 'catastrophic' impacts on the environment.[141]

Taghi Farva and John Milton[142] arrived at the following conclusion: 'The weak link between research and development during the post-independence period was heavy reliance on international funding without which many of the ... projects would be abandoned, leading to closures of the research stations.' It was in this light that Lord Hailsham emphasized that 'international cooperation is no substitute for [building] national excellence' in research.[143] Clearly the East African nations required building new research capacities.

Building African research capacities

After the departure of colonial scientific teams between 1962 and 1964, the shortage of scientific staff could not be addressed by appointing competent African scientific personnel.[144] The lack of capacity and low numbers of African researchers implied that the first decade of independence coincided with the lowest level of scientific productivity in East Africa.[145] The solution was to approach international donor agencies to drive the research agenda; but as already mentioned, their perspectives were often based on experiences in institutions in the donor countries.

In 1960, the Weizmann Institute of Science in Israel invited leaders and scientists from newly independent (and soon-to-be-independent) African countries to the first conference on the role of science in the advancement of the new nations. About 40 countries attended, with 35 representing Africa. The eagerness of African countries was obvious, considering that they intended to forge new directions, at least politically.[146] The pace of change for the newly independent African states needed to be decisive, with demonstrable progress in accordance with their political aspirations; but this implied that research and development activities needed to progress at the same pace. Regrettably, in the early years after independence, the weak local economies did not permit funding on the same scale as had been available during the colonial years. Therefore, despite the aspirations on developing African research capacity, reliance on grants and international aid was not enough to accelerate research, contrary to anticipation.[147] These views were clearly expressed by Thomas Odhiambo,[148] who identified three major weaknesses in the administration of research work in East Africa. The first weakness was the lack of a central body to determine research priorities; the second weakness was limited budgets to support research projects; and the third was the lack of field controls to standardize content of research activities for application in local areas.

In 1964, a symposium on science policy and research administration in Africa was organized by UNESCO in Nairobi—recognizing that research is a multi-disciplinary issue.[149] This was followed in 1965 by the establishment in Nairobi of a UN Regional Centre for Science and Technology in Africa, with two goals: the first was to increase training opportunities for the continent's scientists, and the second was to increase cooperation between research groups across states, using standardized scientific methods and experimental protocols.[150] (More details on this are given in Chapter 10.)

By 1967, independent African states were preparing to establish new economic and political directions. The three East Africa countries had begun to pursue different strategies in their development policies.[151] For example, under the Arusha Declaration of 1967, Tanzanian socialist policy (under President Julius Nyerere) aimed to expand agricultural development to create self-reliance in food production through peasant farming, thereby breaking with the past. This approach was adopted in spite of the fact that a socialist policy attracted limited international funding from western countries, thus forcing Tanzania to lean towards socialist countries for technical and financial backing.[152] Kenya, on the other hand, remained allied to the West and benefited most from multilateral agencies.[153] In Uganda political instability undermined progress in research.[154] In the end, the imperial science research infrastructure did not adequately address why and how the African environmental crisis influenced development policy. Chapter 4 delves into the origin of the hypothesis of the African environmental crisis and presents some practical experiences from development initiatives in the latter part of the twentieth century. In Chapter 10, we will briefly outline the trajectory of the scientific research for development during the latter periods (1970–1990s) of post-independence.

Notes

1 Basalla, G., 'The spread of Western Science,' *Science* 156.3775 (1967): 611–622, 611.
2 Kreike, E., *Environmental infrastructure in African history: Examining the myth of natural resource management in Namibia* (Cambridge: Cambridge University Press, 2013), 22
3 Sayre, N.F., *The politics of scale: A history of rangeland science* (Chicago: University of Chicago Press, 2017), 24, 27.
4 Jacobs, N.J., 'The intimate politics of ornithology in colonial Africa,' *Comparative Studies in Society and History* 48.3 (2006): 564–603.
5 Steel, R.W., 'Problems of population pressure in tropical Africa: Presidential address,' *Transactions of the Institute of British Geographers* 49 (1970): 1–14.
6 Gascoigne, J., *Science in the service of empire: Joseph Banks, the British state and the uses of science in the age of revolution* (Cambridge: Cambridge University Press, 1998), 8–14, 147–148, 179.
7 Van Beusekom, M.M., *Negotiating development: African farmers and colonial experts at the office Du Niger, 1920–1960* (Portsmouth: Heinemann, 2002); Osborne, M.A., 'Science and the French empire,' *Isis* 96.1 (2005): 80–87.
8 Ibid.
9 Wright, H., 'German methods of development in Africa,' *Journal of the Royal African Society* 1.1 (1901): 23–38.
10 Omoree, A., Kurwijila, L. and Grace, D., 'Improving livelihoods in East Africa through livestock research and extension: Reflections on changes from 1950s to the early twenty first century,' *Tropical Animal Health Production* 41 (2009): 1051–1059.

11 Church, A., *East Africa a new dominion: A crucial experiment in tropical development and its significance to the British Empire* (Connecticut: Negro Universities Press Westport, 1927), 35.
12 Meritt, H.P., 'Bismark and the first participation of East Africa,' *English Historical Review* 91.360 (1976): 585–597.
13 Gascoigne, J., 'Science and the British Empire from its beginnings to 1950,' in Bennett, B.M. and Hodge, J.M. (eds.), *Science and empire: Knowledge and networks of science across the British Empire, 1800–1970* (New York: Palgrave Macmillan, 2011), 47–48.
14 Abbott, G.C., 'A re-examination of the 1929 Colonial Development Act,' *Economic History Review* 24.1 (1971): 68–81.
15 Smith, C.T., *An historical geography of Western Europe before 1800* (London: Addison-Wesley Longman, 1978), 23.
16 Beck, A., *A history of the British medical administration of East Africa, 1900–1950* (New York: Harvard University Press, 1970), 35.
17 Brown, K., 'Tropical medicine and animal disease: Onderstepoort and the development of veterinary science in South Africa 1908–1950,' *Journal of Southern African Studies* 31.3 (2005): 513–529; 517, Beck, *A history of the British medical administration*, 35.
18 Ibid., 8, 24.
19 Worthington, E.B., 'East Africa and her neighbours,' *The Geographical Journal* 121.4 (1955): 417–425.
20 Prendergast, D.K. and Adams, W.M., 'Colonial wildlife conservation and the origins of the society for preservation of the wild fauna of the Empire (1903–1914),' *Oryx* 37.2 (2003): 251–260.
21 Christopher, A.J., 'Patterns of British overseas investment in land, 1885–1913,' *Transactions of the Institute of British Geographers* (1985): 452–466, 465.
22 Herderson, W.O., 'The war ecology of German East Africa, 1914–1917,' *Economic History Review* 13.1/2 (1943): 104–110.
23 Conte, C.A., *Highland sanctuary: Environmental history in Tanzania's Usambara mountains* (Athens: Ohio University Press, 2004).
24 Zimmerman, A., 'What do you really want in German East Africa, 'Herr Professor'? Counterinsurgency and the science effect in colonial Tanzania,' *Comparative Studies in Society and History* 48.2 (2006): 419–461.
25 Hailey, W.M. (Baron), *An African survey, revised 1956: A study of problems arising in Africa south of the Sahara* (Oxford: Oxford University Press, 1957), 916.
26 Berry, L. and Janet, T., 'Soil conservation policies in the semi-arid regions of Tanzania, a historical perspective,' *Geografiska Annaler: Series A, Physical Geography* 54.3–4 (1972): 241–253, 251.
27 Wright, M., 'Local roots of policy in German East Africa,' *Journal of African History* 9.4 (1968): 621–630, 621.
28 Losos, G.J. and Ikede, B.O., 'Review of pathology of diseases in domestic and laboratory animals caused by *Trypanosoma congolense, T. vivax, T. brucei, T. rhodesiense* and *T. gambiense*,' *Veterinary Pathology* 9.1_suppl (1972): 1–79.
29 Smuts, J.C., 'East Africa,' *The Geographical Journal* 51.3 (1918): 129–145.
30 Anderson, R., *The forgotten front: The East African campaign* (Cheltenham: Tempus, 2004).
31 Wright, 'Local roots of policy in German East Africa,' 621.

32 Keay, R., 'Scientific cooperation in Africa,' *African Affairs* 75.298 (1976): 86–97.
33 Worthington, E.B., 'Geography and the development of East Africa,' *The Geographical Journal* 116.1/3 (1950): 29–43, 41.
34 Earl of Athlone, 'Proceedings of the Royal African Society 1938; Supplement. Land use and soil erosion in Africa,' *Journal of the Royal African Society* 37.146 (1938): 3–19.
35 Malmsten, N.R., 'British government policy toward colonial development, 1919–39,' *Journal of Modern History* 49.2 (1977): D1249–D1287.
36 Church, A., *East Africa: A new dominion* (H.F. & G. Witherby, 1927).
37 Owen, W.E., 'Some thoughts on native development in East Africa,' *Journal of the Royal African Society* 30.120 (1931): 225–237.
38 Data source from Smith, D., 'Scientific research centres in Africa,' *African Studies Bulletin* 10.3 (1967): 20–47, 23.
39 Berry and Janet, 'Soil conservation policies in the semi-arid regions of Tanzania, a historical perspective.'
40 Hoyle, B.S., 'Gillman of Tanganyika, 1882–1946: Pioneer geographer,' *The Geographical Journal* 152.3 (1986): 354–366; Conte, *Highland sanctuary*, 52.
41 Conte, *Highland sanctuary*, 52.
42 Church, *East Africa a new dominion*, 95, 98;
43 Ibid.
44 Worthington, *Science in Africa*, 316.
45 Ibid., 24.
46 Nowell, W., 'Supplement: The agricultural research station at Amani,' *Journal of the Royal African Society* 33.131 (1934): 1–20.
47 Alter, P., *The reluctant patron: Science and the state in Britain, 1850–1920* (Oxford: Berg, 1987), 6.
48 Bennett, G., 'Patterns of government in East Africa,' *International Affairs* 45 (1969): 80–90.
49 Macleod, R.M. and Andrews, E.K., 'The Committee of Civil Research: Scientific advice for economic development 1925–30,' *Minerva* 7.4 (1969): 680–705.
50 Gluckman, M., 'Seven-year research plan of the Rhodes-Livingstone Institute of Social Studies in British central Africa,' *Journal of Rhodes-Livingstone Institute* 4 (1945): 1–32.
51 Dodd, J.L., 'Desertification and degradation in sub-Saharan Africa,' *BioScience* 44.1 (1994): 28–34; Worster, D., *Dust Bowl: The southern plains in the 1930s* (Oxford: Oxford University Press, 2004).
52 Grove, R. and Vinita, D., 'Imperialism, intellectual networks, and environmental change: Origins and evolution of global environmental history, 1676–2000: Part I,' *Economic and Political Weekly* (2006): 4345–4354, 4349.
53 Bonneuil, C., 'Development as experiment: Science and state building in late and post-colonial Africa, 1930–1970,' *Osiris* 15 (2000): 258–281, 259.
54 Vail, L., 'Ecology and history: The example of Eastern Zambia,' *Journal of Southern African Studies* 3.2 (1977): 129–155, 155.
55 Owen, W.E., 'Some thoughts on native development in East Africa,' *Journal of the Royal African Society* 30.120 (1931): 225–237.
56 Van Zwanenberg, R., 'The development of peasant commodity production in Kenya, 1920–40,' *Economic History Review* 27.3 (1974): 442–454, 451.
57 Jacks, G.V. and Whyte, R.O., *Vanishing lands: A world survey of soil erosion* (New York: Doubleday, Doran and Company, 1939), 68.

58 Worthington, E.B., 'Organization of research in Africa,' *Scientific Monthly* 74.1 (1952): 39–44.
59 Mills, D., 'British anthropology at the end of empire: The rise and fall of the colonial social science research council, 1944–1962,' *Revue d'Histoire des Sciences Humaines* 1.6 (2002): 161–188.
60 Church, *East Africa a new dominion*, 9; Grigg, E., 'Land policy and economic development in Kenya,' *Journal of Royal African Society* 31.122 (1932): 1–14.
61 Masefield, G.B., *A history of the colonial agricultural service* (Oxford: Clarendon Press, 1972).
62 Earl of Athlone, 'Proceedings of the Royal African Society 1938; Supplement. Land use and soil erosion in Africa,' *Journal of the Royal African Society* 37.146 (1938): 3–19.
63 Ibid., 16.
64 Pearce, R.D., *The turning point in Africa: British colonial policy 1938–48* (Frank Cass, 1982), 42, 43.
65 Worthington, 'Geography and the development of East Africa.'
66 Cooper F. and Packard, R.M. (eds.), *International development and the social sciences: Essays on the history and politics of knowledge* (Berkeley: University of California Press, 1997), 17, 18, 30.
67 Constantine, S., *The making of British colonial development policy 1914–1940* (London: Frank Cass, 1984), 2, 5.
68 Mills, 'British anthropology at the end of empire.'
69 Worthington, 'Organization of research in Africa,' 41.
70 Bennett, G. and Smith, A., 'Kenya: From 'White Man's Country' to Kenyatta's state, 1945–1963,' in Low, D.A. and Smith A. (eds.), *Kenya: From 'White Man's Country' to Kenyatta's State, 1945–1963. History of East Africa* III (Oxford: Clarendon Press, 1976).
71 Pereira, H.C., 'Co-operation in research,' *East African Agricultural Journal* 22.2 (1956): 57–59.
72 Worthington, 'Organization of research in Africa,' 40.
73 Clarke, S., 'The research council system and the politics of medical and agricultural research for the British colonial empire, 1940–52,' *Medical History* 57.3 (2013): 338–358.
74 Earl of Athlone, 'Proceedings of the Royal African Society 1938.'
75 Hodge, J.M., 'Science, development and empire: The colonial advisory council on agriculture and animal health, 1919–43,' *Journal of Imperial and Commonwealth History* 30.1 (2008): 1–26.
76 Grischow, J.D., 'Late colonial development in British West Africa: The Gonja Development project in the northern Territories of the Gold Coast, 1948–57,' *Canadian Journal of African Studies* 35.2 (2001): 282–312.
77 Sunseri, T., 'A political ecology of beef in colonial Tanzania and the global periphery, 1864–1961,' *Journal of Historical Geography* 39 (2013): 29–42, 39.
78 Hailey, *An African survey, revised 1956*.
79 Clarke, S., '"The chance to send their first class men out to the colonies": The making of the colonial research service,' in Benette, B.M. and Hodge, J.M. (eds.), *Science and empire: Knowledge and networks of science across the British Empire, 1800–1970* (New York: Springer, 2011).
80 Lee, J.M., and Martin, P., *The colonial office, war, and development policy* (London: Institute of Commonwealth Studies, 1982), 183.

66 *Empire, science, society and development*

81 Pearce, *The turning point in Africa*, 19.
82 Worthington, 'Organization of research in Africa,' 41.
83 Bunting, A.H., 'Land development and large-scale food production in East Africa by the overseas food,' *Economic Botany* 6.1 (1952): 55–68.
84 Baker, S.J.K., 'A background to the study of drought in East Africa,' *African Affairs* 73.291 (1974): 170–177.
85 Cohen, A. (Sir), 'Conference on the medical, agricultural and veterinary aspects of food production in East Africa, opening address by His excellence the Governor of Uganda,' *East African Agricultural Journal* XX.1 (1954): 3–11, 7.
86 Worthington, 'Organization of research in Africa.'
87 Duthie, D.W., 'The application of science,' *East African Agricultural Journal* XIV.4 (1949): 175–176.
88 Mills, 'British anthropology at the end of empire.'
89 Beinart, W., Karen, B. and Daniel, G., 'Experts and expertise in colonial Africa reconsidered: Science and the interpenetration of knowledge,' *African Affairs* 108.432 (2009): 413–433, 430.
90 McCraken, J., 'Experts and expertise in colonial Malawi,' *African Affairs* 81.322 (1982): 101–116, 102.
91 Green, E., 'A lasting story: Conservation and agricultural extension in colonial Malawi,' *Journal of African History* 50.2 (2009): 247–267.
92 Bennett, 'The consolidation and reconfiguration of 'British' networks of science,' 38, 39.
93 Paul, H.W., *From knowledge to power: The rise of the science empire in France, 1860–1939* (Cambridge: Cambridge University Press, 2003).
94 Stanner, W.E.H., 'Observations on colonial planning,' *International Affairs* 25.3 (1949): 318–328.
95 Cooper, F., 'Modernization bureaucrats, backward Africans, and development concept,' in Cooper, F. and Randall, M.P. (eds.), *International development and the social sciences: Essays on the history and politics of knowledge* (Berkeley: University of California Press, 1997), 64–65.
96 Grove, A.T., 'Soil erosion and population problems in south-east Nigeria,' *The Geographical Journal* 117.3 (1951): 291–304.
97 Hailey, *An African survey, revised 1956*, 913.
98 Bradley, K., 'Scientific research in Britain's colonies,' *Scientific Monthly* 70.5 (1950): 332–334, 332, 334.
99 Worthington, 'Organization of research in Africa,' 41.
100 Nyanzi, S., 'A review of the East African common market,' *Transition* 6/7 (1962): 13–14; Smith, C.T., *An historical geography of Western Europe before 1800* (Santa Barbara: Praeger, 1967), 24.
101 Pyenson, L., *Cultural imperialism and exact sciences, 1900–1930*. Vol. 1 (Bern: Peter Lang, 1985), 11.
102 Gluckman, 'Seven-year research plan of the Rhodes–Livingstone Institute of Social studies in British central Africa.'
103 Cowen, M., 'Early years of the Colonial Development Corporation: British state enterprise, overseas during late colonialism,' *African Affairs* 83.330 (1984): 63–75, 63, 68, 74.
104 Swynnerton, J.R.M., 'Kenya's agricultural planning,' *African Affairs* 56.224 (1957): 209–215, 209, 210.

105 Bradley, 'Scientific research in Britain's colonies,' 332.
106 Williams, L.C., 'Enlightened Africa,' *Scientific Monthly* 68.3 (1949): 1999–207.
107 Bradley, 'Scientific research in Britain's colonies,' 332, 334.
108 O'Barr., W.M., Spain, D.H. and Tessler, M.A., 'The history and conduct of survey research in Africa,' in O'Barr, W.M., Spain, D.H. and Tessler, M.A. (eds.), *Survey research in Africa: Its application and limits* (Evanston: Northwestern University Press, 1973).
109 Hoyle, 'Gillman of Tanganyika, 1882–1946,' 364.
110 Cohen, 'Conference on the medical, agricultural and veterinary aspects of food production in East Africa, opening address by His Excellency the Governor of Uganda,' 7
111 Worthington, 'East Africa and her neighbours.'
112 Parker, G.G., 'A summary of British native policy in Kenya and Uganda, 1885–1939,' *Journal of Negro Education* 19.4 (1950): 439–448.
113 Hougham, D., 'The spatial components of Anglo-African development plans, 1943–1956,' *Canadian Journal of African Studies* 15.3 (1981): 527–538.
114 Low, D.A. and Smith, A., *History of East Africa, Vol. III* (Oxford: Clarendon Press, 1976).
115 Žumer, M., 'Natural resources research in East Africa,' *Bulletins from the Ecological Research Committee* 12 (1971): 1–87, 21.
116 Gold, J., 'The reconfiguration of scientific career networks in the late colonial period: The case of the food and agriculture organization and the British Forestry Service,' in Bennett, Brett M. and Hodge, M. (eds.), *Science and empire: Knowledge and networks of science across the British Empire, 1800–1970* (New York: Springer, 2011), 299.
117 Williams, 'Enlightened Africa,' 206.
118 Tate, H.R., 'The report of the joint select committee on closer union in East Africa,' *Journal of the Royal African Society* 31.122 (1932): 38–53.
119 Shrum, W., 'Science and story in development: The emergence of non-governmental organizations in agricultural research,' *Social Studies of Science* 30.1 (2000): 95–124.
120 Worthington, *A survey of research and scientific services in East Africa, 1947–56*, 44.
121 Keay, 'The natural sciences in Africa,' 97.
122 Nurse, K. and Wight, D., 'Development assistance and research capacity strengthening: The commissioning of health research in East Africa,' *Journal of East African Studies* 5.2 (2011): 233–251, 241–242.
123 Bunting, 'Land development and large scale food production in East Africa,' 67.
124 Mackenzie, A.F.D., *Land, ecology and resistance in Kenya, 1880–1952* (Edinburgh: Edinburgh University Press, 1998).
125 Sunseri, T., 'Something else to burn: Forest squatters, conservationists, and the state in modern Tanzania,' *Journal of Modern African Studies* 43.4 (2005): 609–640.
126 Showers, K.B. and Malahleha, G.M., 'Oral evidence in historical environmental impact assessment: Soil conservation in Lesotho in the 1930s and 1940s,' *Journal of Southern African Studies* 18.2 (1992): 276–296, 296.
127 Bunting, 'Land development and large-scale food production in East Africa,' 67.
128 Lane, P., 'Environmental narratives and the history of soil erosion in Kondoa District, Tanazania: An archaeological perspective,' *International Journal of African Historical Studies* 42.3 (2009): 457–483.

68 *Empire, science, society and development*

129 Hailey, *An African survey, revised 1956*, 970.
130 Worthington, 'A survey of research and scientific services in East Africa,' 40.
131 Fairhead, J. and Leach, M., 'Desiccation and domination: Science and struggles over environment and development in colonial Guinea,' *Journal of African History* 41.1 (2000): 35–54.
132 Swynnerton, R.J.M., 'Agricultural advances in Eastern Africa,' *African Affairs* 61.244 (1962): 201–215.
133 Sunseri, T., 'Every African a nationalist: Scientific forestry and forest nationalism in colonial Tanzania,' *Comparative Studies in Society and History* 49.4 (2007): 883–913.
134 Manning, P., 'The prospects for African economic history: Is today included in the long run?' *African Studies Review* 30.2 (1987): 49–62.
135 Saleem, M.A.M, 'Experience gained in the research-to-development continuum: Livestock research for sustainable livelihoods in the East African mountains,' *Mountain Research and Development* 21.2 (2001): 118–122.
136 Lele, U., 'Rural Africa: Modernization, equity, and long-term development,' *Science* 211.4482 (1981): 547–553.
137 Beck, A., 'The East African community and regional research in science and medicine,' *African Affairs* 72.288 (1973): 300–308.
138 Zeleza, P.T., 'The politics of historical and social science research in Africa,' *Journal of Southern African Studies* 28.1 (2002): 9–23, 10, 17.
139 Nurse, K. and Daniel, W., 'Development assistance and research capacity strengthening: The commissioning of health research in East Africa,' *Journal of Eastern African Studies* 5.2 (2011): 233–251, 240.
140 Burton, A. and Jennings, M., 'Introduction: The emperor's new clothes? Continuities in governance in late colonial and early postcolonial East Africa,' *International Journal of African Historical Studies* 40.1 (2007): 1–25, 9, 15.
141 Evers, Y.D., 'Supporting local natural resource management institutions: Experience gained and guiding principles,' in Stiles, D.D. (ed.) *Social aspects of sustainable dryland management* (New York: John Wiley & Sons, 1995), 99.
142 Farva, T. and Milton, J., *The careless technology: Ecology and international development* (Tom Stacey, 1973).
143 Keay, 'Scientific cooperation in Africa,' 87.
144 Clark, W., 'After independence in East Africa,' *African Affairs* 61.243 (1962): 126–137.
145 Nurse and Daniel, 'Development assistance and research capacity strengthening,' 244.
146 Gappert, G., 'An American on science in East Africa,' *Transition* 5 (1962): 28–30.
147 Nunn, G.H., 'Focus on Africa,' *Background on World Politics* 4.2 (1960): 85–87.
148 Odhiambo, T.R., 'East Africa: Science for development,' *Science* 158.3803 (1967): 876–881, 877, 878.
149 Smith, D., 'Scientific research centres in Africa,' *African Studies Bulletin* 10.3 (1967): 20–47.
150 Petitjean, P., 'The joint establishment of the World Federation of Scientific Workers and of UNESCO after World War II,' *Minerva* 46.2 (2008): 247–270.
151 Segal, A., 'The politics of land in East Africa,' *Economic Development and Cultural Change* 16.2 (1968): 275–296.

152 Žumer, 'Natural resources research in East Africa,' 3; Beck, A., 'The East African community and regional research in science and medicine,' *African Affairs* 72.288 (1973): 300–308, 302.
153 Muchena, F.N. and Kiome, R.M., 'The role of soil science in agricultural development in East Africa,' *Geoderma* 67.3–4 (1995): 141–157, 143.
154 Farva and Milton, *The careless technology*.

4 African environmental crisis narratives

Schemes, technology and development, 1904–1960

This chapter examines the origin of African environmental crisis narratives and development solutions provided by imperial science approaches. These narratives inspired colonial development research activities.[1] However, the accuracy of these narratives remain disputed.[2] Chukwumah Ijomah[3] warns that such narratives are the result of misinterpretation due to 'faulty scientific [thinking].' In the context of the crisis narrative, James C. McCann[4] describes a strange 'agreement' in the form of preconceived ideas between researchers and policy makers on historical conditions of the African environment, which although not scientifically corroborated, has persisted. As Rocheau and co-workers[5] suggest '[t]he variety of crisis narratives suggests something other than a single recurring crisis.' The development agents in the African colonies did not consider their actions as contributing to environmental crisis; instead they continued to blame local African communities.[6]

An important question that needs posing is the origin of the crisis narrative. We have previously introduced the environmental desiccation hypothesis that was posed by nineteenth-century European explorers. Three events influenced discussions that had become popular by the 1930s. The first was a global debate that arose from an environmental crisis in the midwest United States that was believed to have had counterparts in other parts of the world. The second event was the global economic slump in the 1930s, followed by extended droughts that exacerbated existing environmental conditions. The third was local methods of agricultural practices and livestock grazing in East African colonies that prompted the colonial governments to embark on large-scale schemes in attempting to solve environmental and economic problems.

Various large-scale experimental developments were designed according to experiences gained from western models of development science.[7] Reliance on technology as an instrument of development concentrated projects in the hands of Europeans, since Africans were perceived to lack the required expertise.[8] Contrasted against indigenous production systems that existed at the time, these schemes were expected to demonstrate development success and environmental conservation.[9] The new development model was also intended to supply raw materials to expanding export markets. According to Commoner Barry,[10] 'decisions [i.e., on large-scale projects] have often been well meaning ... but catastrophic in the ultimate effect on the environment.' Such ecological 'engineering tests' were grounds for disappointment in colonial development ventures, since they were implemented on scales that ignored the potential limitations of the environments and new economic technologies.[11] It is important for the sources of environmental crisis narratives to be identified.

Colonial officials maintained that advancement of any society would be coupled with increased demands for manufactured goods, which in turn required increased agricultural production to meet market demands. They claimed that this would encourage the peasants to shift from subsistence agriculture to growing commercial crops.[12] However, as Van Beusekom[13] convincingly suggests, the discussions focused on changes in development paradigms instead of understanding what actually happened to development projects in the light of stated goals. Although the goals were to reverse anticipated environmental impacts, nothing was said about the effects of development projects on the environment.

In this chapter we first present a theoretical basis for the African environmental crisis. Second, we examine the origins of the environmental crisis hypothesis—in terms of both global and local causes. Third, we analyze how the colonial land-use policy transformed indigenous resource use and created conditions susceptible to land degradation. Fourth, we examine the contribution of development schemes that were viewed as solutions to the environmental crisis.

Theoretical basis for African environmental crisis narratives

We discuss two theories—the 'nature-culture trap' posited by Emmanuel Kreike, and the 'environmental change and policy' conundrum discussed by Melissa Leach and Robin Means—to investigate how environmental crisis narratives might have originated. Emmanuel Kreike[14] proposes three hypotheses to explain changes in the physical environment, which he describes as: *modernization*, *declinist* and *inclinist*, each of which reflects how the physical environment changes and the directions this may take. The *modernization* hypothesis focuses on the rigorous use of science and the application of technology as a solution to manage natural resources and environmental problems. It accepts certain levels of environmental degradation 'as a price of progress and economic growth.' Conversely, the *declinist* hypothesis reasons that the application of modern science is a cause of environmental degradation and explains how human agencies degrade pristine nature. The declinist paradigm claims that the pre-colonial communities lived in harmony with their environment. That changed when colonial involvement led to clearing natural vegetation to provide space for large-scale agricultural and grazing schemes.

More fundamentally, the *inclinist* hypothesis advocates the use of indigenous knowledge to explain adaptations to changes in resource management in order to combat environmental degradation. It rejects the alarmist thesis of extreme environmental degradation which it attributes to prejudice in depicting the African people as agents of environmental crisis. Further, Kreike argues that Africa presents natural and social footprints of human agencies from pre-colonial periods, thus rejecting the idea of 'pristine nature.' That is to say, the African environment has changed in the past and will change in the future. He highlights the varieties of scales at which environmental changes occur, for which the drivers are both natural and human induced. He suggests that dynamic changes in nature–human relations—including the exploitation of natural resources and impacts of natural variability—are likely to continue to control environmental changes.

Melissa Leach and Robin Means,[15] by comparison, are categorical in their opinion that colonial and contemporary environmental policies are the principal forces driving the narrative of environmental degradation. The narrative is a powerful tool that perpetuates the viewpoint that African peasants misused their environments. It was so entrenched and durable that colonial and post-independence administrations used it as a guiding principle in developing environmental policies. We now go on to examine the origin of the narrative.

Origins of the environmental crisis hypothesis

By 1935, E. Stebbing,[16] the professor of forestry at the University of Edinburgh, was advancing a hypothesis that due to the misuse of natural resources, the Sahara Desert was expanding southwards and threatening the West African colonies. Was it a global view of environmental changes, or local land-use events, or both that popularized these African environmental crisis narratives? The origin of the African environmental crisis might be considered as being both global and local, in each case, producing varied narratives. A historical overview has recently been published.[17] We examine the global origin first, followed by local perspectives.

Global environmental narratives

The global environmental discourse has its origin in the US Great Plains during the late nineteenth century and early 1930s. Overgrazing aggravated by extended droughts, overexposed soils blown by winds created the problem referred to as the 'dust bowl,' during the period more colloquially referred to as the 'dirty thirties.'[18] The American Government responded by implementing massive land rehabilitation programs, as well as research to investigate the socio-ecological triggers of the dust bowl. The turning point was the merging of restoration work and increased interest in ecological research.[19] The realization emerged that the problem was prompted by human activities—such as breaking up the soils of the Great Plains and allowing heavy livestock grazing in the rangelands—while ultimate causes were found elsewhere. According to Donald Worster,[20] although the dust bowl appeared in the 1930s, the processes had begun some 50 years earlier. Accordingly, the close link between the dust bowl and the economic recessions of the 1930s might be merely coincidental.

Because of its global implications, the problems related to the dust bowl were considered as 'cascading events' that might have been initiated in small areas but spread to affect larger areas.[21] There was a perception that conditions associated with the 'dust bowl' existed in the newly formed African colonies,[22] thus suggesting that the risk of the global dust bowl that ruined the economies of the American Great Plains was also a possibility in African environments.[23] An important question posed by David Anderson[24] is 'how ... the global science of economic depression, dust bowl and droughts in the USA influenced environmental and development policies' in Africa.

Among extreme ideas that influenced colonial development policy were those of Elspeth Huxley[25] (mentioned earlier in Chapter 1) who called for the deliberate reduction of livestock in the African reserves. We pay attention to her arguments because they were both radical and representative of colonial thinking at the time. In her view, the colonial government should take far-reaching decisions if the grazing lands were to be saved from permanent damage caused by livestock overgrazing. She stated: '[i]f nothing is done—it is certain that within ten years, large areas of pastureland will have been turned into desert, water supplies will have been seriously depleted, and the affected areas will suffer from frequent droughts.' Colonial experts, including Huxley, discounted the possibility that excess stock could be sent to other grazing lands. She added: 'in the first place there is not always suitable land available, and in the second place, the new land would soon be eaten to death like the old.' In her opinion, colonial actions against the problem of livestock overstocking should be resolute, including the use of force where necessary, even if that meant 'calling in the army.' Another of her suggestions was that all the male animals should be castrated for 'the breed [to] die out.' The other equally implausible proposal was 'compulsory culling,' which she argued would somehow raise the living standards of the African peoples. Such proposals appealed to colonial officials who linked land degradation with poor land use by African peasants.

Local environmental crisis narratives

We break down our presentation of local perspectives of African environmental crisis narratives into ecological and development/management and political perspectives. According to the ecological perspective, indigenous land use removed vegetation—through deforestation, use of fire, overgrazing or overcultivation—which created gullies across landscapes. This view went even further, claiming that under the combined consequences of these factors, formerly productive lands would potentially be converted into 'deserts' if interventions failed.[26] A reference point used was the widespread environmental degradation of the 1930s.

In Africa, during the 1930s, the 'dustbowl' was described using different terminology such as 'desertification'—a process linked to human actions that convert productive land into sterile environments.[27] It was suggested[28] that the arid and semi-arid regions inhabited by millions of African herders were prone to the problem of desertification: first, because the regions were overstocked, and second, because the climatic conditions behind the dust bowl were active. In official reports, desertification was used as a proximate cause of land degradation—associated with livestock grazing and indigenous crop cultivation methods.[29]

During this period, there was a major policy focus on African peasant agriculture and livestock husbandry across the East African colonies. There were two reasons for this. First, there was a general perception that the population numbers in African reserves (areas allocated to Africans) were growing rapidly, with the likelihood that land degradation on the scale of the American Great Plains was a potential risk. Second, the European settlers—who were also being criticized for their systems of agriculture—were determined to deflect attention from themselves by campaigning to place African areas under soil conservation programs. This tactic appears to have convinced colonial officials who 'acknowledged the need to impose greater controls on the methods of African husbandry.'[30] Consequently, while previously the practice had been merely to relocate African populations from their lands, the new approach was to encourage African farmers to produce more food and cash crops on the reserves. This was one side of the plan; the other side (from the perspective of the European settlers) was that allowing Africans to expand cultivation would accelerate soil erosion. It was for this contradictory reason that soil conservation developed political significance and it was in this respect that the links with the US experience were made.[31]

Indeed, among the colonial officials, some believed that the links between the US experience and African environmental conditions were definitive. Elspeth Huxley[32] was one such example, as mentioned before. She stated, 'Dust storms in America have provided the most specular example of contemporary wind erosion … a situation 'exactly similar [to the] … affairs' in Africa. Another European presumption was that land degradation in the African reserves was attributable to resources held as a common pool, while the herds were privately owned. This problem—which in later decades came to be known as the 'tragedy of the commons'—underscored the perceived causal relations between land degradation and individual livestock holdings.[33] The presupposition is that individuals will continue to overharvest resources held in common for personal benefits.

Hence, the suggested solution was to control the use of common resources.[34]

Land degradation vs. overgrazing

In considering the ecological explanation of land degradation,[35] we need a definitive understanding of the differences between degradation and overgrazing. Perevolotsky and Seligman[36] define *land degradation* as negative changes based on the use of subjective vegetation indicators (cover, species composition, and biomass and species richness); while *overgrazing* is an operative word that refers to the overuse of plants by herbivores. The same authors state: 'We suggest that traditional heavy grazing, often incorrectly termed "overgrazing" and blamed for many of the landscape ills of the Mediterranean region, is in fact not only an efficient form of land use but one that is ecologically sound.' Although the impression created in the historical literature is that overgrazing would permanently alter the biotic and abiotic components of rangeland ecosystems, this does not in fact happen—and if it does, it occurs only at the scale of landscape patches, as opposed to geographical scales.

We now examine the voice of a proponent of the overgrazing view, Henri-Noël Le Houérou, who spent much of his professional career working on issues of rangeland degradation in the Mediterranean ecosystems of North Africa. He believed that a century's evidence from interdisciplinary teams of scientists confirmed that there was general deterioration of the ecology, and that this was attributable to human actions and livestock grazing. This claim was challenged by the findings of colonial and post-colonial researchers (see Chapters 5 and 10). Le Houérou's sarcasm can be gauged from a statement such as 'livestock consume more feed than the pasture produces.'[37] However, this doesn't sound like a logical preposition, given that supplementary feeding is rarely practiced on a large scale in sahelian Africa.

Returning to the work of Perevolotsky and Seligman[38] in the Mediterranean rangelands—they provide an alternative opinion based on their knowledge of meta-analysis (500 years) of Mediterranean rangelands and grazing systems. They arrive at the following conclusion:

> Herbivores rarely denude plants completely, nor are herbivores completely excluded from the community; ... instead, there is ... an intermediate level of dynamic coexistence.... The high resilience of the Old-World Mediterranean rangelands and the persistence of grazing by small ruminants ... over thousands of years is an example of such dynamic coexistence.

Le Houérou and Host[39] (in another publication) acknowledge the interdependence between rainfall and rangeland production. Other researchers have supported this view, implying that the dynamic interactions between climate variability and vegetation productivity need to be separated from grazing impacts—and this can be achieved only under experimental conditions.[40] The differences of opinions were even more acute regarding African systems of livestock grazing, which the colonial government blamed for land degradation.

The officials appeared to be ignorant of the fact that indigenous land-use systems adeptly set land aside for grazing during different seasons of the year.[41] Another colonial misunderstanding was the use of carrying capacity as a measure for controlling stocking of the rangelands, and that this could be a fixed quantity for any particular landscape. In reality, different rangeland landscapes have different carrying capacities, which depend on several variables and refer to specific conditions, including the amount of forage produced, rainfall, soil type and moisture, grazing history, and the daily food intake required by specific species of livestock.[42] Accordingly, in a drought year when there is no forage production, the so-called carrying capacity can refer only to residue vegetation from previous seasons, which would be insufficient to sustain livestock. Consequently, the order by colonial officials requiring herders to reduce their herds to correspond with carrying capacity was not a practical solution. Archer[43] is even more blunt when he states, 'the concept is discussed without evidential support backed by controlled and pre-grazing trials—[and cannot] be applied in a historical study.'

Consequently, the argument by colonial officials for maintaining stocking rates according to carrying capacity was nothing but a myth, considering that there was no livestock census, neither was any rangeland productivity data available. The reality is that the best utilization strategy for such variable rangelands is according to traditional methods employed by African pastoralists. Therefore, if applied to African rangelands, a statement such as 'when a population is above a system's carrying capacity, environmental degradation occurs'[44] is not factual, since carrying capacities and herd population numbers remained unknown. Thus, it is not an understatement that colonial land-use policies had huge influence on environment impact directly or indirectly.

Changing land-use policies

By the early twentieth century, there was evidence that the colonial government was acquiring large tracts of land that had previously been managed by local African communities.[45] These lands were either transferred to European settlers, set aside as 'Crown land,' used for commercial agricultural production, or for purposes of nature conservation. The colonial policy of removing former inhabitants disrupted local agricultural and pastoral production by indigenous communities[46] and caused land alienation. Another policy was to control the remaining land allocated to African peasants and herders, thereby disrupting flexible land-use systems which had been prevalent during pre-colonial periods.[47] The bulk land use being promoted was plantation agriculture and grazing schemes. However, as will be shown later, the expansion of plantation agriculture did not immediately increase agricultural production.[48]

In some cases, pastoralist societies were displaced from their land altogether. We use the example of the Maasai, who were the greatest losers of land between 1904 and 1911.[49] The treaty to remove them from the northern Laikipia reserves to the southern reserves was agreed by 1904. The land into which they moved was drier than the northern ranges and infested with ticks and tsetse flies.[50] The expansion of the settler population, particularly into these vacated rangelands, was rapid over a short period of time. The European ranches were on an extensive scale (in excess of 50,000 acres apiece).[51] In contrast, the Maasai (estimated at 45,000 people) occupied a reduced area of 93,000 km^2 after their removal, compared to their country which had covered an estimated 200,000 km^2 before colonization. If one considers that their livestock population would have remained at the pre-displacement density, the remaining territory would be stocked at more than five times the previous level.[52] The direct impact of these interventions was a gradual breakdown of the indigenous systems of land use that in turn, resulted in range overgrazing.[53]

Under the circumstances, it became impossible to distinguish between impacts of policies implemented to promote economic progress, and those that resulted in actions that contributed to environmental degradation.[54] Such was the case until the Kenya Land Commission of 1933. In order to resolve issues of land alienation—which was the main bone of contention at that time—the commission focused its attention on investigating colonial criticisms of African methods of land use. The commission's report states: 'African husbandry was typically stigmatized as wasteful and deleterious to the soil,' a fact emphasized by the settlers when giving their views to the commission; they argued that Africans could not be trusted with land management, due to their tendencies to abuse the land.[55] The suggested solution was to implement large-scale development programs.

Large-scale development programs

The solution suggested to combat land degradation was large-scale development schemes, including soil conservation, agricultural and grazing schemes, among which soil conservation received the greatest amount of attention. The problem of soil erosion was perceived to lie at the core of economic and social development. It was linked to soil fertility, crop cultivation and grazing impacts. The solution to combating soil erosion was expected to solve other development problems. Due to the multiple dimensions of soil conservation related to the desired expansion of agricultural production, land-use transformation and rangeland management, the colonial message on the subject was vague as to what specific activities would address the problem. We now examine the multiple dimensions of large-scale soil conservation, agricultural and grazing schemes in turn.

Soil conservation schemes

There was general agreement among colonial officials that the African reserves were at greater risk of soil erosion than other areas.[56] Two issues were raised on the subject. The first issue was the need to find evidence of the benefits of physical control to prevent soil erosion and to protect successfully rehabilitated areas. The second issue was the extent of social acceptance of control mechanisms among local communities (see Chapter 6). In line with these issues, the history of soil erosion control reveals various shortcomings. First, despite the surveys conducted by Professor Robert Scott Troup[57] of Oxford University in Uganda and Kenya on the physical and fertility limitations of tropical soils, his report to the colonial office was not acted upon.[58] Second, the linkages between soil erosion and environmental desiccation were questionable. Third, the scale inferred excluded land protected from local land uses. For example, Lord E.B. Worthington[59] suggested that in some territories, there were areas understocked by livestock over a period of decades, but that the environment 'has systematically [been] destroyed.'

Additionally, the ultimate causes—other than those narrated in this chapter—were unknown. More specifically, early research on soil erosion did not use historical information to reconstruct environmental processes which may have caused it.[60] For example, did the erosion of soils include the loss of biological production potential of the land? Mathew Turner[61] defines 'ecological degradation' as 'persistent reduction in the biological productivity of an area.' It should be borne in mind that biological productivity involves environmental factors such as rainfall, which are not under human control. Therefore, the weakness in this debate is the failure to separate natural processes from those induced by human activities—which would be necessary in order to develop precise prescriptions of the causal factors of soil erosion.

However, even where historical observations were available, interpretations of environmental changes appeared to be imprecise. In the northern Kitui District, Kenya, A.M. Champion[62] reported a personal observation of the area called Mumoni:

> [The area] in 1909 was one of the most flourishing and populated parts of the district. To my great surprise when I visited the place in 1930 [21 years later] the population had almost entirely disappeared and hardly a head of stock was to be seen.... The area had been cultivated and grazed to destruction, where there had been grass and trees and shrubs, the soil was either bare and gravelly or was hard and sealed.... Where water had once been plentiful ... in 1930 it was either absent or only obtained by digging to a great depth.

An interpretation of the above observation is necessary. The earlier visit (which was shortly after the establishment of colonial administration) was during a wet year, when the population had enough pasture for their stock. The second visit in 1930 took place when famine held the district in its grip. This fact is not mentioned by the author. Furthermore, the author does not consider whether the 'disappearance' of the population could have been due to the government policy that removed people and livestock from their lands, or the drought itself.

According to Sabina Häusler,[63] the colonial soil conservation policy rested on four pillars: The first pillar was that soil erosion control had to be made compulsory. The second pillar was the colonial opinion that local peasants and pastoralists degraded soils due to their lack of knowledge of soil conservation and therefore required the colonial officials to educate them. The third pillar was the persistent perception that the main cause of soil erosion was increased populations of people and livestock. The fourth pillar was the thinking that indigenous land use required regulation.

From the mid-1930s, soil conservation programs and the process of building soil erosion control structures were placed under the supervision of the Department of Agriculture in all three East African colonies, overseen by provincial administrators. It was anticipated that desirable results would be achieved with increased use of ordinances to compel the peasant farmers and demonstrations of recommended agricultural technologies.[64] (More on this in Chapter 7.) The officials saw the need for constant demonstrations of rehabilitation methods to help farmers produce more crops.

By 1938, research on soil erosion had become important for government development programs. However, research at station scales was not applied to land use until the next decade (see Chapter 5) and did not therefore translate into increased land productivity.[65] African perceptions of colonial projects were informed by the unproductive time spent on soil erosion control. Furthermore, the technical officials working on large schemes seldom agreed on technical questions and solutions, thus demoralizing the staff involved, which—combined with the lack of repairs to soil erosion control structures—left the schemes in ruins.[66] According to Berry and Townshend,[67]

> The colonial administrators were wrong in their particular approach to the problem and it is here and in the reaction of the Africans to the colonial attitudes that we can find the reasons for failure. Many of the measurements actually adopted in conservation programs were unpopular with the people, because they cut across accepted agricultural practices. The peasants often had practical reasons for disliking measures.

In the Kamba reserves in eastern Kenya, government officials persistently blamed the peasants for keeping large herds, saying that these were responsible for environmental degradation.[68] Between 1937 and 1947, the Kamba districts of Machakos and Kitui received more than 50 percent of the total soil conservation funding.[69] By 1948, the programs involved the construction of terraces, planting alley grasses and manuring to increase soil fertility.[70] In the Kitui district between 1946 and 1949, 3,500 terrace structures were completed.[71] Between 1947 and 1949, colonial officials in Nairobi and London were determined to transform the Akamba rural landscapes through increased cash crop production. However, due to resistance by the Wa Kamba, the soil conservation infrastructure fell into disrepair, dams silted up and the restored gullies became active again. The colonial government found itself desperate[72] and decided that 'a frontal attack on the soil erosion problem' required changes in cultural behavior among the African peasants.[73]

In Tanganyika, the WaGogo and the WaSukuma were confronted with forced destocking programs for the purpose of soil erosion control.[74] However, the removal of stock disrupted their integrated farming-livestock system. The colonial officials ignored the realities, one of which was that the fertility of the crop lands had been maintained through the integration of crop cultivation and livestock manure.[75] Another experimental region was the district of Kondoa, which was known for spectacular gullies and bare ground—one of the most severe cases of land degradation in East Africa. Here, the removal of up to 90,000 head of stock did not produce dramatic results.[76] In the same district by the 1950s, soil erosion was considered to have reached extreme levels. It was proposed that planting sisal could contribute to soil conservation, although no success was reported in this regard.[77] The region attracted much research that continues to this day, still attempting to answer the very question as to whether or not livestock overgrazing was the cause of the severe land degradation. Contemporary research by Christiansson and colleagues[78] has demonstrated that the causes of land degradation in the region were historical, with the suggestion that it was linked to past climate change. Indeed, Paul Lane estimates that environmental degradation in the region of Haubi in Tanzania might have occurred between 600 and 300 years ago, during periods of extremely wet weather.[79] As archeological evidence[80] shows, the severe erosions of the region date back to about 12,500 years ago (during the wet Holocene period). Ecological historians later explained the problem in terms of historical environmental forces, including climatic variability and geological factors.[81] Land use intensifications at any one point in time might simply show spikes in the chronological history of the geological timeline.[82]

Indeed, mechanical methods of soil erosion control failed because colonial research investigated only areas that were utilized—spatial and temporal circumstances associated with the causes of soil erosion were not investigated in territories that had no recent history of use.[83] Any solution to problems of soil erosion would derive only from better understanding of the landscape history, the timing and sequences of land degradation.[84] Rationalizing soil erosion in terms of multiple causative factors, along with historical investigations, might have been the right approach.[85] The next prominent anti-soil erosion activities to be undertaken were agricultural schemes.

Agricultural schemes

As far back as 1923, an imperial conference had been organized to chart the way forward on agrarian development policies in the colonies. However, the British Treasury was not enthusiastic about this step, preferring to fund research as opposed to development programs. They claimed that without proper coverage of the region by Meteorological Services—that has direct influence on agriculture, it would be risky to expand agricultural schemes.[86] On the other hand, the colonial governments were pushing for schemes even in absence of the 'science,'[87] an approach which initiated competing land-use processes. The first process was separating land occupied by European settlers from the African reserves (mainly in Kenya); this created the 'white highlands' as islands, surrounded by African reserves. The second process involved the expansion of plantation agriculture. For example, the booming production of cotton by African farmers in Uganda and Tanganyika found ready global markets after the failure of the cotton crop in the USA. However, after 1925, when American production tripled, the prices in East Africa collapsed. Thus, the colonial policy on commercial crops—intended to enhance food sufficiency—turned out to be misplaced.[88]

In the drier grazing lands in East Africa, the governments experimented with large-scale agricultural production. One such crop was sisal. A marketing initiative called the Sisal Growers of East Africa was established, on the assumption that large-scale sisal plantations would potentially supply global market demands. In Tanganyika, sisal exports increased from 22,000 tons in 1923, to 62,000 tons in 1929,[89] but by 1938, the global price of sisal had slumped.[90] Furthermore, the climate variability and collapsing markets had a crippling effect on cotton grown on a large scale to serve competitive global markets.[91]

During the Second World War, the colonial governments took control of marketing agricultural products.[92] In particular, the governors of the three East African colonies embarked on war-time development programs by promoting regional collaboration for improving the agricultural economy.[93] In Tanganyika, after the 1940s, agricultural exports by African peasants increased in value and were estimated at £150,000 per annum; by 1948 this had increased by 50 percent. In particular, the export of maize from African farms was valued at £400,000 over the same period.[94] These increases in production were achieved without necessarily modernizing African peasant farming methods.

Post-war planning was concerned broadly with social and economic development, so researchers were encouraged to prioritize the problems they were working on according to the two policy directions (i.e., social and economic).[95] The challenge for practical research was the variety of problems that existed, which limited possibilities for investigating and solving within reasonable time frames.[96] With funding enabled by the Colonial Development and Welfare Act of 1945, the colonial office was able to support several large-scale projects.[97] However, the expansion of cash crops[98] required radical policy changes, particularly a move from traditional land tenure practices[99] to commercial agriculture requirements. The African Land Development (ALDEV) project that had invested heavily in soil conservation schemes during the post-war years extended support to agricultural production schemes. Under the British Labour Government in 1945, an amount of $12 million per year was put at the disposal of the colonies, and about £3 million was allocated to the development of African agriculture. Given these opportunities, African farmers successfully applied their own knowledge and low technology to expand agricultural production.

The colonial policy was to transition peasant farmers from subsistence production to commercial crops such as cotton. In this venture, the Sukuma of Tanganyika were willing to move from subsistence to cash crops, buy more stock, and over time, strengthen their mixed economy. By using tractors they increased their capacity to cultivate larger pieces of land.[100] They found that cotton (output estimated at 500,000 bales per annum) was an important source of income, and the second most important export crop in Tanganyika.[101] However, by 1953, the cotton agriculture had declined due to infestations by pests and drought.[102] Between 1954 and 1962, ALDEV provided loans totaling £271,000 to over 3,800 individual farmers in the three East African colonies.[103] These so-called 'model farmers' adopted government farming technologies and soil conservation methods on their farm plots.[104] The most ambitious agricultural project was the groundnut schemes.

Groundnut schemes

During the post-war economic reconstruction period, the British Government began an ambitious scheme to provide vegetable oils that were in short supply globally. In 1946, a new proposal was made to the British Minister, by a Mr. Samuel who was the chair of the United African Company (the Unilever Group) on a visit to East Africa, on new development approaches for increasing food production. According to J. Wakefield[105] it was not until 1947—with the formation of the Overseas Food Corporation—that a new project to produce such oils from groundnuts to be grown in East Africa, justifying it on the grounds that the 'measures are necessary to fill the gap in the world supply of edible fats.'[106] The project enjoyed strong political support and provided the authorities with the prospect of harnessing European technology for large-scale agricultural production. The schemes served as a field laboratory to experiment with new agrarian development that—if successful—would demonstrate that 'prepackaged development schemes' were most appropriate in the colonies.[107] The groundnut schemes were larger than any development initiatives that the colonial governments had previously attempted, far exceeding what could be achieved using indigenous technology and knowledge.

The British Government and colonial authorities realized that growing the crop by African peasants alone would not satisfy global market demands; yet they knew that African labor was vital for the success of the project. Therefore, they argued that if African labor was utilized and the project was successful, the benefits to the African population would exceed anything that they could expect from traditional farming systems. A note in the *East African Agricultural and Forestry Journal* was emphatic about the potential outcomes, stating: 'If the groundnut scheme is successful, the productive power of every African employed in it will be unbelievably greater than under the present agricultural methods.'[108] The report did not clarify how this success would be achieved. In contrast, a few agricultural researchers had cautioned against such optimism.[109]

Earlier field observation work by John Wakefield[110] reported that African farmers had grown groundnuts on a small scale, producing from 544 kg to 908 kg per acre. The only reason that had prevented African peasants from growing the crop on a large scale was the difficult of clearing thick bush with their limited technology. The British Government gave its final approval in 1947 to the groundnut schemes. The cabinet mission was ferried across East Africa in a Royal Air force plane, covering 18,630 km of potential areas for the schemes in Tanganyika, Northern Rhodesia (present day Zambia), Uganda and Kenya. Later the Kenyan sites were left out due to their unsuitability. The project—at a cost of £23 million—was approved by the British cabinet and included the construction of a railway line to the sites to transport the produce more efficiently. The scale of land clearing planned required the use of heavy machinery.[111] Using caterpillar tractors pulling chains, a total of 3,210,000 acres of natural vegetation across the three colonies were designated for clearing. The colonial officials used standard American machinery that was not suitable for the soils of East Africa. Unfortunately, by removing the vegetation, the tractor blades also removed the source of soil organic matter that promotes soil fertility.[112] The schemes eventually cost some £37 million, instead of the approved amount.[113]

The British Overseas Food Cooperation had forecast the yields of groundnuts in Tanganyika and Uganda sites at 56,000 tons per annum in 1948, increasing to 609,000 tons per annum by 1951. Contrary to this optimistic forecast, however, the yield at the end of 1951 was a paltry 9,162 tons of nuts after an expenditure of £35 million.[114] In Tanganyika, the expected 128,000 acres per annum of land to be cleared of vegetation and planted with groundnuts in 1947, turned out to be only 60,000 acres. Furthermore, in the planted areas, yields were dismal, despite the high costs of planting. Havinden and Meredith[115] report that the mechanical harvesting of the nuts also failed: 'After the rains, the denuded ground baked hard in the sun and proved too difficult for the harvesters, with the result that many of the groundnuts were left in the ground or had to [be] dug up by hand.' During the planting season of 1948 only 15,000 acres, plus an additional 20,000 acres were planted, bringing total land cleared to 35,000 acres. In south Busoga in Uganda, an area of 750 acres was cleared of vegetation for the project, but was abandoned after spending £100,000, without planting any nuts.[116] By 1950, the Kongwa scheme—for which three farm units of 6,000 acres, 3,000 acres and 1,500 acres had been cleared—remained unplanted with groundnuts and was converted into grazing schemes.

These failures were due, first, to inadequate rainfall that resulted in poor crop yields and, second, the problem of working the soil with mechanized equipment incurred high operational costs. During the 1950–1951 growing season, about 35,000 acres could not be harvested due to hard baked soils using the machines.[117] By 1954, indigenous pests had ruined the remaining crops and the schemes were abandoned.[118]

Although the groundnut schemes had initially served as a model of mechanized farming in tropical Africa, they were never able to solve the problems of soil conservation that appeared to be the central thinking behind the colonial policy. It was argued that the misapplication of 'scientific knowledge to the African bush' had exacerbated the ecological and economic problems introduced by the groundnut schemes.[119] The motivation for investing in groundnut schemes had been economic, but the impacts were noticeably environmental, for example, the clearing of bush exposed soils to torrential rains that washed away the top soil.[120] Arguably, the greatest failure was the application of unsuitable mechanized farming technologies in African savanna environments.[121]

The technical difficulties of clearing large areas using heavy machinery and planning rotational cropping appear to have been insurmountable. Moreover, the lack of equipment repair facilities meant that the planned expansions of the crop were never achieved.[122] Consequently, despite the availability of funding, the groundnut production schemes failed.[123] Inasmuch as the groundnut schemes had been a publicity stunt, their failure brought the viability of large-scale schemes into question for the first time. Analysts would later suggest that the schemes were 'white elephants.'[124] Despite the British Government spending £36 million in Tanganyika alone,[125] the disastrous failures of the groundnut schemes vindicated those who had cautioned against investments in large-scale agricultural schemes in Africa, where scientific knowledge of the environment was lacking. The failures resulted in the subsequent dissolution of the British Overseas Food Corporation. We next analyze experiences from grazing schemes—which turned out to be another disappointment for the colonies.

Grazing schemes

Grazing schemes were introduced as part of the economic reconstruction activities during the post-war years.[126] The schemes countered what was

African environmental crisis narratives   85

perceived as the African herders' tendencies to overstocking the rangelands, thus accelerating soil erosion.[127] Four main approaches were used. The first was the development of water supplies, and the second was the improvement of veterinary services and livestock marketing. The third approach involved changes in land tenure, and the fourth concerned stocking control.

The grazing programs used water as a mechanism for dispersing the stock, thereby regulating the herds in relation to the available pastures. The schemes were planned for above-average rainfall years but lacked preparedness for drought management—thus making them ecologically and economically fragile in the face of recurrent droughts. The grazing schemes and development activities between 1936 and 1959 in the three East African territories (i.e., Kenya, Tanganyika and Uganda) are summarized in Table 4.1.

Table 4.1 Grazing schemes in the East African territories, 1936–1959

Year	Country/District	Development activities
1936–1945	Kenya: Samburu	Grazing schemes to promote livestock marketing. Quarantine interfered with livestock marketing.[139]
1946	Kenya: Nandi	A betterment scheme fenced 27,500 acres from which livestock was removed.[141]
1946–1958	Kenya: Kaputei	The Kaputei Maasai experimental ranch of some 22,000 acres. Compulsory cattle dipping against tick-borne diseases. Fixed stock numbers, which increased from a total of 1,400 head to 2,300 head by 1954, and to 2,400 head by 1958, instead of the 1,700 head as stipulated in the official agreement.[145] The Maasai moved en masse out of the scheme to resist compliance.
1949	Kenya: Machakos	32 dam units built to supply water for livestock.[140]
1953	Kenya: Machakos	Furrows to ferry water over 310 km, constructed by the Mau Mau detainees at a cost of £300,000. About 200 boreholes sunk and over 1,300 dams constructed at a cost of £400,000 to £500,000. Resettled 1,209 families on the grazing schemes.[140]
1954–1961	Kenya: Ilkosongo	A 1.3-million-acre ranch subdivided into 110,000- and 120,000-acre grazing pasture units. Grazing was intended to mimic traditional Maasai movements within the ranches. Fixed stock numbers for each herder to bring onto the pasture. By the end of 1959, the pastures were heavily grazed. Mass cattle mortality during the drought of 1961. The schemes were abandoned.[147]

continued

Table 4.1 continued

Year	Country/District	Development activities
1946–1949	Tanganyika: Sukuma	Carried the largest cattle populations by the 1940s. Mixed farming, but drought was common. Crop residues used as supplementary cattle feed, and livestock manure to fertilize farms. Land rehabilitation involved removal of livestock and fining individuals who did not comply. During the drought of 1949, 1.5 million head of cattle were lost. The scheme collapsed.[149]
1946–1952	Tanganyika: Kisongo	Mixed economy during famine periods. Land shortages disrupted traditional grazing movements. Successful disease control and additional water sources improved cattle recovery, with the population increasing by 50%. Excessive alterations of the Maasai land-use practices resulted in the collapse of the program.[153]
1953–1958	Tanganyika: Imbulu	Government ordered destocking. The Iraqwi chief used grazing certificates to bring more stock onto the scheme, claiming that they complied with the regulations. The scheme failed to bring any tangible economic benefits and was abandoned by 1958.[154]
1953–1959	Tanganyika: Shinyanga	An estimated £900,000 was allocated for water development, building 58 earth dams and 135 boreholes. Following the 1955 to 1959 drought, an estimated 200,000 cattle died. Although a pilot project, it was abandoned due to lack of flexibility in dealing with the variable climate.[155]
1948–1956	Uganda: Karamojong	Between 1948 and 1952, 10,556 km^2 of rangelands were rehabilitated. Veterinary services and cattle marketing were improved. Authorities miscalculated rangeland carrying capacities, so by 1956, the program had broken down and was abandoned.[158]

In the northern arid rangelands of Kenya, during dry years, shortages of water and pasture caused much hardship for livestock and people. When the herds died in large numbers, the colonial officials considered it 'as nature's way of maintaining a balance between animals and available pasture.'[128] Nevertheless, the grazing schemes did not improve the shortage of grazing for the livestock, nor did they reduce livestock mortality during drought years.[129] More importantly, the officials were unable to regulate livestock numbers according to the carrying capacities that they imposed on the rangelands. Since the nomads did not allow the officials to count their stock by direct methods, livestock numbers remained unknown.[130]

Due to the high variability of climate, and scarcity of forage and water, it was impossible to fully control herd movements according to official grazing plans, even with the use of armed guards who patrolled tribal boundaries. Despite heavy fines imposed by the officials,[131] the nomads used every available opportunity to disregard the grazing lines. The colonial officials were aware that part of the problem was that the pastoralists managed multi-species livestock, each with different forage requirements.[132] Some areas were suitable for groups that managed browsers (such as camels) and small stock, while the same group would seek different grazing areas for their cattle—often across administrative borders.[133]

During the post-war years, the most significant source of capital for grazing schemes was the African Land Development (ALDEV). In the Machakos District in Kenya, one project involved protecting 500 ha of a formerly degraded site from livestock grazing.[134] However, such trials lacked proper experimental design for comparing different grazing systems and controls in order to assess the performance of rangelands under protection from grazing.[135] Expecting the pastoralists to respond to grazing management in a prescribed manner failed to work, and therefore a new approach had to be found. In the Nandi district during 1946, the colonial government removed livestock from large areas[136] and, during the same period, the colonial government allocated £189,000 over six years for development in the Makueni District in Kenya—a model scheme according to which all other future schemes would be designed. The officials operated the schemes by what they called 'Makueni rules' which the African residents signed to indicate their compliance. The plan involved clearing natural vegetation and supplying each area with surface dams to water stock.[137]

In order to increase acceptability of the scheme, the programs were 'sweetened' by the provision of social and veterinary services. However, the types of projects and their roles in improving the social welfare of the African herders were often overrated.[138] In many cases, the project outcomes were not reported.[139] Again, many such projects failed. For example, the Kaputei Maasai[140] were provided with veterinary services and dipping facilities against tick-borne diseases, on the understanding that they were not allowed to increase the cattle population on the schemes beyond fixed numbers. However, years later (in the 1950s), the cattle population had increased by 50 percent above the recommended figures (Table 4.1). When confronted with destocking rules, the Maasai simply decided to move out of the schemes. A similar experience occurred among the Ilkisongo Maasai in 1954.[141]

Allowing the Maasai to practice their indigenous grazing system within block ranches did not meet official specifications. Initial increases in the livestock population were followed by a crash during subsequent droughts (between 1956 and 1959), when the schemes had become heavily grazed. Perhaps exaggerated, Talbot[142] describes the impact on the environment as follows: 'the destruction was so bad that the scheme was visible from a highflying airliner (if the ground was visible through the blowing dust) as a jagged, bared, red earth scar in the savanna landscape.'

In the Sukumaland in Tanganyika land was claimed to have been heavily degraded.[143] However, the planners of the scheme did not take into consideration the indigenous systems of land use in the Sukumaland.[144] The Sukuma traditionally practiced a mixed farming economy with crop cultivation and livestock management being equally important. Crop residues provided food supplements after harvest and livestock manure fertilized the farm plots. However, contrary to the expectations of colonial officials, grazing protection did not improve forage quality.[145] At Kalo in the Kondoa region of Tanganyika, pilot areas were also set aside for controlled rotational grazing schemes. These two schemes—the Sukumaland development scheme established in 1946 and the Kalo rehabilitation scheme established in 1948—were intended to improve soil conservation. The local people who failed to implement the project requirements were fined heavily for contravening grazing rules, which contributed to the breakup of the schemes.[146] In the Mbulu district the agro-pastoralists devised ingenious methods to circumvent the government destocking program.[147] Comparable experiences were reported among the Kisongo Maasai in Arusha, Tanganyika. The Kisongo maintained high densities of livestock through seasonal transhumance until 1945, when land shortages disrupted their traditional livestock movements.[148]

Between 1953 and 1959 large sums of money were used to develop water schemes in Shinyanga[149] (Table 4.1). Dorothy Hodgson,[150] reporting on the Maasai Development Plan (MDP), suggests that the program used heavy machinery to remove bushes that harbored tsetse flies. A total area of 128,000 acres of bush country was cleared. The design of that program suggested that community participation was encouraged by scientists and other technical staff, leading the officials to believe that unlike past projects, they had finally developed a sustainable and cost-effective plan. With a total budget of £265,000, the scheme was alleged to be successful. However, in the years following the project, the livestock quotas that the Maasai were expected to sell were not realized. Hodgson concludes that by 1955, 'less than half the estimated acreage of tsetse infested bush had been cleared.... The Maasai were not just disappointed, but angry by the end of the project.'

In Karamoja, Uganda, schemes were frustrated by rainfall failures, forcing the government to shift its attention from development projects to the provision of famine relief.[151] A long-term vision held by the colonial government was destocking the grazing lands and settling the pastoralists to cultivate crops.[152] The policy anticipated that if the grazing areas were supplied with sufficient water and the herds reduced, the rangelands would be able to recover from past overgrazing.[153] However, prior to the colonial period, the regular use of fire had maintained the landscape in the savanna—creating mosaics rich in grass cover, with reduced bush cover. The deterioration reported during the colonial period was caused by alterations in the traditional systems of rangeland management—including banning the use of range fire.[154] In addition, development planners made a fundamental error by basing the calculation of the carrying capacities of the rangelands on tax registers instead of on actual livestock populations. By 1956, when the livestock population census had been completed, this major error was realized, and the administration used it as an excuse to abandon the Karamoja scheme.[155]

From the forgoing discussions, the local causes of the environmental crisis were colonial land-use policies and inappropriate development projects, as opposed to indigenous land use. The lessons are clear: compulsory and often half-hearted government programs did not restore degraded lands.[156] From the evidence available, African environmental crisis was not the product of indigenous land use alone but development programs and changes in land-use policies. Chapter 5 tests the veracity of the environmental crisis hypothesis.

Notes

1 Hoben, A., 'Paradigms and politics: The cultural construction of environmental policy in Ethiopia,' *World Development* 23.6 (1995): 1007–1021.
2 Showers, K.B., 'Soil erosion in the Kingdom of Lesotho and development of historical environmental impact assessment,' *Ecological Applications* 6.2 (1996): 653–664, 654, 656.
3 Ijomah, B.I.C., 'Some problems of quantitative research in Africa,' in Tessler, M.A., O'Barr, W.M. and Spain, D.H. (eds.), *Survey research in Africa: Its applications and limits* (Evanton, IL: Northwestern University Press, 1973), 52, 53, 54.
4 McCann, J.C., 'The plow and the forest: Narratives of deforestation in Ethiopia, 1840–1992,' *Environmental History* 2.2 (1997): 138–159.
5 Rocheleau, D.E., Steinberg, P.E. and Benjamin P.A., 'Environment development, crisis and crude: Ukambani, Kenya, 1890–1990,' *World Development* 23.6 (1995): 1037–1051.
6 Stafford, R.A., *Scientist of empire: Sir Roderick Murchison, scientific exploration and Victorian imperialism* (Cambridge: Cambridge University Press, 1989), 189.
7 Phillips, J., 'Ecology in the service of man in British territories in Africa: Selected aspects and examples,' *Vegetatio* 5/6 (1956): 72–82.
8 Latour, B., *Science in action: How to follow scientists and engineers through society* (Cambridge Massachusetts: Harvard University Press, 1988).
9 Thurnwald, R.C., 'The crisis of imperialism in East Africa and elsewhere,' *Social Forces* 15.1 (1926): 84–91; Jacks, G.V. and Whyte, R.O., *The rape of the earth: A world survey of soil erosion* (London: Faber & Faber, 1939).
10 Commoner, B., 'Summary of the conference: On the meaning of ecological failures in international development,' in Farva, M.T. and Milton, J.P. (eds.), *The careless technology: Ecology and international development* (Tom Stacey, 1973), xviii.
11 Bonneuil, C., 'Development as experiment: Science and state building in late colonial and postcolonial Africa, 1930–1970,' *Osiris* 15 (2000): 258–281.
12 Van Rensburg, H.J., 'The role of pasture development in soil conservation, Tanganyika territory,' *East African Agricultural Journal* XIII.1 (1947): 23–26.

13 Van Beusekom, M.M., 'Disjunctures in theory and practice: Making sense of change in agricultural development at the office du Niger, 1920–60,' *Journal of African History* 41.1 (2000): 79–99.
14 Kreike, E., 'The nature-culture trap of the late 20th century global paradigms of environmental change in Africa and beyond,' *Global Environment* 1.1 (2008): 114–145.
15 Leach, M. and Means, R., 'Environmental change and policy,' in Leach, M. and Means, R. (eds), *The lie of the land: Challenging received wisdom on the African environment* (Oxford: James Currey, 1996).
16 Stebbing, E.P., 'The encroaching Sahara: The threat to the West African colonies,' *The Geographical Journal* 85.6 (1935): 506–519.
17 Benjaminsen T.A. and Hiernaux, P., 'From desiccation to global climate change: A history of the desertification narrative in the West African Sahel, 1900–2018,' *Global Environment* 12 (2019): 206–236.
18 Louis, B.R., 'Dust bowl era,' *Encyclopedia of Water Science* (2003): 187–191; Worster, D., *Dust bowl: The Southern plains in the 1930s* (Oxford: Oxford University Press, 2004).
19 Ormerod, S.J., 'Restoration in applied ecology: Editor's introduction,' *Journal of Applied Ecology* 40.1 (2003): 44–50.
20 Fairhead, J. and Leach, M, 'Desiccation and domination: Science and struggles over environment and development in colonial Guinea,' *Journal of African History* 41.1 (2000): 35–54, 41.
21 Peters, D.P.C, Sala, O.E., Alan, A.C.D.C. and Brunson, M., 'Cascading events in linked ecological and socioeconomic systems,' *Frontiers in Ecology and the Environment* 5.4 (2007): 221–224.
22 Sunseri, T., 'A political ecology of beef in colonial Tanzania and the global periphery, 1864–1961,' *Journal of Historical Geography* 39 (2013): 29–42.
23 Cohen, D.W., 'Agenda for African economic history,' *Journal of Economic History* 31.1 (1971): 208–221.
24 Anderson, D., 'Depression, dust bowl, demography, and drought: The colonial state and soil conservation in East Africa during the 1930s,' *African Affairs* 83 (1984): 321–343.
25 Huxley, E., 'The menace of soil erosion,' *Journal of the Royal African Society* 36.144 (1937): 357–370, 368.
26 Jacks, and Whyte, *The rape of the earth*, 20, 62, 73.
27 Stebbing, 'The encroaching Sahara.'
28 Tuhin, G. and Indrajit, P., 'Dust storm and its environmental implications,' *Journal of Engineering Computers and Applied Sciences* 3.4 (2014): 30–36.
29 Stebbing, 'The encroaching Sahara.'
30 Anderson, D. and Throup, D., 'Africans and agricultural production in colonial Kenya: The myth of the war as a watershed,' *Journal of African History* 26.4 (1985): 327–345.
31 Anderson, 'Depression, dust bowl, demography, and drought.'
32 Huxley, 'The menace of soil erosion.'
33 Hardin, G., 'The tragedy of the commons,' *Science* 162.3859 (1968): 1243–1248.
34 Becker, C. Dustin and Ostrom, Elinor, 'Human ecology and resource sustainability: The importance of institutional diversity,' *Annual Review of Ecology and Systematics* 26 (1995): 113–133, 115.

35 Backer, S.J.K. 'A background to the study of drought in East Africa,' *African Affairs* 73.291 (1974): 170–177.
36 Perevolotsky, Avi and Seligman, No'am G., 'Role of grazing in Mediterranean rangeland ecosystems,' *BioScience* 48.12 (1998): 1007–1017.
37 Le Houérou, Henri Noel, 'Man and desertification in the Mediterranean region,' *Ambio* 6.6 (1977): 363–365.
38 Perevolotsky and Seligman, 'Role of grazing in Mediterranean rangeland ecosystems,' 1014.
39 Le Houérou, H.N. and Hoste, C.H., 'Rangeland production and annual rainfall relations in the Mediterranean Basin and in the Sahelo–Sudanian zone,' *Journal of Range Management* 30.3 (1977): 181–189.
40 Anderson, G.D. and Talbot, L.M., 'Soil factors affecting the distribution of the grassland types and their utilization of wild animals on the Serengeti plains, Tanganyika,' *Journal of Ecology* 53.1 (1965): 33–56.
41 Phillips, J., 'Aspects of the ecology and productivity of some of the more arid regions of southern and eastern Africa,' *Vegetatio* 7.1 (1956): 38–68.
42 Murray-Rust, D.H., 'Soil erosion and reservoir sedimentation in a grazing area west of Arusha, Northern Tanzania,' *Geografiska Annaler* 54.3/4 (1972): 329, www.jstor.org/stable/520772, accessed 14 October 2016.
43 Archer, S., 'Technology and ecology in the karoo: A century of windmills, wire and changing farming practice,' *Journal of Southern African Studies* 26.4 (2000): 675–696.
44 Brian, O., 'Overgrazing: Is solution available?' *Nebarska Anthropolist Paper* 99, (1996), http://didgitalcommons.und.ed/nebanthro/99, accessed June 2018.
45 Morgan, W.T.W., 'The 'White highlands' of Kenya,' *The Geographical Journal* 129.2 (1963): 140–155; Mwangi, E., 'The footprints of history: Path dependence in the transformation of property rights in Kenya's Maasailand,' *Journal of Institutional Economics* 2.2 (2006): 157–180.
46 Neumann, R.P., 'Ways of seeing Africa: Colonial recasting of African landscape in Serengeti National Park,' *Ecumene* 2.2 (1995): 149–169.
47 Phoofolo, P., 'Face to face with famine: The BaSotho and the rinderpest 1897–1899,' *Journal of Southern African Studies* 29.2 (2003): 503–527.
48 Grigg, E., 'Land policy and economic development in Kenya,' *Journal of Royal African Society* 31.122 (1932): 1–14.
49 Tidrick, K.K., 'The Masai and their masters: A psychological study of District Administration,' *African Studies Review* 23.1 (1980): 15–31, 24.
50 Hughes, L., *Moving the Maasai: A colonial misadventure* (Oxford: Palgrave Macmillan, 2006).
51 Morgan, 'The "White highlands" of Kenya,' 146; Tidrick, 'The Masai and their masters: A psychological study of District Administration,' 25.
52 Neumann, 'Ways of seeing Africa.'
53 Sindiga, I., 'Inducing rural development in Kenya Maasailand,' *Journal of Eastern African Research and Development*, 14 (1984): 162–177.
54 Shutt, A.K., 'The settlers' cattle complex: The etiquette of culling cattle in colonial Zimbabwe, 1938,' *Journal of African History* 48.2 (2002): 263–287.
55 Anderson, 'Depression, dust bowl, demography, and drought.'
56 Chambers, R., *Settlement schemes in tropical Africa: A study of organizations and development* (London: Routledge & Kegan Paul, 1969), 20, 24.

92 Empire, science, society and development

57 Troup, R.S., *Colonial forest administration* (Oxford: Oxford University Press, 1940).
58 Church, A., *East Africa a new dominion: A crucial experiment in tropical development and its significance to the British Empire* (Connecticut: Negro Universities Press Westport, 1927), 103.
59 Worthington, E.B., *Science in Africa: A review of scientific research relating to tropical and southern Africa* (Oxford: Oxford University Press, 1938), 138.
60 Showers, 'Soil erosion in the kingdom of Lesotho,' 658, 659.
61 Turner, M., 'Overstocking the range: A critical analysis of the environmental science of sahelian pastoralism,' *Economic Geography* 69.4 (1993): 402–421.
62 Champion, A.M., 'Soil erosion in Africa,' *The Geographical Journal* 82.2 (1933): 130–139.
63 Häusler, S., 'Listening to the people: The use of indigenous knowledge to curb environmental degradation,' in Stiles, D. (ed.), *Social aspects of sustainable dryland management* (New York: Wiley, Chichester, 1995), 181.
64 Anderson and Throup, 'Africans and agricultural production in colonial Kenya.'
65 McNall, P.E., 'Economic phases in soil erosion control,' *Journal of Farm Economics* 22.3 (1940): 613–630.
66 Beinart, W., 'Soil erosion, conservationism and ideas about development: A southern African exploration, 1900–1960,' *Journal of Southern African Studies* 11.1 (1984): 52–83.
67 Berry, L. and Townshend, J., 'Soil conservation policies in the semi-arid regions of Tanzania: A historical perspective,' *Geografiska Annaler: Series A, Physical Geography*, 54.3–4 (1972): 241–253.
68 Gadsden, F., 'Further notes on the Kamba destocking controversy of 1938,' *International Journal of African Historical Studies* 7.4 (1974): 681–687.
69 Frost, R.A., 'Sir Philip Mitchell, Governor of Kenya,' *African Affairs* 78.313 (1979): 535–553.
70 Bernard, F.E. and Thom, D.J., 'Population pressure and human carrying capacity in selected locations of Machakos and Kitui districts,' *Journal of Developing Areas*, 15.3 (1981): 381–406.
71 Munger, E.S., 'Water problems of Kitui District, Kenya,' *Geographical Review* 40.4 (1950): 575–582.
72 Ward, E.W., 'Kenya's greatest problem,' *Journal of the Royal African Society* 38.152 (1939): 370–380; Bernard and Thom, 'Population pressure and human carrying capacity in selected locations of Machakos and Kitui districts,' 386.
73 Huxley, 'The menace of soil erosion'; Mackenzie, A.F., *Land, ecology and resistance in Kenya, 1880–1952* (Edinburgh: Edinburgh University Press, 1998).
74 Maddox, G.H., 'Njaa: Food shortages and famines in Tanzania between the wars,' *International Journal of African Historical Studies* 19.1 (1986): 17–34.
75 Berry and Townshend, 'Soil conservation policies in the semi-arid regions of Tanzania.'
76 Christiansson, C., Sikula, I.S. and Östberg, W., 'Man-land interrelations in semi-arid Tanzania: A multi-disciplinary research program,' *Ambio* 20.8 (1991): 357–361.
77 Christiansson, C., 'Notes on morphology and soil erosion in Kondoa and Singida Districts, central Tanzania,' *Geografiska Annaler* 54.3/4 (1972): 319–324.
78 Payton, R.W., Christiansson, C., Shishira, E.K, Yanda, P. and Eriksson, M.G., 'Landform, soils and erosion in the north-eastern Irangi Hills, Kondoa, Tanganyika,' *Geografiska Annaler* 7.2/3 (1992): 65–79.

79 Lane, P., 'Environmental narratives and the history of soil erosion in Kondoa District, Tanzania: An archeological perspective,' *International Journal of African Historical Studies* 42.3 (2009): 457–483.
80 Fleitmann, D., Dunbar, R.B., McCulloch. M., Mudelsee, M., Vuille, M., McClanahan, T.R., Cole, J.E. and Eggins, S., 'East African soil erosion recorded in a 300-year-old oral colony from Kenya,' *Geographical Research Letters* 34.4 (2007): 4401.
81 Christiansson, C., 'Degradation and rehabilitation of agro-pastoral land: Perspectives on environmental changes in semiarid Tanzania,' *Ambio* 17.2 (1988): 144–152.
82 Hobley, C.W., 'Soil erosion: A problem in human geography,' *The Geographical Journal* 82.2 (1933): 139–146.
83 Pereira, H.C., 'The research project,' *East African Agricultural and Forestry Journal* XXVIII (Special issue) (1962): 107–109.
84 Sheridan, M.J., 'The environmental consequences of independence and socialism in north Pare, Tanzania, 1961–88,' *Journal of African History* 45.1 (2004): 81–102.
85 Sleger, M.F.W. and Stroosnijder, L., 'Beyond the desertification narrative: A framework for agricultural drought in semi-arid East Africa,' *Ambio* 37.5 (2008): 372–380.
86 Grigg, 'Land policy and economic development in Kenya,' 1–4.
87 Malmsted, N.R., 'British government policy toward colonial development, 1919–39,' *Journal of Modern History* 49.2 (1977): D1249–D1287.
88 Church, A., *East Africa: A new dominion* (H.F. & G. Witherby, 1927), 248.
89 Westcott, N., 'The East African sisal industry, 1929–1949: The marketing of a colonial commodity during depression and war,' *Journal of African History* 25.4 (1984): 445–461.
90 Ibid.
91 Tosh, J., 'Lango agriculture during the early colonial period: Land and labour in a cash-crop economy,' *Journal of African History*, 19.3 (1978): 415–439.
92 Westcott, 'The East African sisal industry, 1929–1949.'
93 Lee, J.M. and Petter, M., *The colonial office, war, and development policy: Organisation and the planning of a metropolitan initiative, 1939–1945*, Institute of Commonwealth Studies (London: University of London, 1982).
94 Sunman, H., *A very different land: Memories of empire from the farmlands of Kenya* (London: The Redcliffe Press, 2014), 198.
95 Lee and Petter, *The colonial office, war, and development policy*, 165, 189.
96 Keay, R.W.J, 'The natural sciences in Africa,' *African Affairs* 64 (1965): 50–54, 51, 52; Baker, S.J.K., 'A background to the study of drought in East Africa, *African Affairs* 73.291 (1974): 170–177.
97 Schumaker, K.B., 'Soil erosion in the kingdom of Lesotho and development of historical environmental impact assessment,' *Ecological Applications* 6.2 (1996): 653–664.
98 Eckert, A., 'Useful instruments of participation? Local government and cooperatives in Tanzania, 1940 to 1970s,' *Journal of African Historical Studies* 40.1 (2007): 97–118.
99 Harbeson, J.W., 'Land reforms and politics in Kenya, 1954–70,' *Journal of Modern African Studies* 9.2 (1971): 231–251.
100 Tanner, R.E.S., 'Land tenure in northern Sukumaland, Tanganyika,' *East African Agricultural Journal* XXI.2 (1955): 120–123.

101 Mcloughlin, P.F.M., 'Some observations on the preliminary report of the culture and ecology in East Africa project,' *American Anthropologist* 68.4 (1966): 1004–1009.
102 Nyambara, P.S., 'Colonial policy and peasant cotton agriculture in southern Rhodesia, 1904–1953,' *International Journal of African Historical Studies* 33.1 (2000): 81–111.
103 Sunman, *A very different land*, 157–158; Swynnerton, R.J., 'Agricultural advances in Eastern Africa,' *African Affairs*, 61.244 (1962): 201–215.
104 McWilliam, M., 'The managed economy: Agricultural change,' *Development and Finance in Kenya 1945* (1963): 268–269.
105 Ibid.
106 'Agricultural development,' *East African Agricultural Journal* XIII.3 (1948): 129–130.
107 Bouneuil, C., 'Development as experiment: Science and state building in late colonial and post-colonial Africa, 1930–1970,' *Osiris* 15 (2000): 258–281, 281.
108 'Agricultural development.'
109 Ibid., 129.
110 Wakefield, A.J. 'The groundnut scheme,' *East African Agricultural Journal* XIII.3 (1948): 131–134.
111 Bunting, A.H., 'Land development and large-scale food production in East Africa by the overseas food corporation,' *Economic Botany* 6.1 (1952): 55–68.
112 Bunting, 'Land development and large-scale food production in East Africa'; Pearce, R.D., *The turning point in Africa: British colonial policy 1938–48* (London: Frank Cass, 1982), 186.
113 Wakefield, 'The groundnut scheme.'
114 Hailey, W.M. (Baron), *An African survey, revised 1956: A study of problems arising in Africa south of the Sahara* (Oxford: Oxford University Press. 1957), 844.
115 Havinden, M. and Meredith. D., *Colonialism and development* (London: Routledge, 1993), 279.
116 Chambers, R., *Settlement schemes in tropical Africa: A study of organizations and developments* (London: Routledge & Kegan Paul, 1969), 29.
117 Bunting, 'Land development and large-scale food production in East Africa.'
118 Phillips, 'Aspects of the ecology and productivity of some of the more arid regions.'
119 Van Rensburg, 'The role of pasture development in soil conservation, Tanganyika territory.'
120 Bunting, 'Land development and large-scale food production in East Africa.'
121 Phillips, J., *Agriculture and ecology in Africa: A study of actual and potential development south of the Sahara* (London: Faber & Faber, 1959), 339, 352.
122 Stanner, W.E.H., 'Observations on colonial planning,' *International Affairs* 25(3): 318–328; Phillips, *Agriculture and ecology in Africa*, 331.
123 Twining, 'The situation in Tanganyika.'
124 Havinden, M.A., and Meredith, D., *Colonialism and development: Britain and its tropical colonies, 1850–1960* (London: Routledge, 2002), 281, 282.
125 Low, D.A. and Lonsdale, J.M., 'Introduction: Towards the new order 1945–1963,' in Low D.A. and Smith A. (eds.), *History of East Africa, Vol III*, (Oxford: Clarendon Press, 1976).
126 Kakwenzire, P., 'Resistance, revenue and development in northern Somalia, 1905–1939,' *International Journal of African Historical Studies* 19.4 (1986): 659–677.

127 Van Beusekom, 'Disjunctures in theory and practice,' 98.
128 Ibid.
129 PC/NFD/5/5/10, W.N.B. Loudon 1945, Notes on the Development of grazing control in Samburu 1936–1945.
130 DC/GRA/2/2, From R.S. Winser to Mr. A.J. Stevens, Garissa District, handing-over report, 1946.
131 At 20 percent of the value of the trespassing stock.
132 DC/GRA/2/2, From R.S. Winser to Mr, A.J. Stevens, Garissa District handing-over report, 1946.
133 WAJ/17, From Mr. F.P.B. Derrick to Mr. V.G. Hardy, Wajir District handing-over report, 1947
134 Hailey, An African survey, revised 1956, 993.
135 Pereira, Riney, Dasgupta, and Rains, 'Land use in semi-arid southern Africa [and Discussion],'
136 Youé, C.P., 'Settler capital and the assault on the squatter peasantry in Kenya's Uasin Gishu District, 1942–63,' African Affairs 87.348 (1988): 393–418.
137 Osborne, M., 'Controlling development: 'Martial race' and empire in Kenya, 1945–59,' Journal of Imperial and Commonwealth History, 42.3 (2014): 464–485.
138 Ibid., 474.
139 Phillips, Agriculture and ecology in Africa, 369.
140 Hedlund, H., 'Contradiction in the peripheralization of a pastoral society: The Maasai,' Review of African Political Economy 15/16 (1979): 15–34.
141 Skovlin, J.M., 'Ranching in East Africa: A case study,' Journal of Range Management, 1971: 263–270.
142 Talbot, L.M., 'Ecological aspects of aid programs in East Africa, with particular reference to rangelands,' Bulletins from Ecological Research Committee 13 (1971): 21–51, 21–24.
143 Malcolm, D.W., Sukumaland: An African people and their country: A study of land use in Tanganyika (IAI: Oxford University Press. 1953).
144 Ibid.
145 Worthington, Science in Africa, 139; Allan, W., The African husbandman (Münster: LIT Verlag, 2004), 192.
146 Berry and Townsend, 'Soil conservation policies in the semi-arid regions of Tanzania,' 244.
147 By sharing grazing tickets with their neighbors outside the scheme, more stock was brought on to the scheme.
148 Lawi, Y.Q., 'Tanzania's operation Vijiji and local ecological consciousness: The case of Eastern Iraqwland, 1974–1976,' Journal of African History 48.1 (2007): 69–93.
149 Berry and Townsend, 'Soil conservation policies in the semi-arid regions of Tanzania.'
150 Hodgson, D.L., 'Taking stock: State control, ethnic identity and pastoralists development in Tanganyika, 1948–1958,' Journal of African History 41.1 (2000): 55–78, 55, 58.
151 Munger, E.S., 'Water problems of Kitui district, Kenya,' Geographical Review 40.4 (1950): 575–582.
152 Gartrell, B., 'Searching for the "roots of famine": The case of Karamoja,' Review of African Political Economy 33 (1985): 102–110.

153 Thomas, A.S., 'The vegetation of the Karamoja District, Uganda: An illustration of biological factors in tropical ecology,' *Journal of Ecology* 31.2 (1943): 149–177.
154 Mamdani, M., 'Karamoja: Colonial roots of famine in North-East Uganda,' *Review of African Political Economy* 25 (1982): 66–73.
155 Quam, M.D., 'Cattle marketing and pastoral conservation: Karamoja District, Uganda 1948–1970,' *African Studies Review* 21.1 (1978): 49–71, 57.
156 Sindiga, 'Inducing rural development in Kenya Maasailand,' 29.

Part II
Ecological and social research

5 Experimental science and development

A re-evaluation of the environmental crisis hypothesis, 1939–1960

Introduction

The African environmental crisis hypothesis (based on equilibrium ecological model) has been popularized by colonial and post-independent development and land-use policies.[1] The crisis hypothesis is closely associated with the general desiccation hypothesis discussed in Chapter 2 and historical patterns of land use discussed in Chapter 4. Although specific processes that defined the environmental crisis have not been clearly described—perhaps mainly due to lack of verification—the hypothesis has developed a life of its own.[2]

The current chapter presents a meta-analysis of published proxy environmental indicators (sediment production, crop yields, stream discharge, range production and livestock production performances, reseeding and bush clearing) from agronomic and range science grazing experiments to investigate if the outcomes of experiments may be interpreted according to the equilibrium or the alternative disequilibrium hypothesis (the following section discusses these two hypotheses). The experiments are those published in issues of the *East African Agricultural and Forestry Journal* between the 1930s and 1960s. We selected experimental reports that met the following conditions: (1) the experiments were scientifically designed (i.e., with replications of treatments and controls);[3] (2) the experiments simulated different land-use intensifications;[4] (3) the experiments were conducted for at least two years.

We specifically selected reports in which the data had been clearly displayed according to treatments, controls and time—which made it easy to summarize for visual comparisons. We used the interpretations of the authors and our own to re-appraise and verify the contrasting ecological hypotheses (equilibrium vs. disequilibrium). We present our findings in the following sections: (1) ecological theoretical framework—describing the features and assumptions of the equilibrium and disequilibrium hypotheses; (2) rationalizing experimental protocols; (3) agronomic research; (4) range science research; and (5) testing the environmental crisis hypothesis from the perspectives of the opposing ecological models.

Ecological theoretical framework

The history of imperial science in Africa has been framed around environmental degradation—associated with indigenous land use, particularly in arid and semi-arid environments. As introduced in Chapter 1, the ecological basis for considering land degradation is the succession model (also called the equilibrium model). This model assumes that environmental events are self-regulating unless the processes are disrupted by disturbances often associated with land-use activities. It proposes that land-use intensification serves as a trigger to prompt environmental indicators to change unless management initiatives intervene. Land-use intensifications include the perceived overcultivation of agricultural lands and overgrazing of grazing lands. The model further supposes that rangelands—including those in Africa—have fixed carrying capacities which provide a ceiling for allowable stocking rates, beyond which the range degrades.

While imperial science has focused on the proximate causes of land degradation (i.e., human actions), the ultimate causes (e.g., rainfall variability) that trigger different processes described by the disequilibrium model have been overlooked.[5] We have mentioned before that rainfall variability would influence land-use changes in arid and semi-arid regions, including those in Africa.[6] Thus, when during later years, the thinking about land degradation shifted from proximate to ultimate causes, this represented a paradigm shift in considering ecological processes that influence land degradation.[7] According to this alternative disequilibrium model—which clearly includes the functioning of the drylands—carrying capacity of the rangelands are highly variable in space and time in accordance with rainfall variability. The disequilibrium model is scale-dependent—this implies that land-use impacts at the scale of land units (i.e., local landscapes) will respond differently from those at geographical scales. Putting it another way, it would be inappropriate (without adjustments) to apply scientific results from research stations that pronounce problems of land degradation at restricted scales to indigenous land use on a larger geographical scale.

Further, the equilibrium model advocates rest and rotational grazing as alternatives to continuous rangeland grazing.[8] Fallow periods, reseeding and bush clearing were expected to improve rangeland production, while continuous grazing by livestock was expected to aggravate the problem of range restoration. In the context of these opposing views, we now rationalize a selection of proxy environmental indicators in selected experimental protocols to test the environmental crisis hypothesis.

Rationalizing experimental protocols

Testing the equilibrium model (which precipitated the environmental crisis hypothesis) requires an upfront definition of proxy environmental indicators of land-use intensification that have been investigated across East

Africa. These include sediment production, soil moisture, soil fertility, storm discharge, stocking rates, range production and conditions, and trends.[9] Land-use intensification may be described broadly as the expansion of agronomic and rangeland production, with associated changes in land-use gradients and the performance of corresponding proxy environmental indicators.[10] The response of the proxy indicators is inferred from their direction of change (i.e., increasing, decreasing or no response) as a result of land-use intensification. We have framed the relationships between land-use intensification and changes in the proxy environmental indicators using a schematic scenario model[11] (Figure 5.1). Each scenario provides an ecological explanation (either equilibrium or disequilibrium) in relation to changing land-use intensification. Considering that different proxy environmental indicators behave differently, each scenario might represent varieties of land-use intensification independently—that is, an increase in one type of indicator might not necessarily imply a decrease in another and vice versa.

In Figure 5.1, scenarios A and D might imitate the presumed environmental crisis hypothesis, while scenario C represents the alternative disequilibrium hypothesis. Scenario A corresponds with increasing trends of the proxy indicators with increasing land-use intensification (e.g., increasing sediment production). Conversely, scenario D shows declining trends of the proxy indicators (e.g., diminishing soil fertility) in response to land-use intensification. Scenario B is controlled by factors other than land-use

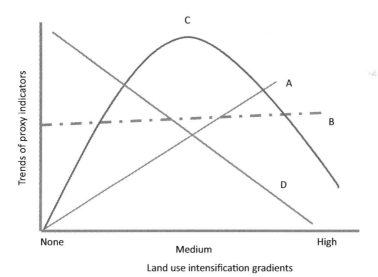

Figure 5.1 Scenarios of hypothetical intensities of land use and corresponding proxy environmental indicators.

Note
The scheme shows the predictions of equilibrium (environmental crisis hypothesis) (A and D) and (C) disequilibrium hypothesis. Line B corresponds with an independent gradient.

intensification (i.e., it is independent). In scenario B, the lack of response does not imply that the proxy indicators are not suitable for decision making in cases where environmental variables are appropriate for measuring changes. Scenario C (disequilibrium) corresponds with the 'intermediate disturbance' hypothesis[12] that suggests that potential responses reach a maximum at the level of medium land-use intensification. In our representation it might also suggest spatial and temporal variability of the indicators that would be necessary to calibrate to the scales of management.[13]

Colonial officials perceived that intensification of crop cultivation and overstocking of the rangelands would cause spiraling degradation due to increased soil erosion (Scenario A). In both cases, the proxy indicators respond in a feedback, namely that increased land-use intensification is followed by positive (scenario A) or negative (scenario D) changes in the indicators. In the view of imperial science, the African herders managing multi-species livestock would allow them to graze the vegetation closely. Accordingly, it was perceived that

> if not systematically controlled [the livestock] will crop an area so closely that the grass is not even permitted to come to flower and sheep will even pull up and eat the roots of many kinds of grass, whilst the goats will do untold damage to the trees and shrubs.[14]

However, two parallel processes might be operating in the grazing system. In the first process, until the level of medium land-use intensity (scenario C), grazing promotes rangeland productivity.[15] For scenario C, a decrease in the indicator with higher land-use intensity assumes that animals would continue to nibble at individual plants. Yet, in practice this rarely happens in African savannas where plants are highly adapted to herbivory. Therefore, in the second process, perennial plants use defensive mechanisms (such as thorns and spines) to protect the stubble biomass.[16] Hence, the grazers adapt their behavior by moving from one plant to another. Scenario D is rarely achieved in the field. The final outcome is influenced by rainfall variability rather than by grazing. It would therefore be imprudent to ignore factors such as droughts that might depress plant biomass, or sediment production from a watershed. We now apply some of these scenarios to the topic of agronomic research.

Agronomic research

In terms of agronomic research, we selected six experiments that reported rates of change in the following proxy environmental indicators: soil erosion, soil moisture days, storm intensity, river discharge, soil fertility and the application of commercial and domestic manure fertilizers to boost crop production. Our re-interpretation of the data is to inform readers to view the outcomes from the opposing ecological models. We discuss the findings of these experiments in turn.

Soil erosion

Soil erosion control had remained a major preoccupation for agricultural development in the East African colonies. However, in our perusal of the articles published in the *East African Agricultural and Forestry Journal*, between 1930s and 1960s, we found less than 5 percent of the total number of articles reporting some aspects of soils research (Table 5.1). We found even fewer experiments that investigated soil erosion at the watershed scale.[17]

In a Tanzanian study, historical rates of soil erosion across different land-use systems were estimated at 200–600 m^3 km^{-2} per year^{-1}.[18] An aspect of soil erosion with which the colonial authorities were mostly concerned was the

Table 5.1 Rates of soil loss, soil moisture and soil fertility based on research studies conducted in Kenya and Tanganyika, 1950s–1960s

Year	Country	Problem	Experiments
1950s	Tanganyika: Mpwapwa	Soil loss	Four treatments: Tr1: entire plots cultivated; Tr2: entire plot under grass; Tr3: top-half plot cultivated; Tr4: plots entirely under cover. Measurements, water runoff and sediment yields. The sediments were dried and weighed.[21]
1967–1969	Kenya: Buchuma and Mutara	Soil moisture days	Crop yields vs. good moisture days and grazing. Rainfall had stronger effects on plant growth than grazing.[33]
1954–1957	Tanganyika	Soil fertility	Application of commercial and organic fertilizers and crop yields.[44]
1955–1960	Tanganyika	Soil fertility	Six treatments: O, A3, M3, M1, M2, M4. Applied organic fertilizer with sulphur phosphate to determine yields of four crop types.[44]
1956	Tanganyika	Soil nutrients	In 1956, sulphur phosphate was mixed with manure. Nine trials conducted across different agro-ecological zones.[44]
1960	Tanganyika	Soil moisture	Investigated effects of soil moisture reserves on forage plants and grazing.[44]

formation of gullies. The available opinion then is that the gullies—once formed—are difficult to stop.[19] At the Mpwapwa research station[20] in central Tanganyika, the amounts of water run-off and sediments yield from experimental plots were measured over an eight-year period. The cultivated plots yielded an equivalent of 58.85 tons ha^{-1} of sediments, compared to plots planted with bulrushes that yielded 40.35 tons ha^{-1}, while the plots with grass cover yielded 22.28 tons ha^{-1} of sediments.[21] The annual run-offs from the treatment plots—up-scaled at watershed scales—are summarized as percentages of runoff and soils lost (Figures 5.2A and 5.2B). The limitations of the scale notwithstanding, the important finding was that vegetation cover was necessary for soil conservation.

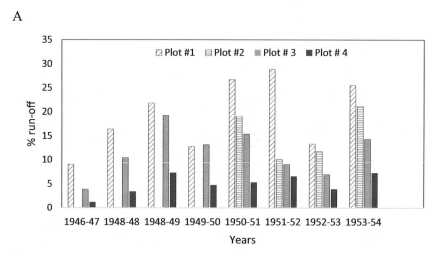

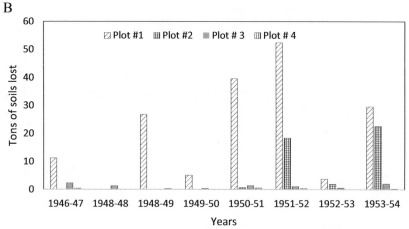

Figure 5.2 (A) Percentage run-off and (B) soil erosion in tons per acre per year, from treatment plots.

It should be noted that the experiment was conducted on a research station that did not reflect outcomes from a watershed or African farms. Thus, the results might be examined from two perspectives. The first is that data collected from micro-plots has limitations.[22] At the watershed scale—which represents real land-use conditions, rainfall provides a coarse scale in which the runoff and sediment production reflect the status of land-use intensification.[23] Investigations at the scale of plots would not divulge effects of land-use intensification at scales of indigenous land use. Second, at the watershed scale, soils eroded from a site are not lost but are redistributed downstream.[24] The experiment may be compared with storm discharge and sediment production by flash floods.

Storm intensity and stream discharge

Sediment yields may be related to the amounts, duration and intensity of rainfall (Figure 5.3). Despite the limited data, the volume of water discharged at the watershed scale has a direct relationship with the volume of sediments in the stream discharge—which in turn might be influenced by the intensification of land use within the watershed.[25] From the relationships in the studies we identified (based on the limited data available), increase in rainfall resulted in corresponding increase in stream discharge. This relationship is an example of scenario A in Figure 5.1. Other factors such as existing soil moisture would also influence the volume of stream discharge.[26]

The findings of various investigations[27] show that vegetation cover plays an important role in influencing stream flows. The removal of vegetation, for whatever reason, is likely to increase the amounts of stream discharge, thus incurring potential soil loss. Large-scale land clearing is often carried

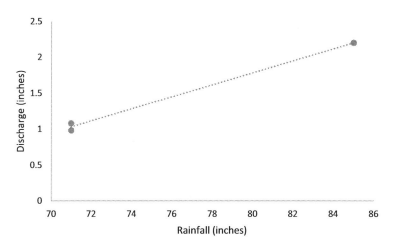

Figure 5.3 Relationship between storm intensity and discharge in an experimental watershed.

out by development projects but is not part of indigenous land-use practices (see Chapters 7 and 8). Considering that the East African region experiences erratic rainfall—varying between periods of drought and deluge—the amounts of sediment yield would also vary.[28] Investigations by other researchers[29] concluded that factors such as droughts and therefore moisture deficits would influence the effectiveness of rainfall in a watershed. Conversely, soil moisture days are crucial for crop production.

Soil moisture days and crop yield

In terms of crop production, the most important variable that requires monitoring is soil moisture, which is determined by the balance of water in the soil between rainfall and evaporation.[30] We use the example of experiments that measured relationships between good soil moisture days and crop yields at two sites in Kenya[31] (one in a low rainfall area and the other in a higher rainfall zone), conducted over a three-year period. The site with less soil moisture days produced fewer crops than the site that sustained higher soil moisture days that produced more crops over the three years.[32] This finding suggests that rather than relating total rainfall to crop yields, it would be more effective to relate soil moisture days to crop yields.

In another study, conducted in southern Tanganyika involving nine trial plots distributed across different agro-ecological zones, forage production was greatly influenced by rainfall and soil moisture reserves, as opposed to grazing practices.[33] Soil moisture days of between 100 and 120 days per annum have been shown to produce significant amounts of crops[34]—the challenge remains the scarcity of research on soil moisture field capacity.[35] Soil moisture days are independent of land-use intensifications (see scenario B in Figure 5.1), but they are associated with soil fertility,[36] which we discuss in the following subsection.

Effects of land use on soil fertility

An experiment in Tanganyika in 1954 investigated the efficacy of inorganic and organic fertilizers on crop yields over a period of four years. It assessed the effects of residual phosphate on soya, groundnuts, sorghum and maize production (Table 5.1 and Figure 5.4). Over the four years, the yields by different crops showed fluctuating responses. Among the four crops, maize and groundnuts showed superior responses to applications of phosphates during some of the years, whilst soya beans showed the least response. Evans[37] pointed out that the crops were grown on two different types of soils—however, this failed to be reported. G.H. Gethin Jones[38] reported that there are no absolute scales of soil fertility; instead, soil fertility is relative to the types of crops under given climatic conditions. This is contrary to the perceived universal decline in soil fertility according to environmental crisis hypothesis (see scenario D in Figure 5.1).

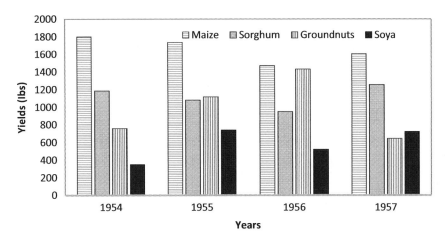

Figure 5.4 Effects of phosphate fertilizer on two grain crops (maize and millet) and two legume crops (groundnuts and soya beans) over four years.

The indigenous African farmers augmented soil fertility by making use of fallow periods and rotational cropping. Organic fertilizers were more accessible to the peasant farmers than costly inorganic fertilizers.[39] They applied cattle manure regularly in order to sustain crop yields.[40] Such responses are likely to be represented by scenario C in Figure 5.1. However, it is the inorganic fertilizers that were popularized but their disadvantages were often not explained to farmers. First, inorganic fertilizers have optimum levels above which soil nutrients will be promoted no further. In fact, repeated applications over longer periods might harm the crops. Second, legumes for example, do not require heavy use of fertilizers. Therefore, contrary to the environmental crisis hypothesis, inorganic fertilizers are of limited use in promoting soil nutrients. We now compare these outcomes with a second series of experiments.

In a Tanganyika study between 1955 and 1960, R.C. Grimes and R.T. Clarke[41] investigated six fertilizer application treatments (see Table 5.1) comprising mixtures of super-phosphates and cattle manure. Cattle manure promoted better grass yields than inorganic fertilizers.[42] The combinations with super-phosphate produced the highest yield in 1956 across the six treatments (Figure 5.5). Conversely, the residual effects of the farm manure—the first crops grown were preceded by a year of applications, and the second were planted two years after the manure application—showed that the soil fertility had declining tendencies after a peak (representing scenario C in Figure 5.1).

The findings did not disclose why soil fertility is generally low. In this regard, Sir Bernard Keen, Director of the East African Agriculture and Forestry Organization (EAAFRO) suggested in his annual address in 1954, that

108 *Ecological and social research*

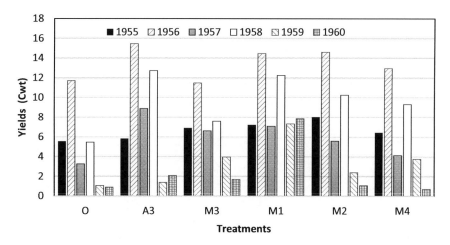

Figure 5.5 Responses of maize grain in cwt/acre (1 cwt = 0.05 ton UK) to fertilizer applications.

the low fertility of tropical soils could not be attributed to indigenous land use. The low soil fertility according to him was 'simply because the higher average temperatures cause a rapid oxidation of vegetation organic matter.' He advised the authorities and researchers that they should not attempt to 'force tropical agriculture into a system that is alien to it, but to develop one that fits the environmental factors.'[43] Unfortunately, colonial officials did not acknowledge this fact, and continued to attribute the loss of soil fertility to African systems of land use.

Overall, none of the agronomic experiments that we reviewed fully verify the equilibrium model (that is, the implied environmental crisis hypothesis). There was always the possibility of alternative explanations of environmental degradation. Since the experiments were not conducted on African farms, any conclusions that relate the outcomes to land use by African peasants would be invalid. Unlike the agronomic experiments, all the range science experiments were conducted on grazing lands used by the African herders.

Range science research

We examine ten range science experiments conducted across East Africa from 1948 to the 1960s (Table 5.2). The aims under general range science research were: first, to determine the relationship between rainfall variability and grazing capacities and carrying capacities; second, to determine whether grazing systems influence rangeland productivity; third, to determine if (according to expectations) indigenous continuous rangeland grazing practices perform poorly compared to the alternative rotational and rest grazing system; fourth, to determine if rehabilitation of degraded rangelands—through bush clearing and reseeding—promotes grass production; fifth, to determine if the range conditions and trends are declining (according to the environmental crisis hypothesis). Finally, our aim was to determine if the responses in both agronomic and range science reflect equilibrium (again inferring an environmental crisis) or the alternative hypothesis. We discuss individual experiments in turn.

Rainfall variability and grazing capacity

In the Machakos grazing experiments that related rainfall and grazing capacity, and measured rangeland carrying capacity,[44] the results show that grazing capacity forms mirror images of rainfall patterns (Figure 5.6A). By contrast, the carrying capacity (animals/unit area/unit time) varied over time (Figure 5.6B). During the last year of data collection (1957), the

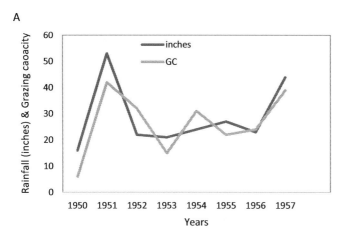

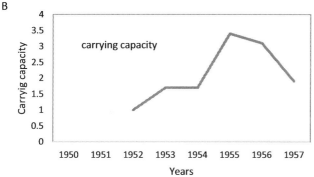

Figure 5.6 (A) Data showing relationships between rainfall and grazing capacity (GC) and (B) carrying capacity and time.

Source: H.C. Pereira, "Lessons gained from grazing trials at Makavete, Kenya," *East African Agricultural Journal* XXV.1 (1959): 59–62.

carrying capacity declined slightly when both rainfall and grazing capacity remained high. From the data alone, we are unable to explain the inverse response of carrying capacity to the variable rainfall. There are two possible reasons why carrying capacity did not respond to rainfall. First, the experiment would have excluded any biological data, for example, if the rangelands had been attacked by pests such as locusts (see Chapter 9). Second, there was possibility of inaccuracies in the calculations of carrying capacity. Both theoretical and practical knowledge of rangeland research in East Africa show that rainfall variability is the main driver of carrying capacity.[45] Nonetheless, the view of colonial officials was that livestock grazing diminished rangeland productivity. Accordingly, the rainfall factor was downplayed when colonial officials and researchers promoted the use of rotational grazing as opposed to indigenous grazing practices.

Rotational grazing

Rotational grazing (i.e., moving livestock between different pastures at fixed periods) is compared with the indigenous method of continuous grazing in terms of changes in plant production and animal weights. The purpose of rotational grazing is to rest some pastures while grazing other pastures, compared to the indigenous practice of continuous grazing over all pastures. The environmental crisis hypothesis perspective is that rangeland productivity would be improved under rotational as opposed to continuous grazing.[46] The assumption is livestock grazing is the dominant influence on changes in vegetation. Considering that the grazing locations and timing are fixed, the folly of the rotational grazing plan becomes apparent when rainfall fails in pastures scheduled for grazing but falls in distant areas. Researchers[47] found either 'no significant difference,' or that the continuously grazed pastures demonstrated superior grass production compared to rotational grazing, contrary to the environmental crisis hypothesis. In the indigenous system, the grazing was uniform across pastures and the grass swards had remained palatable to cattle. The differences were also reflected in changes in cattle weights (see below).

Other researchers were more forthright,[48] concluding that resting the pastures frequently was undesirable as it failed to promote pasture production compared to continuously grazed pastures. This finding demonstrates that the African rangelands—having co-evolved with herbivores—produce more forage when closely grazed than when grazing is deferred.[49] This is clearly contrary to the claims of the environmental crisis hypothesis.

Brian Walker[50] conducted grazing trials involving rotational (R), continuous grazing (CG), and grazing and rotational (GR) systems (Table 5.2). These trials showed that—contrary to the expectation that rotational grazing would yield superior forage production than continuous

Table 5.2 Impacts of rotational grazing, fire, bush clearing and reseeding on rangeland rehabilitation, 1948–1960s

Year	Country	Problem	Experiments
1948–1954	Tanganyika: Iringa	Rangeland overgrazing	Controlled grazing, bush clearing and application of fire.[55]
1950s	Kenya: Machakos	Land degradation	Restoration experiment using three treatments: bush clearing, reseeding and ploughing. The objective was to provide information on the productivity of the eroded landscapes over a seven-year period. The paddocks were stocked at 15 bulls per pasture. Rainfall during the period was above average.[55]
1951–1959	Uganda: Karamojong	Bush clearing	Controlled grazing experiments, aimed at rehabilitating grass production.[56]
1953–1955	Kenya: Kitui	Land rehabilitation	Tested the cost and efficiency of bush clearing using arboricides to kill bushy vegetation. The cleared areas were subdivided into paddocks of 150 acres each for trials with rotational grazing. Cattle in the grazing experiments were regularly weighed since weight was used as an indicator of growth performance.[56]
1954	Kenya: Baringo	Bush clearing	Investigated loss of grass cover, bush encroachment and high stocking densities. Modified season of grazing and reduced stocking density.[59] Bush clearing using mechanical means. The experiments involved the use of 'Holt rollers' pulled by a tractor to crush bushy plants. This was followed by burning the woody residue and then reseeding to regenerate grass. The area was rested for some time before being grazed.[60]
1950s	Kenya: Kitui	Land rehabilitation	Two grazing treatments were attempted. The first involved subdivision of the land in accordance with individual farms that were fenced to protect them from livestock grazing in order to allow recovery. In the second experiment, all bushy plants were cleared and the areas ploughed and sown with perennial grasses before arrival of the rains. The treatments comprised sowing seed on bare ground and ploughed up ground and sowing seeds. The controls were areas which had been cleared of bushes and left unseeded.[58]

continued

Table 5.2 continued

Year	Country	Problem	Experiments
1957–1961	Kenya: Baringo	Land rehabilitation	The Njems plains had been grazed by 36,000 stock in 1957 and were reported as being completely bare of any herbaceous cover. Three of the experimental sites were fenced to exclude livestock entry. Treatments included reseeding, and ploughing followed by reseeding. The growth performance of the reseeded plots was evaluated at the end of every growing season.[60]
1957–1961	Kenya: Kitale	Rotational/ traditional grazing	The grazing experiment involved a scheme of 29,780 acres stocked with 3,000 head of cattle. The area was subdivided into four blocks designed for cattle to spend about four months in each paddock before moving to the next paddock. The blocks were rested for at least 12 months. All the blocks, including the control ones that were open to continuous grazing, had their soil surfaces ploughed using tractors to embed the seeds. All the grazing blocks were protected from illegal grazing by being fenced and patrolled by armed guards. The experiments were abandoned in 1960.[60]
1960s	Tanzania: Sukumaland	Rotational grazing	Five-year grazing/rest treatments in grazing trials involving rotational and continuous traditional systems. Rotational grazing plots in four replications, each grazed for eight weeks: two weeks of grazing and six weeks of rest. During the same period, three paddocks were rested for one-third of the time in a three-year grazing cycle. The paddocks were rested during the early growing seasons to allow them to recover from previous grazing seasons. The treatments were then compared with continuous grazing. The effects of grazing and resting of the pastures were measured in terms of sward production and changes in livestock body weights on the different grazing systems.[62]
1967	Kenya: Kedong	Rotational grazing	Conducted grazing trials involving rotational (R), grazing and rotational (GR) and continuous grazing (CG) at Ukiriguru. The different grazing treatments were compared for changes in botanic composition and productivities of the natural pastures.[55] The grazing experiments were completed by EAAFRO in 1967. The design included two–four acres per steer rotational and continuous grazing, seven acres per steer rotational grazing, and seven acres per steer continuous grazing, compared to 13 acres per steer rotational and continuous grazing. Each replicate was stocked at six Borana breed steers, grazed for six months and rested for 12 months. The rotational grazing pastures were burned in year 3. The continuously grazed pastures were not burned.[55]

grazing—the former grazing system performed poorly, leading Walker to conclude:

> The botanic composition of the three treatments ... remained very much the same over the period of experiment.... Except for the increase in stocking rate, the continuous grazing treatment remained the same as in the two [other] treatments.... What would this mean ... is that at low grazing pressures continuous grazing is favoured over rotational grazing, because the pasture on that treatment is ... kept at a more nutritive stage than the pasture on the rotational [grazing system where grass was of a poor quality].

The conclusion would be a surprise to the colonial officials who advocated for rest and rotational grazing as opposed to the traditional continuous grazing system. Grazing seasons added another dimension to the outcomes of the experiments—that is, whether grazing takes place during periods of plant dormancy or during a growth season. Heavy stocking during dormancy would have little or no long-term effects on forage plants.

In another experiment, Walker and Scott[51] reported that continuous grazing at low stocking densities on the hard pan soils of Sukumaland tended to redistribute grazing pressure over the pasture. They recommended continuous grazing over rotational grazing for beef cattle production at low stocking rates.

In 1969, the steers in each treatment plot were slaughtered and the total carcass weights were measured (Table 5.2). Rotational grazing at 4 acres per steer and 7 acres per steer (i.e., high stocking density) showed lower weight gains than their continuous grazing counterparts (Figure 5.7). At the stocking rate of 13 acres per steer (i.e., low stocking density), the rotational and continuous treatments showed comparable results. The carcass grades under the rotational treatments had lower weights compared to those under continuous grazing.[52] Bearing these results in mind, we now compare the findings of experiments on range restoration.

Range restoration

Researchers in East Africa claimed that in some areas 'overgrazing and destruction of vegetation has gone beyond the possibility of restoration.'[53] This is precisely what the environmental crisis hypothesis would predict. But what does the statement actually mean? We will examine the issue from the perspectives of range rehabilitation and restoration methods: rangeland reseeding and bush clearing. In the 1950s, major land rehabilitation programs were implemented across the Karamojong district in Uganda[54] and the Kamba reserve in eastern Kenya. Some experiments compared bush cleared paddocks with those that remained under traditional grazing and those that had been ploughed and re-seeded (Table 5.2). The ploughed and

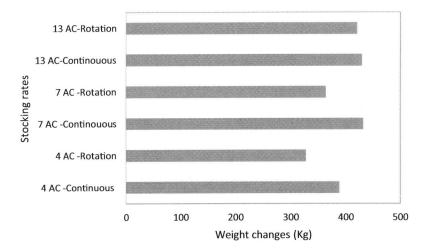

Figure 5.7 Rotational grazing experiments stocked at 4 acres per steer, 7 acres per steer and 13 acres per steer compared to continuous grazing.

Data source: A.D. McKay, "Range management research at E.A.A.F.R.O." *East African Agricultural and Forestry Journal* XXXV.4 (1970): 346–349.

reseeded treatments did not show superior productivity. Accordingly, Pereira[55] concluded that there was no economic rationale for breaking the soil to reseed in order to improve pastures. Again, it should have been acknowledged that the success of reseeding experiments was dependent on rainfall.[56] Moreover, this is another fallacy of imperial science, considering that there was no evidence of any lack of a soil seedbank in the first place.

In second reseeding experiments in the Baringo area, researchers assumed that the potential for the growth of grass cover had been lost,[57] based on reports of nineteenth-century European travelers. The soil surfaces were ploughed to create micro-environments where the grass seeds would be embedded to avoid being blown by wind or washed away by surface runoff water (Table 5.2). The first series of experiments failed to demonstrate any establishment of grass. David Pratt[58] made the following remarks:

> In view of the great influence of seasonal chance on reseeding, it is dangerous to place too much importance on the precise quantitative results obtained from a reseeding experiment.... [T]he most striking feature of the experiment is the extent of the differences between sites ... the results ranged from virtual failure to reasonable successes.

The performance of the reseeded sites—when compared with those stocked at 8.4 acres per head of animal unit—showed that the latter treatment exhibited better plant growth. The paradox may be explained by the role played by livestock in assisting natural reseeding—through trampling and breaking the soil crust, thereby improving water infiltration through the soil. This is an evolutionary role that ungulate herbivores have played in the establishment of savanna grasslands in Africa.[59]

In third reseeding experiments, the methods and seasons of reseeding were influenced by climate variability and site potentials.[60] That experiment required time for proper recovery of the grass cover. The main challenge was bush regeneration after one-time bush clearing. The trials failed for a variety of reasons, including attacks by army worms, locusts and harvester ants;[61] range restoration projects were therefore required, to focus on this multiplicity of issues.

Environmental restoration

Several restoration experiments were concerned with testing methods of bush clearing to deal with bush encroachment. Aerial photographs taken in 1947 through to the 1950s show that vast areas of the East African savannas were covered by bushy plants.[62] In the three East African territories, an estimated 241,402 km^2 were at risk of bush encroachment.[63] By associating bush encroachment with overgrazing, the colonial science perspective failed to understand the historical processes involved. From other historical sources, we know that bush encroachment has been a problem from the late nineteenth century after the rinderpest epizootic wiped out 90 percent of the herbivore populations. However, following colonial intervention, the traditional control method of using fire was banned, thus allowing the bush cover to expand, displacing the grasslands. Research experiments were therefore planned to test if removal of the bush cover would contribute to restoration of the rangelands.[64]

Both ecological restoration and grazing experiments were conducted over a period of five years.[65] Large areas of bush lands were cleared and subdivided into grazing paddocks. The experiments showed that low ground cover was due to bush encroachment, and not livestock grazing as suggested by the environmental crisis hypothesis.[66] Various methods of bush clearing were applied—such as manual and mechanical clearing, stumping, and fire, in combination with ploughing up the soils and reseeding,[67] followed by grazing.[68] The outcomes of the experiments showed variabilities.[69] For example, in bush clearing experiments using Holt roller tractors in the Baringo district in Kenya (Table 5.2), the areas from which bushes had been cleared were reseeded and planned for later grazing. However, reseeding was unsuccessful.[70]

In the same region, between 1955 and 1956, P.E. Glover and colleagues[71] conducted three controlled experiments (Table 5.2). In the first experiment, A.V. Bogdan[72] reported the removal of livestock from an area that was highly degraded and encroached by bush. One hundred acres of bushland were cleared and divided into pastures stocked with small stock and cattle.

116 *Ecological and social research*

The experiment compared cutting treatments, grazing and rest from grazing. While cattle-grazed paddocks experienced the most thriving regeneration of the bush, bushes were suppressed in the goat-browsed paddock. The impact on bush regeneration varied according to the season when treatment was applied.

In the second experiment, H.W. Bougall and A.V. Bogdan[73] reported that bush thinning by selective clearing and the application of fire increased grass production. This result had been demonstrated earlier by W.P. Bewg and Van Rensburg,[74] who showed that the selective clearing of bushes improved grazing. It would be recalled that the environmental crisis hypothesis held that the conditions and trends of the East African rangelands were on a downward trend (scenario D in Figure 5.1) due to disturbance to the environment.

Range conditions and trends

The methods of assessing range conditions and trends relied on the succession model (equilibrium hypothesis) which was developed in the USA and applied to the East African rangelands. The methods used perennial grass species (called decreasers—because they decline under heavy livestock grazing) as a key indicator of favorable range condition. Conversely, the weedy and annual forage species (called increasers—because they tend to increase under heavy grazing pressures) were considered as indicators of a decline in range condition. Yet again, the methodology ignored the role played by erratic rainfall in controlling plant growth. Thus, the absence of the decreaser species was not due to historical overgrazing, but instead to low site potential and rainfall variability. Therefore, an incorrect diagnosis was used to determine range condition and trends (scenario D in Figure 5.1).

The situation was a concern among grassland researchers in East Africa, who organized a conference in 1964 to try and reach consensus on methods of rangeland condition and trend assessments. The following definitive agreement was reached at the conference:

> [F]or sound quantitative and ecological premises to prevent further deterioration of East African rangelands, and to devise management practices for their reclamation and economic utilization, we must find a compromise between the desirable and the achievable under present conditions.... Objective and critical information on the carrying capacity of the different range types and their response to different management is the prerequisite for the determination and classification of range condition.... This could be done only in those locations where information on previous grazing and burning history, stocking rates, and livestock movements are available, and where future management could be controlled.[75]

Experimental science and development 117

According to the conference, these practices could be 'done only' in areas where there was a history of range research and some information on vegetation composition and soil conditions under a variety of treatments. Thus, the approach would not be applicable to rangelands where research had not been conducted—namely the majority of the grazing lands in East Africa. The second important phrase in the above quotation is the 'compromise' between various options—the 'desirable and the achievable.' This implies that the proposed methods for calculating stocking rates and grazing capacities were based on practical considerations instead of on exact science.

The conference agreed on the need to establish monitoring methods such as grazing trial plots and permanent transects to be continuously sampled. According to the conference, '[t]his could be done ... without preconceived ideas, until more critical information will have been gathered on the ecological status and production potentials of the [range types].'[76] Thus, the conference was finally questioning 'preconceived ideas,' such as the use of the environmental crisis hypothesis for guiding research activities. From the series of agronomic and range science experiments that we have analyzed, we may now reach concrete conclusions questioning the veracity of the environmental crisis hypothesis.

Testing the environmental crisis hypothesis

In our hypothetical scenario scheme (Figure 5.1), we indicated that changes in land-use intensification induce a variety of responses by proxy environmental indicators, which may reflect the function of equilibrium or disequilibrium ecological model. When applying this scheme to existing research studies, we have cautioned against research conducted at small scales to preferences of watershed or indigenous land-use scales. Whereas most of our scenarios can be confirmed by experimental outcomes, in most cases the outcomes were contrary to those predicted by the environmental crisis hypothesis.

We may summarize our findings as follows.

1 Vegetation cover plays an important role in controlling soil erosion. This interpretation needs to be broad enough to include all forms of land clearing, including by development projects.
2 Experimental research using micro-plots does not ideally represent soil erosion at the watershed scale. At the watershed scale, rates of soil erosion are influenced by soil moisture conditions, and the size and frequencies of storms that directly influence the extent of stream discharge.
3 Soil moisture days influence crop yields, more than direct rainfall.
4 Soil fertility is dependent on factors other than tilling of the land. Applications of inorganic and organic fertilizers improved crop yields,

but the responses were short-term, requiring repeated applications of the fertilizer. Thus, the general lower soil fertility in the tropics is not a function of land use.

5 The definitive core of the environmental crisis hypothesis prompted experiments that were intended to restore degraded rangelands. It suggests that rangeland problems were associated with stocking densities, and grazing and range carrying capacities, which were assumed to be fixed in time and space. However, without exception, the outcomes of the range science experiments rejected the hypothesis. Rainfall variability was crucial in rangeland reseeding programs that showed greater responses to rainfall and grazing than controlled grazing. In all experiments, rotational grazing—contrary to the hypothesis—performed poorly compared to the indigenous continuous grazing which demonstrated superior performance in pasture productivity, quality and increased weight of steer carcasses.

6 There were mixed responses in environmental rehabilitation experiments. Bush clearing improved pasture production, but reseeding experiments did not. Reseeding was influenced more by rainfall than by grazing. Goats were found to be more capable of keeping down bush regeneration after clearing than cattle.

7 Finally, the assessment of range conditions and trends—which according to the hypothesis were deteriorating—resulted in an incorrect prognosis that misled development projects. Thus, we have demonstrated that findings from experiments reported here do not support the environmental crisis hypothesis suggesting the misapplication of ecological theories.

Chapter 6 investigates the extent to which social science research may explain how African peasants and herders responded to development projects and whether their behavioral responses were influenced by government development initiatives.

Notes

1 Hoben, A., 'Paradigms and politics: The cultural construction of environmental policy in Ethiopia,' *World Development* 23.6 (1995): 1007–1021.
2 Grove, A.T. and Rackham, O., *The nature of Mediterranean Europe: An ecological history* (New Haven: Yale University, 2001), 11.
3 Keya, N.C.O., 'Grass/legume pastures in western Kenya: I. A comparison of productivity of cut and grazed swards,' *East African Agricultural and Forestry Journal* XXXIX.3 (1974): 240–246.
4 Fernow, B.E., 'Applied ecology,' *Science* 17.433 (1903): 605–607; McPherson, G.R. and DeStefano, S., *Applied ecology and natural resource management* (Cambridge: Cambridge University Press, 2003).
5 Oba, G., Weladji, R.B., Lusigi, W.J. and Stenseth, N.C., 'Scale-dependent effects of grazing on rangeland degradation in northern Kenya: A test of equilibrium and non-equilibrium hypothesis,' *Land Degradation and Development* 14 (2003): 83–94.

6 Oba, G., Stenseth, N.C. and Lusigi, W., 'New perspectives on sustainable grazing management in arid zones of sub-Saharan Africa,' *BioScience* 50.1 (2000): 35–51.
7 Kiage, L.M., 'Perspectives on the assumed causes of land degradation in the rangelands of Sub-Saharan Africa,' *Progress in Physical Geography* 37.5 (2013): 664–684.
8 Müller, B., Frank, L. and Wissel, C., 'Relevance of result periods in non-equilibrium rangeland systems: A modelling analysis,' *Agricultural Systems* 12 (2007): 295–317.
9 Ormerod, S.J., Barlow, N.D., Marshall, E.J.P. and Kerby, G., 'The uptake of applied ecology,' *Journal of Applied Ecology* 39.1 (2002): 1–7.
10 Freckleton, R.P., Hulme, P., Giller, P. and Kerby, G., 'The changing face of applied ecology,' *Journal of Applied Ecology* 42.1 (2005): 1–3.
11 See also Oba, Weladji, Lusigi, and Stenseth, 'Scale-dependent effects of grazing on rangeland degradation.'
12 Connell, J.H., 'Diversity in tropical rain forest and coral reefs,' *Science* 199 (1978): 1302–1310.
13 Oba, Weladji, Lusigi, and Stenseth, 'Scale-dependent effects of rangeland degradation.'
14 Champion, A.M., 'Soil erosion in Africa,' *The Geographical Journal* 82.2 (1933): 130–139.
15 See McNaughton, S.J., 'Compensatory plant growth as a response to herbivory,' *Oikos* 40: 329–336.
16 Some plants grow spines that detracts animals from continuously nibbling at them. See Oba, G., Mengistu, Z. and Stenseth, N.C., 'Compensatory growth of the African dwarf shrub *Indigofera spinosa* following simulated herbivory,' *Ecological Applications*, 10.4 (2000): 1133–1146.
17 Pereira, H.C., 'The research project,' in 'Hydrological effects of changes in land use in some East African catchment areas,' Special issue of *East African Agricultural and Forestry Journal* XXVII (1962): 107.
18 Christiansson, C. 'Degradation and rehabilitation of agropastoral land: Perspectives on environmental changes and ecological imbalance,' *Ambio* 17.2 (1988): 44–52.
19 Van Rensburg, H.J., 'Gully utilization and erosion control,' *East African Agricultural Journal* XXIII.3 (1958): 190–192.
20 Bewg, W.P. (reported by H.J. Van Rensburg), 'Iheme stock farm, Iringa, southern highland province, Tanganyika,' *East African Agricultural Journal* XXI.3 (1956): 169–170.
21 Van Rensburg, H.J., 'Run-off and soil erosion tests, Mpwapwa central Tanganyika,' *East African Agricultural Journal* XX.4 (1955): 228–231.
22 Holme, R.V., 'Soil examination by the microplot technique,' *East African Agricultural Journal* XV.4 (1950): 189–191.
23 Pereira, 'The Research Project.'
24 Duckham, A.N., 'Soil conservation and food production,' *East African Agricultural Journal* XV.2 (1950): 115–118.
25 Pereira, H.C., Dagg, M. and Hosegood, P.H., 'The water balance of both treated and control valleys,' in 'Hydrological effects of changes in land use in some East African catchment areas,' Special issue of *East African Agricultural and Forestry Journal* XXVII (1962): 36–37.
26 Dagg, M., 'Physical properties of the surface soils, infiltration and availability of soil moisture,' in 'Hydrological effects of changes in land use in some East African catchment areas,' Special issue of *East African Agricultural and Forestry Journal* XXVII (1962): 68–70.
27 Ibid.
28 Van Rensburg, H.J., 'Land use in semi-arid parts of Tanganyika,' *East African Agricultural Journal* XX.4 (1955): 247–253.

29 Pratt, M.A.C., 'Relationship of runoff to rainfall,' in 'Hydrological effects of changes in land use in some East African catchment areas,' Special issue of *East African Agricultural and Forestry Journal* XXVII (1962): 73–75.
30 Dagg, M., 'A rotational approach to the selection of crops for areas of marginal rainfall in East Africa,' *East African Agricultural and Forestry Journal* XXX.3 (1965): 296–300.
31 Cassady, J.T. 'The effect of rainfall, soil moisture and harvesting intensity on grass production on two rangeland sites in Kenya,' *East African Agricultural and Forestry Journal* 39.1 (1973): 26–36, 26.
32 Taerum, R. and Gwynne, M.D., 'Methods for studying grass roots under East African conditions and some preliminary result,' *East African Agricultural and Forestry Journal* XXXV.1 (1969): 55–65.
33 Anderson, G.D. and Naveh, Z., 'Promising pasture plants for northern Tanzania V: Overall comparisons of promising plants,' *East African Agricultural and Forestry Journal* XXXIV.1 (1968): 84–105.
34 Evans, A.C., 'A study of crop production in relation to rainfall reliability,' *East African Agricultural Journal* XX.4 (1955): 263–267.
35 Glover, P.E., 'Rain-water penetration in British Somaliland soils,' *East African Agricultural Journal* XV.1 (1950): 26–33.
36 Jones, P.A., 'Response of mature Napier grass to fertilizers and cattle manure in Kenya,' *East African Agriculture and Forestry Journal* XXX.3 (1965): 276–285.
37 Evans, A.C., 'Soil fertility studies in Tanganyika II: Continued applications of fertilizer on the red and red-brown loams of the Nachinwea series,' *East African Agricultural and Forestry Journal* XXVIII.4 (1963): 228–230.
38 Jones, G.H., 'Some aspects of the relationships between climate, soil type, nutrient-status and other factors, and crop production,' *East African Agricultural and Forestry Journal* XX.1 (1954): 13–14.
39 Evans, A.C., 'Soil fertility studies in Tanganyika III on the Kikungu and Luseni soil types of the lake and western regions,' *East African Agricultural and Forestry Journal* XXVIII.4 (1963): 231–239.
40 Wilson, F.B., 'A system of composting farm and village waste,' *East African Agricultural Journal* XIV.2 (1948): 82–85; Grimes, R.C. and Clarke, R.T., 'Continuous arable cropping with the use of manure and fertilizers,' *East African Agricultural and Forestry Journal* XXVIII.2 (1962): 74–80.
41 Ibid.
42 Jones, 'Response of mature Napier grass to fertilizers and cattle manure in Kenya.'
43 Keen, B., Director of EAAFRO, 'Presidential address,' *East African Agriculture and Forestry Journal* XX.1 (1954): 5–11.
44 Pereira, H.C., 'A physical basis for land use policy in tropical catchment areas,' *Nature* 184.4701 (1959): 1768.
45 Oba, Stenseth and Lusigi, 'New perspectives on sustainable grazing management in arid zones of sub-Saharan Africa.'
46 Mckay, A.D., 'Rangeland productivity in Botswana,' *East African Agricultural and Forestry Journal* XXXIV.1 (1968): 178–193.
47 Jacks, G.V. and Whyte, R.O., *The rape of the earth: A world survey of soil erosion* (London: Faber and Faber, 1939).
48 Ibid.
49 Van Rensburg, H.J., 'Grass burning experiments on Msima River farm, southern highlands, Tanganyika,' *East African Agricultural Journal* XVII.3 (1952): 119–129.
50 Walker, B., 'Grazing experiments at Ukiriguru, Tanzania II: Comparisons of rotational and continuous grazing systems on natural pastures of hardpan soils using an extra-period Latin-square change-over design,' *East African Agricultural and Forestry Journal* XXX IV.1 (1968): 235–244.

51 Walker, B. and Scott, G.D., 'Grazing experiments at Ukiriguru, Tanzania III,' *East African Agricultural and Forestry Journal* XXX IV.2 (1968): 245–255.
52 Ibid.
53 EAAFRO, 'Rehabilitation with grass,' *East Africa Agricultural Journal* XVIII.4 (1953): 137–158.
54 Jordan, S.M., 'Reclamation and pasture management in the semi-arid areas of Kitui District, Kenya,' *East African Agricultural Journal* XXIII.2 (1957): 84–88; Philip, M.S., 'Costs and efficiency of bush clearing by arboricides in Karamoja,' *East African Agricultural and Forestry Journal* XXVIII (1962): 49–50.
55 Pereira, H.C., 'Lessons gained from grazing trials at Makavete, Kenya,' *East African Agricultural Journal* XXV.1 (1959): 59–62.
56 Jordan, 'Reclamation and pasture management in the semi-arid areas of Kitui District, Kenya.'
57 Pratt, D.J., 'Reseeding denuded land in Baringo district, Kenya,' *East African Agricultural and Forestry Journal*, 29.1 (1963): 78–91.
58 Pratt, 'Reseeding denuded land in Baringo district, Kenya'; Pratt, D.J. 'Bush-control studies in the drier areas of Kenya: II. An evaluation of the Holt IXA "Bush Breaker" in *Tarchonthus/Acacia* thicket,' *Journal of Applied Ecology* 3.1 (1966): 97–115.
59 Savory, A. (with Jody Butterflied), *Holistic management: A new framework for decision making* (Washington, D.C.: Island Press, 1999).
60 Pratt, 'Reseeding denuded land in Baringo district, Kenya.'
61 Leach, R.J., 'Pasture development on the intensive reclamation area,' *East African Agricultural and Forestry Journal* XXVIII (1962): 53–54.
62 Wilson, J.G., 'Opportunities for pasture improvement in the various ecological zones of Karamoja,' *East African Agricultural and Forestry Journal* 27.Sup. 1 (1962): 47–48; Jones, P.E., 'Costs and efficiency of mechanical bush clearing in Karamoja,' *East African Agricultural and Forestry Journal* XXVIII (192): 51–52.
63 Swynnerton, J.R.M., 'Kenya's agricultural planning,' *African Affairs* 56.224 (1956): 209–215.
64 Pratt, 'Reseeding denuded land in Baringo District, Kenya.'
65 Ibid., 137.
66 Heady, H.F., 'Influence of grazing on the composition of *Themeda triandra* grassland, East Africa,' *Journal of Ecology* 54.3 (1966): 705–727.
67 Wilson, 'Opportunities for pasture improvement.'
68 Ibid.; Jones, 'Costs and efficiency of mechanical bush clearing in Karamoja.'
69 Northwood, P.J. and Macarthey, J.C., 'Pasture establishment and renovation by direct seeding,' *East African Agricultural and Forestry Journal* XXXV.2 (1969): 185–189.
70 Pratt, 'Bush-control studies in the drier areas of Kenya.'
71 Glover, P.E., Trump E.C. and Williams, R., 'Note on mechanical bush clearing,' *East African Agricultural Journal* XXV.1 (1954): 18–22.
72 Bogdan, A., 'Bush-clearing and grazing trial at Kisokon, Kenya,' *East African Agricultural Journal* XIV.4 (1954): 253–259.
73 Bougall, H.W. and Bogdan, A.V., 'Browse plants of Kenya: With special reference to those occurring in south Baringo,' *East African Agricultural Journal* XXIII.4 (1958): 236–245.
74 Bewg, (reported by H.J. Van Rensburg), 'Iheme stock farm, Iringa, southern highland province, Tanganyika.'
75 Naveh, Z., 'The determination of range condition and trend on East African rangelands,' *East African Agricultural and Forestry Journal* XXXII.2 (1966): 159–162.
76 Ibid.

6 Social science research
Behavioral responses to development, 1919–1950

The application of social science research for development was first mentioned in the early twentieth century, but implementation did not start until the 1950s.[1] In re-appraising the history of social science research in East Africa, we might therefore need to understand the processes and extent to which African societies responded to development changes.[2] The fundamental question of social science research was to understand whether or not the responses by African societies to development initiatives were predetermined by their social, ecological and cultural conditions, which in turn influenced their decisions.[3] We investigate this question in the current chapter.

Our analysis focuses on four perspectives in turn. The first perspective is understanding the history of social science research in the light of the economic behavior of East African societies. In doing so, we hope to unravel the socio-ecological factors that might explain the reasons why and how societies responded to development initiatives in different ways.[4] The second perspective is understanding how the responses of African societies to development initiatives may be influenced by socio-cultural ecology. The third perspective is understanding the impact of colonial policies on the responses of African societies. In particular, we investigate how close links between the work of social scientists and technical and administrative officials informed development policies that in turn transformed African systems of production.[5] In this case, it is interesting to understand the scientific rationality used by colonial officials in dealing with development endeavors that affected a variety of social-cultural systems.[6] The fourth perspective is understanding comparative responses to development initiatives by various African societies—that is, those who practiced agricultural, agro-pastoral and pastoral economies. In each case, implications for environmental crisis associated with social responses to development will be identified.

History of social science research in East Africa

The history of social science research in East Africa can be traced back to 1919 when practical applications of social science were first mentioned. In 1928, the International African Institute developed a five-year plan to coordinate scientific research activities with practical applications of the findings. The Rhodes-Livingstone Institute in what was Northern Rhodesia (present-day Zambia) proposed the coordination of social science research activities across southern and eastern Africa.[7] The driving force behind this initiative was to respond to discontent among African people over land that had been transferred to European settlers (e.g., in Kenya), land tenure changes, and the introduction of new policies—including settling mobile herders into grazing schemes.[8] The complex webs of African subsistence economies—and colonial ideas about economic progress and environmental conservation—influenced African people's social behavior and their attitude towards development. These factors received attention from the 1930s through the war years and the post-war periods. At the time in the 1930s, social anthropologists conducted in-depth studies of individual communities to interpret how African societies in general responded to colonial development interventions.[9]

The goal of social science research in that context was to facilitate the identification of individual or collective social behaviors towards new projects, and thus facilitate decision making. From 1944 to 1962 the British Colonial Social Science Research Council (CSSRC) provided budgetary allocations of £500,000 per annum to develop research that had direct applications in support of processes of social change across the East African colonies.[10] However, the application of social science research faced two contrasting viewpoints about promoting development.

The first viewpoint was to expect social science researchers to develop universal theories and methods that would investigate social problems objectively. The second viewpoint associated social science research with project implementation (see Chapter 7). By training colonial administrators in social sciences it was perceived that they would be better facilitators of government programs to meet the social and development needs of the colonized people.[11] The proponents of the latter view proposed that the training of social scientists should be tailor-made to the needs of the colonial governments. The opponents of this viewpoint (i.e., the first viewpoint) expressed their displeasure that government demands would force social scientists to focus more on practical problems and less on building theories and new scientific methods. They claimed that this would run the risk of lowering standards in social science research.[12] Conversely, the proponents of the second viewpoint added that social anthropologists working with colonial officials would benefit from transitioning from theoretical to practical actions prompted by lessons learned from development projects.[13] For social anthropologists the priority was in ethnographic encounters with African societies.[14]

Ethnographic encounters with African societies

Walter Goldschmidt[15] describes 'ethnographic encounters' in our context as anthropological investigations into how cultural practices influenced peasants, pastoralists and agro-pastoralists in their responses to development changes. We consider case studies by anthropologists in East Africa by briefly reviewing the ideas of H. Schneider and colleagues[16] who investigated the so-called 'resistance to change' by pastoralists and the comments on their work by other anthropologists who had opposite views. In their analysis, the anthropologists attempted to classify communities on a scale of development receptivity; this varied from agriculturalists being the most receptive groups to pastoralists being the least receptive. In his comments, Francis P. Conant considers the views of Schneider about responses by farming and herding societies to development change as being incompatible. In Conant's view, pastoralists have always accommodated changes such as occasional cultivations during perturbations when environmental and economic conditions warranted it. In response to H. Schneider and colleagues'[17] analysis, Andras Csanedy views the responses in terms of how different societies regard livestock as a medium of exchange. Conversely, in the view of Lenora Greenbaum[18] one needs to differentiate between development and economic change. Pastoralists may have shown resistance to development programs, but not necessarily to economic changes. Greenbaum opines that pastoralists showed no resistance to development if the venture was based on the indigenous economy. Kendall Blanchard,[19] in the same discussion, considers that since pastoralism operates within narrow ranges of environmental constraints to optimize livestock production, pastoralists were genuinely suspicious of changes that could jeopardize their production.

If as Schneider and colleagues suggest, 'development occurs when a change in any of the variables related to [spreading risks] between production costs and ... new investment capital,' then what changes would be required to bring about development among African economies? How would these changes influence wealth accumulation of herds (among pastoralists) or expansion of crop production (by peasants)? These types of questions have interested cultural ecologists who compared different communities pursuing different economic strategies.[20] In particular, anthropologists working in East Africa were interested in how diverse pastoral, agro-pastoral and agricultural communities responded positively to development innovations in the adoption of new technologies. As we show in the remaining part of this chapter, social resistance to development might be a colonial myth. What was referred to as 'resistance' was in fact simply the processes that African societies used when responding to colonial development initiatives.

We begin by focusing on pastoralist and farming societies and the various ways in which these two production systems responded to development changes. The responses of pastoral production systems towards development (including behavioral changes) were influenced by variables such as the ecology of the pastoral environment and herders' relationships with the livestock that they owned. Pastoralists need to make decisions contingent on the requirements of their herds and prevailing environmental conditions, which often oblige them into mobility. A herder's loss of capacity to manage livestock mobility constituted major risks to his economy. Under the transformed land-use policies, herd growth was no longer under the management of herders. Henceforward, herd growth would reflect the environmental and political situations.

Conversely, crop cultivation practices were influenced differently, since crops are viewed as fixed assets (as opposed to mobile assets). Among African peasants, an individual loses access to his fixed land assets when displaced but has the possibility of adjusting in a new environment. Additionally, although farming cycles are subject to seasonal variations, farmers simply must accept losses during adverse environmental conditions. Therefore besides crop cultivation, African peasants maintained small herds as an adaptive strategy to highly variable environments[21]—in order to spread their risks, as it were. Taken in this context, risk aversion is an inbuilt part of indigenous strategies in variable environments.

Thus, for African herding communities, shifting production to western types of economies was unlikely to offer incentives; instead it would involve changes in land tenure from communal to private land holdings, and reduction of herds without providing alternative economic opportunities. The foregoing discussion offers an idea of what to expect in terms of societies' responses to development programs based on socio-ecological systems of production.

Socio-ecological systems of production

Socio-ecological systems refer to relations between societies and nature in terms of food production. The relationship is noticeably complex, involving social adaptations, local ecologies and indigenous knowledge that, when combined, influence social change. Historical analyses of social change have revealed that a variety of processes were involved. Bernard Magubane[22] identifies two stages of change. The first stage is change by 'acculturation,' when African societies were exposed to changes introduced by colonial policies. The second stage is a period of 'acquiescence,' when traditional systems of production were compelled to adapt to the changes that had been introduced. For indigenous communities and their methods of organizing resource management, decision making, and prudent economic opportunities served as a cultural model. Consequently, how particular communities responded to the state's production innovations informed how societies made decisions under changing political and economic conditions. Whether the changes were by 'acculturation' or by 'acquiescence,' social science researchers were able to analyze societies' reactions to development. The processes of change might have varied from one society to another—each serving as a model for understanding how social science research may be applied in the context of socio-ecological systems.[23]

Anthropologists have described responses to development according to two viewpoints: instrumentalists and functionalists.[24] The instrumentalist approach views development as a good thing and considers that it benefits societies. This approach justifies the use of advanced technologies in improving production, compared to those that rely on indigenous technologies. Taking the mobile pastoralist production system as an example, the pro-development argument claims that pastoralists would be integrated into state political and economic programs; in this way, it shifts attention to transformative state interventions compared to indigenous, mobile production systems.[25] By comparison, the functionalist viewpoint contends that social and cultural variations reflect cultural adaptations by a given group. Thus, adaptations of new technologies might be culturally predetermined.[26] For this reason, the functionalist view is that some groups respond positively to development initiatives, while others respond negatively.

In any case, such social theories tend to caricature social behavior. Social patterns were developed as part of adaptive strategies to survive in highly variable environments. For example, pastoralists maintain large herds wherever possible to help them cope with variable environments, with livestock numbers serving as insurance against adverse climatic conditions such as droughts. These circumstances may have influenced the behavior of societies in certain ways, including their attitudes towards social and economic transformations. Thus, pastoralists may have resisted destocking programs either directly or indirectly, reflecting their cultural adaptations to avoiding disasters.

Conversely, cultural structures as instruments of change are not necessarily deterministic, whether societies accept new economic technologies. Change is a necessity of life to cope with new environmental, social, political and economic vicissitudes, implying that social behavior is fluid, as opposed to fixed. Therefore, the argument that social behavior and social boundaries enclosed African societies in some primordial environment sounds illogical. On the contrary, social behavior in response to economic and socio-political changes introduced by outsiders might require some imagination and understanding. In indigenous societies, there are no sudden instigators of change, except where societies have made such decisions themselves, or have been removed from their territories by the authorities.[27] We are interested in understanding if cultural behavior responses toward development may be influenced by cultural ecology.

Cultural ecology of East Africa

Ecological anthropologists[28] investigated how various economic and cultural pursuits influenced the way that communities responded to development changes. If it was cultural traditions that influenced how different African societies responded to colonial development interventions, then one might assume that there would have been some sort of correspondence between development initiatives and social-cultural responses.

Cultural responses would obviously be influenced by ecological adaptations, suggesting that there is a blend of ecological adaptations and social decisions.

A common theme is that the majority of the African peasants were not averse to economic empowerment.[29] Conrad Kottak[30] goes even further, claiming that environmental hazards stimulated environmental awareness and actions taken by officials, to which societies responded (either voluntarily or by coercion), thereby suggesting that there are 'pervasive linkages' between societal responses and development interventions. Thus, according to the same author, cultural practice 'enables human populations to optimize their adaptations.' This would suggest that those introducing development programs needed to combine variations of ecology and culture in their plans. Development planners focusing on livestock programs, for example, assumed that the technology introduced is general enough to be applied under various environmental conditions. In each case a positive response from the local communities was expected. We can give the example of animal health and destocking of rangelands. Acceptance of livestock health projects would be reflected by universal cooperation among individual households and communities.[31] On the other hand, forced destocking would not have been favored by any cultural groups. We now examine how social-cultural behavior influenced responses by African societies to development programs.

Socio-cultural responses towards development

Work by anthropologists[32] in East Africa hypothesized that responses to development programs by African communities occurred along varying ecological and economic gradients—from those who managed livestock to those whose economies were dominated by crop cultivation as mentioned before. The hypothesis was that those groups who were willing to take chances were bound to be more receptive to development changes than those who showed a high degree of independence.[33] Walter Goldschmidt— in his theoretical article on cultural adaptation—explains the flexibility of hoe-farming African peasants and less flexibility to change among pastoralists.

As mentioned before, pastoralists were hypothesized to be most resistant to change, due to their cultural predilections towards livestock ownership. Yet, social theory seems to negate non-economic values of livestock. We use a case example here. In the memorandum by the Chief Veterinary officer in Tanganyika cited by Archibald Church:[34]

> The chief value of the livestock in the country is to the native owner and cannot be over-appreciated in terms of export ... it is impossible to over-estimate the extent to which the health, welfare, and child-birth of the population depend on the meat and milk of the flocks and herds....

> Livestock represent more to the native than mere money. His flocks are not only his banking account.... They also feed his wives and children, while the sale of his surplus provides the wherewithal to meet his liabilities and taxes. The very fact that two-thirds of the best agricultural land in the territory lies idle because of the tsetse-fly infestation and prevents the keeping of cattle, lends added testimony to the importance of livestock.

According to the 'cattle complex' theory postulated by Melville Herskovits,[35] the attachment of various cultural groups to cattle would influence the outcome of any development programs that focused on destocking interventions. According to this theory, herding societies are bound to resist programs if they sense that the changes would be contrary to their social and economic values. However, due to this perceived 'resistance,' colonial officials had described the communities as being 'irrational' because they appeared to resist programs that would benefit them.[36] Accordingly, the colonial officials argued that the cultural value of cattle outweighed any economic rationale, and resulted in the accumulation of poor quality animals, which became a 'self-defeating' exercise.[37] The theory continued to inform colonial destocking policies, resulting in great divergence of views between the European officials and African herders. We will use an example here.

In a dialogue between a colonial official and a pastoralist in the Samburu District in Kenya, the official reported: 'It was utterly useless to explain that fifty fat cattle produced more milk and ate less grass than a hundred bags of skin and bones,' to which the pastoralist replied 'If I have a hundred cattle and fifty die, I still have fifty left. But if I have only fifty cattle and fifty die, I have none left.'[38] In a similar vein, Harold Schneider[39] citing the Kenya Land Commission report of 1932 stated:

> In the midst of plenty, the natives in pastoral and semi-pastoral areas are ... living under conditions of extreme poverty.... In a country such as Kenya, where the native looks on his stock as currency, and not as a productive asset, and where mere numbers count for more than quality, where ... the question of stock is interwoven in every direction with native habitats and customs, the solution of the problem is indeed difficult.

What the commission report failed to mention was that pastoralist societies have always supplemented their diets with grains, either grown themselves or bartered from neighboring agricultural communities. Livestock *is* therefore an asset that can be exchanged for other assets. The goal of every pastoral household is to provide a safety net for the family in terms of food security. With livestock being their most valuable assets, herding societies would clearly be unwilling if development projects failed to meet the basic requirements of their pastoral economy and livelihoods.[40] We now consider some of the hypotheses that describe changes in cultural behavior towards development.

Hypothesis of change

We have already introduced the discussion why some groups resisted change, others adapted quickly, while others took time to adjust their responses and practices.[41] Symanski and co-workers[42] suggest three hypotheses of change along the mobility–sedentary continuum. The first hypothesis proposes that mobile pastoral herders combined animal husbandry with opportunistic shifting cultivation, with the latter livelihood being more transient than animal husbandry (which is more reliable). In the second hypothesis, the authors predict adjustments along the continuum, each representing more stable livelihood sources, according to patterns of transitory cultivation or herding, depending on environmental conditions. In the third hypothesis, the degree of movement between the two economic opportunities is proposed to depend on reliability of the resource base, the availability of new technologies, population growth, and the types of livestock managed—which is also an important determinant of alternative adaptations.

Based on today's knowledge of pastoral production systems, we propose two additional hypotheses (different from those stated above). The first additional hypothesis proposes that the levels of transition along the mobility–sedimentary continuum can be regional—that is, the source of movement is determined by environmental and political situations. The second additional hypothesis proposes that the two systems operate simultaneously in response to internal and external factors. If political factors are taken into consideration, then colonial interventions would have affected the fluidity of the situation. Under colonialism, changed land-use systems created shortages of agricultural lands and those suited for livestock grazing; and in both cases, the population was restricted in their choice of land-use systems. Naturally, in such a system, when societies lost security in their access to land, opportunities for self-regulation were removed.[43]

Accordingly, the impact of colonial development cannot be explained by one set of changes, but a series of structural changes even among groups that showed no resistance to development initiatives.[44] The colonial authorities had underestimated the extent of attachment African peasants had to their land, but also their herds as just mentioned; and considering that the new technologies and practices adversely affected indigenous production systems, resistance to such programs should not come as a surprise.[45] We may consider agro-pastoralists as an example.

It has been shown that expansion of cash crops among agro-pastoral African communities was rapid.[46] The practice among agro-pastoralists is to utilize parts of the same landscape for livestock grazing and crop cultivation.

However, the colonial officials—aiming at soil conservation—did not see it this way. Instead, with that aim in mind, they forced the removal of livestock or the abandonment of crop cultivation.[47] The removal of livestock undermined farming systems by forcing families to abandon some of their economic pursuits and livelihood diversifications. A society under such radical economic change might shift from indigenous animal husbandry to settled crop cultivation. Such a decision might also occur through rational choices, they might have decided that it was more advantageous to settle and cultivate crops.[48] In a similar scenario, a nomadic pastoral community might combine mobility of herds and a shift to cultivation when environmental conditions allowed. By comparison, agricultural communities would have received new farming technologies more favorably, particularly where commercial crops would bring them additional income. We now contextualize these perspectives in terms of colonial development policies.

Impact of colonial development policies

There were two important aims of the colonial development policies. The first was stimulating the economy to finance the colony and produce surplus products for export. The second was building administrative infrastructure in order to implement development programs.[49] The colonial authorities perceived that closer contacts with African societies would be important for translating their policies into development activities.[50] By attempting to balance political stability and demands for intensification of economic production, the colonial governments hoped that environmental conservation would simultaneously be achieved.[51] As a result, these initiatives focused on the perceived environmental problems[52] and did not necessarily aim to improve small-scale farming systems or subsistence pastoralism.

In fact, it was perceived that small-scale African agricultural subsistence production was incapable of fulfilling the economic goals of the colonies. What was in contention was land—the colonial governments preferred allocating land to large-scale schemes for economies of scale. Consequently, the commercialization of farming was aimed at transforming the African peasant economies.[53] Thus the African societies were merely a 'cog in the development wheel'—relevant, but considered unnecessary for moving development plans forward.[54] This would explain why colonial development policies became so unpopular among local societies.

Colonial officials in East Africa had selected specific areas for development. The colonial development policy was to de-link one type of production from all others, in contrast to the indigenous practice of mixed economies. In making land-use changes, for example, the officials had an acuity regarding indigenous systems of land use. They perceived that because land was held in common at a tribal level, there were no incentives for African societies to protect their environment, which consequently contributed to environmental degradation. Hence, land-use ordinances were promulgated, allocating pieces of land to individual families or clans and limiting their stock numbers (see Chapter 7). It was further assumed that if implemented according to the plans, these land-use changes would improve local economies and reverse environmental degradation.[55] However, the greatest disappointment in development planning was the failure to take into consideration environmental variability.[56]

We examine two development approaches. First, most projects lacked alternative plans when rains failed, other than leaving the pastoralists alone to fend for themselves.[57] Second, the agro-pastoralists due to their sedentary nature participated in the soil conservation projects only grumblingly. In addition, soil conservation programs—such as building terraces across farmlands—were unpopular because they took up too much of the farming land. Such structures also required regular maintenance, which utilized labor that was required for crop production.[58]

In other cases, where the official policy displaced populations to allow construction with the aim of soil conservation, the peasants were forced into areas with low farming potential, which had serious consequences for their food production.[59] Furthermore, in planning large-scale agricultural and grazing schemes, development planners overlooked the ecological potential of the land.[60]

In the case of pastoralists, reactions to new development initiatives were varied. From the 1930s, there were limited efforts to understand livestock feed requirements, since the stock grazed on indigenous pastures. More specifically, there were few experiences from mixed livestock and agricultural systems. In Kenya, the absence of definitive policy was blamed for the lack of economic progress, especially in the African reserves. In any case, a uniform land-use policy to incorporate both farming and livestock herding was not feasible. Pastoralists needed more expansive lands for seasonal grazing, while cultivators needed higher potential lands where crop cultivation was possible. Still, among the communities that practiced mixed economies, land losses had the greatest adverse effects on the local economy.[61] Where land use became intensive, the communities were obliged to adopt erosion control technologies.[62]

By the 1940s, there was a perception among colonial officials that the populations of livestock and people had outgrown available land resources in the African reserves.[63] Due to these limitations of available land, any land-use changes would undoubtedly have sociological and ecological consequences.[64] The problem was that development planners continued to approach solutions from simple cause-and-effect relationships.[65] Therefore, when destocking programs were introduced with the anticipation that environmental conservation would be improved, the economic consequences suffered by African herders were not taken into serious consideration.[66]

The situation was even worse among peasant farmers, for whom the colonial researchers and officials assumed that indigenous methods of cultivation were lacking any inbuilt soil conservation methods.[67] On the contrary, as already mentioned, African mixed farming systems and their rudimentary methods are most appropriate in terms of environmental conservation. The practice of mixed farming allows individual farmers to use crop residues to feed their livestock after harvest, as well as livestock manure to maintain soil fertility. The colonial officials' fixation on African peasants as being a cause of land degradation ignored the potential for promoting land productivity.[68]

In summing up this section, we note that the adoption of new agricultural technologies was a process—initial resistance, followed by gradual acceptance. A comparative system permits understanding about complementary social and ecological systems that support the subsistence economies of African peasants and herders—by investigating why one group responded to development changes in a particular way and others responded in different ways.[69] In our analysis, we seek to identify key social, ecological and political drivers that brought about such different responses. The drivers of change altered socio-ecological relations, including political and development processes. Some of the changes—such as dislocation of local populations—reverberated throughout the region, putting greater pressure on resources elsewhere.[70] Next we examine comparative analyses of research conducted by social anthropologists among East African peasants and herding communities, showing relative behavioral responses to development changes.

Comparative social responses to development initiatives

Walter Goldschmidt[71] presented a proposal on how development interventions influenced changes in cultural adaptations of selected African societies. The societies were sampled across Kenya, Tanzania and Uganda. The communities showed a continuum of livelihoods, on the one extreme, hoe-cultivating farmers, and on the opposite economic gradient, pastoralists who adopted agriculture. The farming societies maintained small herds in mixed farming systems, while pastoralists occasionally fell back on crop cultivation when disasters decimated their herds. Conversely, agro-pastoralists adopted new agricultural technologies to expand economic opportunities. We are interested in how and why development changes were accepted or rejected by African societies. We will use some examples.

Colonial development initiatives had introduced cotton as a cash crop as early as 1908. By 1914, the Teso community on the Kenya–Uganda border was harvesting 8,000 tons of cotton annually. They had traditionally practiced a mixed economy dominated by indigenous agriculture. They represent a community that rapidly accepted newly introduced crops and were eager to try them out. This may be compared with the responses by the Nandi and the Kipsigis to development initiatives. From the middle of the 1920s, the European settlers—and later the colonial governments—observed that squatting on European farms by African peasants was a barrier to progress. The excuse was that the herds kept by the squatters overgrazed and caused soil erosion. The policy was therefore to eliminate African livestock squatting on European farms, but this left them without any other options.[72] The Nandi had resented the loss of their land to European settlers, but the pressure forced them to transform their indigenous economy into one of cash crops.[73] The Kipsigis and Nandi, after losing their land to European settlements, changed their economies from mixed agriculture/animal husbandry to one driven by market demands.[74] The traditional value of cattle had changed among this group to become a commoditized economy; cattle products such as milk were sold to creameries as an alternative to building up capital in terms of cattle alone.

In Kigezi in southwestern Uganda, there were concerns from the 1930s that indigenous farming systems were contributing to soil erosion. The peasants combined crop cultivation and animal husbandry, with cattle grazing on communal lands, while crops were cultivated on private plots.[75] The colonial officials claimed that the problem had been exacerbated by high human population density. The local peasants then combined indigenous and modern technical methods of soil conservation, and by 1949 it was reported that the soil had been stabilized and the conservation program had been a spectacular success.[76]

During the 1950s, social responses to government programs exhibited two trends, which we illustrate with two contrasting examples. The first trend was serious political agitation against colonial policies in East Africa—the Mau Mau rebellion was active in Muranga (part of the Kikuyu land), where people were utterly opposed to land terracing after the communities had been displaced from their lands. By comparison, the second trend was that this period witnessed governments winning over some of the societies to the idea of practicing soil conservation.[77] The Akamba of Kitui and Machakos who, before the Second World War had resisted government forced soil conservation programs, had been swayed by government propaganda. The Akamba set aside some 30,000 acres of hillsides for protection against grazing and crop cultivation.[78]

In Sukumaland (in Tanganyika), the society incorporated their indigenous institution of collective action into cooperatives for growing cotton, where indigenous rules were applied to promote participation in the schemes. Individual members who failed to cooperate were fined or ostracized. Thus, it was pressure from within that influenced participation in the schemes, rather than coercive action by colonial officials.[79] By 1954, the soil conservation program in Sukumaland had become highly politicized, which forced the government to abandon its coercive policy.[80]

In Kenya, some communities adjusted their traditional systems of land use in response to colonial government development programs. The Elgeyo traditionally grazed communal pastures, but following changes in land tenure, they allowed their members to enclose plots and plant crops. The proximity of this community to European farms transformed their systems of land use, and they demonstrated far greater adaptations to economic transformation than many others. Internally, too, their land-use systems were altered. Traditionally, they had used different landscapes in their territories for different purposes—the highlands were allocated to crop cultivation and the lowlands to grazing. And, by moving the stock between different ecological zones during different seasons, they avoided putting pressure on the grazing lands. However, following the establishment of colonial land borders which divided land-use types, the movement of livestock between different ecological zones was curtailed. The first casualty was the breakdown of livestock grazing movements between the highland and lowlands. The Elgeyo were forced to subdivide the highland areas into cultivated plots, where they were introduced to planting potatoes as a cash crop and were organized into cooperatives to grow pyrethrum. They also purchased European breeds of dairy cattle to supply milk to local creameries.[81]

The Tugen lowlands in Kenya had previously been shared for livestock grazing among various communities. However, due to increased demand for land, the grazing blocks broke down and were subdivided into individual plots by 1958. Despite their small sizes (varying between 45 and 120 acres), the government used the ranches to promote high-grade cattle to replace indigenous breeds. Within a period of less than two decades, the community had shifted from subsistence to a commercial pastoral economy.[82] Thus in the long-term, these changes transformed indigenous land use into private systems of production.[83]

Among the Karamojong in Uganda, who were branded by the colonial administration as being the most conservative, development focused on livestock disease control and livestock marketing, both of which were supported by the pastoralists. Prior to the colonial period, the Karamojong had had contact in the late nineteenth century with European and Ethiopian game hunters who visited their country to barter firearms for cattle and ivory. The Karamojong's positive responses to colonial intervention did not refute their view that cattle served as their source of wealth, which they used as a medium of exchange with their agro-pastoral neighbors to purchase grain.[84] The evidence shows that the Karamojong responded to external demands by making internal adjustments to accommodate changes as new opportunities became available.[85]

We may compare the Karamojong with the agro-pastoral Pokot community in northwestern Kenya. The Pokot utilized both the highlands and the lowlands, which also corresponded with different economic systems. During the wet season, people and livestock moved into the lowlands and during the dry season they returned to the highlands.[86] The highlands were cultivated, while the lowlands were allocated to pastoralism. The Pokot of the lowlands depended on the grains obtained from the highlands.[87] The colonial government campaigned to establish new agricultural methods, accompanied by orders to cull livestock in the highlands—this forceful destocking was justified on the basis of environmental conservation. The policy was further influenced by pressure from the adjacent European settlers, demanding the quarantining of pastoralists' herds to avoid the spread of diseases. In 1941 after the quarantine was broken, the Pokot protested the forced sales, accusing the colonial government of having the intention to render them poorer. The Pokot violently resisted the imposition of bylaws that restricted their livestock numbers in what they considered to be unacceptable methods of stock population control. The administration justified their actions as aiming to 'improve the conditions of the range.'[88]

In the Iraqwi highlands of Mbulu in Tanganyika, where the community had also traditionally combined crop cultivation on the highlands with grazing on the lowlands, development schemes attempted to rehabilitate the hilly areas by forcing the population to the lowlands. The families who were pushed into the lowlands responded by clearing the vegetation to grow crops and make new homesteads. Regarding stocking regulations, the Iraqwi found ways to short-change the directives of colonial officials—such as hoarding stock or tricking the officials through multiple uses of grazing certificates. Others, accordingly, by using destocking certificates of their friends, showed that they had complied with the orders and returned the excess stock into the scheme. In terms of soil conservation, the colonial officials used propaganda about environmental degradation to emphasize the benefits of protecting the environment. The Iraqwi representatives were taken to demonstration sites in other parts of East Africa, such as Kondoa in Tanzania and the Kamba districts in Kenya, where extreme levels of environmental degradation had been witnessed. The Iraqwi were warned that their country would suffer similar consequences if they did not act soon.[89]

Among the Chaga, who practiced mixed farming of coffee and bananas, indigenous land-use systems played complementary roles.[90] In the case of the Maasai who relied principally on livestock, the loss of grazing lands was a disaster. Previously, the Maasai had been blamed for overstocking their land, risking problems of land degradation.[91] Part of the development intervention was experimentation with group ranches, which titled a few individuals under specific rules of management.[92]

In summing up, we return to the question, which was whether the responses of African peasants and herders to development initiatives were predetermined by some aspects of their environment and culture. Our conclusion is that this was not the case. The African communities showed varied responses to development programs. Chapter 7 discusses dialogue between official colonial personnel regarding African people's participation in development.

Notes

1 Goody, J., *The expansive moment: The rise of social anthropology in Britain and Africa 1918–1970* (Cambridge: Cambridge University Press, 1995), 82.
2 Van Beusekon, M.M. and Hodgson, D.L., 'Lessons learned? Development experiences in the late colonial period,' *Journal of African History* 41.1 (2000): 29–33.

136   Ecological and social research

3 Radding, C., *Landscapes of power and identity: Comparative histories in the Sonora Desert and the forests of Amazonia from colony to Republic* (Durham: Duke University Press, 2005), xviii.
4 Schumaker, L., 'A tent with a view: Colonial officers, anthropologists, and the making of the field in Northern Rhodesia, 1937–1960,' *Osiris* 11 (1996): 237–258.
5 Chambers, R., 'Conference of the East African Institute of Social Research,' *Journal of Modern African Studies* 3.1 (1965): 127–129.
6 Nell, D., ' "For the public benefit": Livestock statistics and expertise in the late nineteenth-century Cape Colony, 1850–1900,' in Dubow, S. (ed.), *Science and society in southern Africa* (Manchester: Manchester University Press, 2000).
7 Beck, A., 'The East African community and regional research in science and medicine,' *African Affairs* 72.288 (1973): 300–308.
8 Beck, A., *A history of the British medical administration of East Africa, 1900–1950* (Cambridge, Massachusetts: Harvard University Press, 1970), 71.
9 Goody, *The expansive moment*, 8.
10 Mills, D., 'British anthropology at the ends of empire: The rise and fall of the colonial social science research council, 1944–1962,' *Revue d'Histoire des Science Humaines* 6 (2002): 161–188.
11 Ibid.
12 Ibid.
13 For relations between anthropologists and colonial administrations work, see Evans-Pritchard, E.E. and Firth, R., 'Anthropology and colonial affairs,' *Man* 49 (1949): 137–138.
14 Mills, 'British anthropology at the ends of empire.'
15 Goldschmidt, W. 'Independence as an element in pastoral social systems,' *Anthropological Quarterly*, 1971: 132–142.
16 Schneider, H.H. [and comments and replies, Blachard, K.I., Carlisle, R.C., Conant, F.P., Csandy, A., Greenbaum, D.J., Greenwood, D.J., Hazard, T., Hosley, E., Huber, H., Knight, G.G., Levin, M.D., Mckean, P.F., Newton, M.B., Robbins, L.H., Vansina, J. and Winans, E.V.], 'Economic development and economic change: The case of East African cattle,' *Current Anthropology* 15.3 (1974): 259–276.
17 Ibid.
18 Ibid.
19 Ibid.; Court, D., 'The ideal of social science in East Africa: An aspect of the development of higher education,' *Minerva* 17.2 (1979): 244–282.
20 Edgerton, R.B., *The individual in cultural adaptation: A study of four East African peoples* (Berkeley: University of California Press, 1971).
21 Ibid.
22 Magubane, B., 'A critical look at indices used in the study of social change in colonial Africa,' *Current Anthropology* 12.4/5 (1971): 419–445.
23 Kottak, C.P., 'The new ecological anthropology,' *American Anthropologist*, 101.1 (1999): 23–35.
24 Schofer, E., 'Cross-national differences in the expansion of science, 1970–1990,' *Social Forces* 83.1 (2004): 215–248.
25 Fumagalli, C.T., 'An evaluation of development projects among East African pastoralists,' *African Studies Review* 21.3 (1978): 49–63.
26 Soltis, J., Boyd, R. and Richerson, P.J., 'Can group-functional behaviors evolve by cultural group selection? An empirical test,' *Current Anthropology* 36.3 (1995): 473–494.
27 Low, D.A. and Londsdale, J.M., 'Introduction: Towards the new order 1945–1963,' in Low, D.A. and Smith A. (eds.), *History of East Africa, Vol. III* (Oxford: Clarendon Press, 1976), 25.

28 Goldschmidt, 'Independence as an element in pastoral social systems.'
29 Shantz, H.L., 'Agricultural regions of Africa. Part III: Present and potential productivity of the land,' *Economic Geography* 18.4 (1942): 343–362.
30 Kottak, 'The new ecological anthropology,' 25.
31 Bates, D.G. and Lees, S.H., 'The role of exchange in productive specialization,' *American Anthropologist*, 79.4 (1977): 824–841, 828, 829.
32 Schneider, 'Economic development and economic change.'
33 Spencer, P., 'The individual in cultural adaptation: A study of four East African peoples,' *Bulletin of the School of Oriental and Africa Studies* 35.3 (1972): 680–681.
34 Church, A., *East Africa: A new dominion* (London: H.F. and G. Witherby, 1927), 86.
35 Herskovits, N.J., 'The cattle complex in East Africa,' *American Anthropologist* 28.4 (1926): 633–664.
36 Gösta, C., 'The rationale of nomad economy,' *Ambio* 4.4 (1975): 146–153.
37 Hutchison, H.G., 'Extension aspects of beef cattle management in Tanganyika,' *East African Agricultural and Forestry Journal* XXX.3 (1965): 265–267, 265.
38 Chenevix, T.C., *Men who ruled Kenya: The Kenya administration, 1892–1963* (Oxford: Caledonian Press, 1993), 285.
39 Cited in Schneider, H.K., *The Pokot (Suk) of Kenya with special reference to the role of livestock in their subsistence economy*, A dissertation, in partial fulfilment of the requirements for the degree Dr of Philosophy (Evanston Illinois: Northwestern University, 1953), 8, 151.
40 Harbeson, J.W., 'Land reforms and politics in Kenya, 1954–70,' *Journal of Modern African Studies*, 9.2 (1971): 231–251.
41 Low and Lonsddale, 'Introduction: Towards the new order 1945–1963,' 22; Radding, *Landscapes of power and identity*, 163.
42 Symanski, R., Manners, I.R. and Bromley, R.J., 'The mobile-sedentary continuum,' *Annals of the Association of American Geographers*, 65.3 (1975): 461–471.
43 Gulliver, P.H., 'Land shortage, social change, and social conflict in East Africa,' *Journal of Conflict Resolution* 5.1 (1961): 16–26.
44 Leys, C., 'Politics in Kenya: The development of peasant society,' *British Journal of Political Science* 1.3 (1971): 307–337.
45 Beinart, W., 'Soil erosion, conservationism and ideas about development: A southern African exploration, 1900–1960,' *Journal of Southern African Studies*, 11.1 (1984): 52–83.
46 Tosh, J., 'Long agriculture during the early colonial period: Land and labour in cash-crop economy,' *Journal of African History* 19.3 (1978): 415–439, 415.
47 Darling, F.F. and Farva, M.A., 'Ecological consequences of sedentarization of nomads,' in George, C.J., Farvar, M.T. and Milton, J.P. (eds.), *The careless technology: Ecology of international development* (Tom Stacey, 1973), 671.
48 Oba, G., *Herder warfare in East Africa: A social and spatial history* (Winwick: White Horse Press, 2017).
49 Leslie, B.L., 'Coercive development: Land shortage, forced labor, and colonial development in the Chiweshe Reserve, colonial Zimbabwe, 1938–1946,' *International Journal of African Historical Studies* 25.1 (1992): 39–65.
50 Fleming, W.G., 'Authority, efficiency, and role stress: Problems in the development of East African bureaucracies,' *Administrative Science Quarterly* 11.3 (1966): 386–404.
51 Hodge, J.M., 'Science and empire: An overview of the historical scholarship,' in Bennet, B.M. and Hodge, J.M. (eds.), *Science and empire: Knowledge and networks of science across the British Empire 1800–1970* (New York: Palgrave Macmillan, 2011), 211.
52 Connelly, W.T., 'Colonial era livestock development policy: Introduction of improved dairy cattle in high-potential farming areas of Kenya,' *World Development* 26.9 (1998): 1733–1748.

53 Berry, S. 'Debating the land question in Africa,' *Comparative Studies in Society and History* 44.4 (2002): 638–668.
54 Edgerton, *The individual in cultural adaptation*, 150.
55 Bennett, J.W., Lawry, S.W. and Riddel, J.C., *Land tenure and livestock development in sub-Saharan Africa: AID evaluation special study No. 39*, U.S. Agency for International Development, May 1986, 134, 135.
56 Kenworthy, J.M. and Glover, J., 'The reliability of the main rains in Kenya,' *East African Agricultural Journal* XXIII.4 (1958): 267–271, 267.
57 Thompson, A.B., 'The water-supply of British Somaliland,' *The Geographical Journal* 101.4 (1943): 154–160.
58 Conklin, H.C., 'The study of shifting cultivation,' *Current Anthropology* 2.1 (1961): 27–61.
59 Berry, L. and Townshend, J., 'Soil conservation policies in the semi-arid regions of Tanzania: A historical perspective,' *Geografiska Annaler* 54.4 (1972): 241–253.
60 Darling and Farvar, 'Ecological consequences of sedentarization of nomads,' 681.
61 Speller, C., 'Land policy and economic development in Kenya,' *Journal of Royal African Society*, 30.121 (1931): 377–385, 377, 378.
62 Murton, J., 'Population growth and poverty in Machakos District, Kenya,' *Geographical Journal*, 1999: 37–46.
63 Talbot, L.M., 'Demographic factors in resource depletion and environmental degradation in East African rangeland,' *Population and Development Review* 12.3 (1986): 441–451.
64 Briske, D.D., Sayre, N.F., Huntsinger, L., Fernandez-Gimenez, M., Budd, B. and Derner, J.D., 'Origin, persistence, and resolution of the rotational debate: Integrating human dimensions into rangeland research,' *Rangeland Ecology and Management* 64.4 (2011): 325–334.
65 Turner, M., 'Overstocking the range: A critical analysis of the environmental science of Sahelian pastoralism,' *Economic Geography* 69.4 (1993): 402–421.
66 Waller, R., and Sobania, N.W., 'Pastoralism in historical perspective,' in Fratkin, E., Galvin, K.A. and Roth, E.A. (eds.), *African pastoralist systems: An integrated approach* (Boulder: Lynne Rienner, 1994), 54.
67 Pereira, H.C., Riney, T. Dasgupta, B. and Rains, A.B., 'Land-use in semi-arid southern Africa [and discussion],' *Philosophical Transactions of the Royal Society of London* (Series B) 278.962 (1977): 555–563.
68 Dorana, M.H., Low, A.R.C. and Kemp, R.L., 'Cattle as store of wealth in Swaziland: Implications for livestock development and overgrazing in Eastern and southern Africa,' *American Journal of Agricultural Economies* 61.1 (1979): 41–47.
69 Waller, R., 'Ecology, migration, and expansion in East Africa,' *African Affairs*, 84.336 (1985): 347–370.
70 Kottak, 'The new ecological anthropology.'
71 Goldschmidt, W., 'Introduction: The theory of cultural adaptation,' in Edgerton, R.B. (ed.), *The individual in cultural adaptation: A study of four East African communities* (Berkeley: University of California Press, 1971), 16.
72 Youé, C.P., 'Settler capital and the assault on the squatter peasantry in Kenya's Uasin Gishu District, 1942–63,' *African Affairs* 87.348 (1988): 393–418.
73 Ellis, D., 'The Nandi protest of 1923 in the context of African resistance to colonial rule in Kenya,' *Journal of African History* 17.4 (1976): 555–575.
74 Schneider, 'Economic development and economic change.'
75 Kerkham, R.K., 'Livestock improvement in the Buganda province of Uganda,' *East African Agricultural Journal* XIII.2 (1947): 116–119.
76 Carswell, G., 'Multiple historical geographies: Responses and resistance to colonial conservation schemes in East Africa,' *Journal of Historical Geography* 32 (2006): 398–421.

77 Neumann, R.P., 'Ways of seeing Africa: Colonial recasting of the African landscape in Serengeti National Park,' *Ecumene* 2.2 (1995): 149–169.
78 Gadsden, F., 'Further Notes on the Kamba destocking controversy of 1938,' *International Journal of African Historical Studies* 7.1 (1974): 681–687.
79 Eckert, A., 'Useful instruments of participation? Local government and cooperatives in Tanzania, 1940s to 1970s,' *International Journal of African Historical Studies* 40.1 (2007): 97–118.
80 Berry and Towshend, 'Soil conservation policies in the semi-arid regions of Tanzania,' 244,
81 Swynnerton, R.J., 'Agricultural advances in Eastern Africa,' *African Affairs*, 61.244 (1962): 201–215.
82 McLoughlin, P.F.M., 'Some observations on the preliminary report of the culture and ecology in East Africa project,' *American Anthropologist* 68.4 (1966): 1004–1009.
83 Ibid.
84 Quam, M.D., 'Cattle marketing and pastoral conservation: Karamoja district, Uganda 1948–1970,' *African Studies Review* 21.1 (1978): 49–71.
85 Barbour, J.P., 'The Karamoja district of Uganda: A pastoral people under colonial rule,' *Journal of African History* 3.1 (1962): 111–124.
86 Schneider, *The Pokot (Suk) of Kenya with special reference to the role of livestock in their subsistence economy*.
87 Goldschmidt, 'Introduction: The theory of cultural adaptation.'
88 Schneider, H.K., 'Pokot resistance to change,' in Bascom, W. and Herskovits, M.J. (eds.), *Continuity and change in African cultures* (Chicago: University of Chicago Press, 1959).
89 Lawi, Y.Q., 'Tanzania's operation Vijiji and local ecological consciousness: The case of Eastern Iraqwland, 1974–1976,' *Journal of African History* 48.1 (2007): 69–93.
90 Sunseri, T., 'A political ecology of beef in colonial Tanzania and the global periphery, 1864–1961,' *Journal of Historical Geography* 39 (2013): 29–42.
91 Hodgson, D.L., 'Taking stock: State control, ethnic identity and pastoralist development in Tanganyika, 1948–1958,' *Journal of African History* 41.1 (2000): 55–78.
92 Wylie, D., 'Confrontation over Kenya: The colonial office and its critics 1918–1940,' *Journal of African History* 18.3 (1977), 427–447.

7 Administrative science for development dialogue
Three Kenyan case studies, 1943–1954

In this chapter, we will show why expert knowledge and administrative science is preferred over scientific knowledge for planning and implementing development projects. We aim to understand the motives of administrative science for development dialogue. The driving force behind administrative science was 'moral imperialism'—a philosophy that the colonial power had 'a moral duty to "civilize" the colonized peoples.'[1] The vision of the British administration was, however, that the African peoples 'should be made good Africans rather than a poor imitation of a European.'[2] Underlying the process of 'making good Africans' was the assumption by colonial officials that the African peasants lacked the knowledge required to progress economically. This was until, during the post-Second World War period, that the colonial officials discovered that some African communities practiced advanced methods of indigenous agriculture and soil conservation. Disregarding those indigenous skills, the officials continued to promulgate ordinances or bylaws to mandate compliance in implementing development projects. This attitude is reflected in the way they organized hierarchical authorities that were often in dialogue among experts and administrators about single or multiple development issues. In each colony, the highest colonial authority concerned with land management was the colonial secretary. At the provincial level, the administration was headed by provincial commissioners, assisted by district commissioners with a supervisory role. At lower administrative tiers, technical departments of agriculture and veterinary services were responsible for project implementation. Research departments and organizations charged with the management of environmental or agricultural schemes played an advisory role on technical matters.[3]

In the implementation of most projects were the concerns of land rights. In colonial Kenya, there were three categories of land rights. The first was customary land, traditionally owned by clans or tribal units. These were the land units in the African reserves, administered by a Local Native Council (LNC). The second type of land rights was what was called 'Crown land.' This type of land classification enabled the government to decide on how the land would be used in the future. The third category was the 'white highlands' allocated exclusively to European settlers. Land use in the European 'white highlands' was under the authority of a lobby group called the European Board.

This chapter presents three case studies from Kenya to reflect the management of agricultural schemes in the colony. The first case study concerns conflicts over the transfer of ancestral land to the European land category by means of a long lease. After lengthy communications among the colonial officials, the local community sought adjudication by a Crown court. We will examine the use of the British justice system, providing a dialogue between the victimized African community and provincial officials. The second case study examines the application of ordinances that forced the peasants to implement agricultural schemes to promote soil conservation. The third case study involves clearing bush for the control of tsetse flies and resettling displaced populations. In each case, we examine the dialogues conducted among officials and representatives of the African peasants (based on archival sources), focusing on the western Rift Valley and the Lake Victoria Basin in Kenya (Figure 7.1).

We structure the discussions as follows. First, we describe briefly the notion of administrative science as a source of expert knowledge for development planning and implementation. Second, we discuss how administrative science was applied in the three above-mentioned case studies: (1) solving land conflicts between the Kipsigis people and the colonial state; (2) applying ordinances on agricultural schemes; and (3) bush clearing for tsetse fly control and agricultural settlement.

Administrative science

Strictly speaking, administrative science is an applied form of social science. It is action-oriented and relies on expert knowledge for planning and implementing programs. In principle, administrative science attempts to bridge imperial science approaches and local development initiatives. It integrates the practical administration and management of African societies and practices using social science methods.[4] Unlike imperial science, administrative science is flexible in terms of space and time, allowing officials to shift development priorities in accordance with colonial policies. Another reason why administrative science differs from imperial science is that it was applied across hierarchical power structures and administrative boundaries—thus enabling information to be shared between technical and administrative departments.[5]

At local community level in the African reserves, government-appointed chiefs and headmen supervised development activities.[6] The provincial commissioners and district commissioners coordinated all development programs within their jurisdictions—directly influencing the welfare of local African societies.[7]

142 *Ecological and social research*

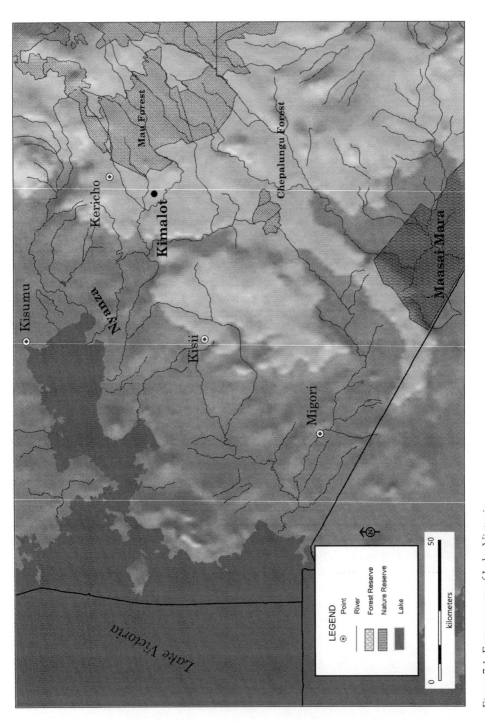

Figure 7.1 Eastern part of Lake Victoria.

In communications between technical departments and the administration, land remained central to the colonial land-use politics from the 1920s. Large pieces of land were alienated from African peasants, as mentioned before. The remaining land consisted of fragmented pieces, which the colonial administration consolidated by moving African peasants and pastoralists into African reserves.[8] The most contentious issue was the alienation of tribal land by the state, for European settler agricultural production, which is referred to in the archives as 'the Kimulot land case' (hereafter referred to as Kimalot).

Case 1: the Kimalot land case, 1920–1956

The conflict concerns the Kimalot area in the Kericho District, which had been inhabited by the Kipsigis (Figure 7.1). The Kipsigis' land case was complicated by their proximity to the European tea estates. The Kipsigis resisted the transfer of customary land under lease to the European tea plantations, which had been conducted by government officials without consulting the Kipsigis. This was also the view of some of the provincial administrators who supported the Kipsigis in the conflict. At the time, in 1925, the District Commissioner (DC) Mr Hemsted wrote a letter to the Provincial Commissioner, stating:

> I have always held opinion ... that the [Kipsigis] have not been fairly treated as regards land, with the result that many thousands of them have been forced to go onto [the European farms] to find grazing for their cattle. Many of the farms should never have been alienated, but this cannot be remedied now.[9]

A local lawyer launched a complaint on behalf of the Kipsigis in 1927. According to the letter received by the Provincial Commissioner, the claim was that the government had destroyed 1,641 homesteads. Consequently, 'All helpless men, women and children and all the new born babies ... died of [unpredictable] heavy storm of rain and cold' after their houses had been burnt down.[10] The administrative officials dismissed the complaint as being factually incorrect, stating that it was 'wilfully inaccurate and misleading.' The new District Commissioner reduced the case to African political propaganda but did not dispute the fact that Kimalot belonged to the Kipsigis.[11]

Whereas the ordinance of the 1920s had placed the Kimalot area within the African reserve, by which the Kipsigis were guaranteed land security, the Morris Carter Land Commission of 1932 placed the same land under the 'Crown land' category, even though it was administratively under the LNC. The Chief Colonial Secretary—knowing that this was a controversial decision—preferred not to raise the matter anew.[12]

The status of the contested leasehold land

The Provincial Commissioner (PC) of Nyanza was willing to give his opinion on what had actually transpired. He stated:

> In their interest I advance the suggestion that in 1920 the Kipsigis were so unsophisticated that they could have taken practically no part in the agreement to lease that land ... and I consider the government cannot avoid responsibility for that lease. If my view is accepted, I endorse [return of the land to the Kipsigis] for generosity in this settlement.

Under the lease agreement, the Kipsigis had to relinquish use of the 7,000 acres of Kimalot land for some 969 years—the arrangement that would have no 'practical value' for coming generations.[13] Promoting the same view as DC Hemsted, DC Kericho (whose administration included Kimalot) made another proposal in 1947. In his opinion, the area had been an integral part of the Kipsigis' tribal land to which they held ancestral rights. In his view, the return of the land to the Kipsigis could play an important public relations role by allaying their fears over the introduction of development programs.[14] Further, the land's suitability was limited, suggesting that it would be of little value to European settlers who might want to use it for tea plantations or dairy ranches.[15]

The problem was of an administrative and political nature, as opposed to one of land suitability. Supporters of both sides attempted to exploit the lacunae in the land law provisions. In order to separate areas that were contested from those that were not, an agricultural official in the Kericho District presented a map (Figure 7.2) showing the subdivisions of the contested land. The land parcels marked A, B and C had varied topography and covered a total area of 12,000 acres. According to the agricultural official, section C would be shifted to the African reserve, while section B would revert to Crown land. The official was however doubtful if transferring section A to the Africans was a fair deal. In the view of the agricultural official, the land parcel was part of a forestland, heavily wooded and received high rainfall. The area was remote and lacked an access road to market the produce. Additionally, clearing the thick forest would be a huge task for which the peasants lacked financial resources.[16]

The Chief Secretary was however insistent that the European Board's decision on the contested land was final, subject to the following conditions: '(a) that the exchange [of land] should be regarded as a settlement of all outstanding claims [by the Kipsigis]; (b) that no settlement would be allowed until the area was free of [tsetse] fly.'[17] The Kipsigis were determined to resist the land transfer. Generally, the matter had worried the agricultural department which blamed the land wrangles for the delays in land improvements.[18]

In his 1948, communication, the DC of Kericho, while being sympathetic to the tribal community, made an additional proposal on how the

Administrative science for development   145

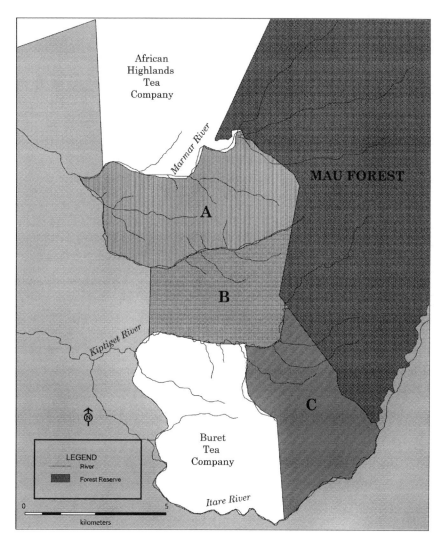

Figure 7.2 Sketch of Kimalot area in conflict with the European Tea estates.

exchange of land should be conducted. In his opinion, the Kimalot problem was extremely complex. First, the area was historically part of the customary land of the Kipsigis, over which they had hereditary land rights. Second, if the Kipsigis were agreeable about swapping the land, they should not lose any of the benefits of their ancestral land. Rather, they should receive an equal piece of land from the unalienated Crown land, suggesting that offering them less would be a discriminatory deal. A fair deal would be if the LNC in Kimalot agreed to be compensated for the total of 12,000 acres.[19]

146 *Ecological and social research*

However, the Provincial Commissioner of Nyanza did not view swapping of the land as being impartial. Symbolically, he compared the proposals of land swapping by European settlers and the Kipsigis to 'attempting to compensate a Welsh farmer for land lost with a piece of land in England or Scotland.' Regardless of the different values of the land in these principalities, the message was that the deal would be unfair for one of the parties. Accordingly, in his view, the proposal should take note of the suggestion made by the District Commissioner of Kericho, mentioned above.[20] Nevertheless, according to a Member of the Agriculture and Natural Resources office, certain facts about the size of the land in the various land parcels were inaccurate. The total contested land was less than the figures given above and the parcels were of different sizes; therefore swapping would not address the problem of land complaints.[21]

Still, the office of the Colonial Secretary was firm, arguing that the Kipsigis had been given a final solution to their complaints through a lease which would not be relinquished for purposes of 'reversionary interest' for land for which they had been fully compensated. The secretary emphasized:

> I am to make it clear that the 5,000 acres was decided upon as a generous compensation for the loss of a reversionary right to 6,500 acres at the end of 969 years and the government cannot under any circumstance consider the allocation to the whole 12,000 acres of land.

In the event, the Kipsigis rejected the offer, so the final decision was to return the whole extent of the land to Crown land.[22] This was a powerful warning to the Kipsigis.

The firm response from the Colonial Secretary did not discourage the DC Kericho under whose responsibility the Kimalot land fell, in again making a new proposal. His argument was that the Kipsigis were never party to the land lease. Indeed, in his opinion, much of the land dealings remained a mystery, considering that he had found no correspondence on how the land lease was made and who had signed it. The LNC, that was legally the body responsible on behalf of the peasants, was not even in existence when the lease had been finalized. In subsequent years, the LNC supported the Kipsigis.[23]

The DC's new plea to the government was premised on his faith that he could persuade the members of the LNC to change their minds on some of the land questions, while appreciating that the Kipsigis' claims were genuine. In his opinion, a better way to approach the problem was to comprehensively solve other outstanding land questions that the Kipsigis had, such as in the areas which bordered the Trans-Mara District (see case study 3). The commissioner reminded the government that, as a community, the Kipsigis were among the most loyal of the African people and their contributions to the war efforts were well known. Besides, they were recognized for their extraordinary skills in land conservation. Considering these factors, the DC pleaded that the government should be more sympathetic to their case.[24] Even so, the administrative dialogue which supported the Kipsigis on the one hand and the government on the other, still did not involve the community directly.

Administrative dialogue

Publicly, the issue was gaining political momentum. This was probably the reason why the Colonial Secretary had to pitch for the government position once again. This time, he supported the new proposal (despite rejecting it outright earlier), whilst at the same time taking a firm position. It is worthwhile looking at part of his argument:

> I am directed to say that the highlands board [i.e., the European Board] has given its approval to the following modifications of the terms of exchanges of land: (a) that the area to be excised from the Kimulot block and added to the Native Land Unit be increased from 5,000 to 6,000 acres, (b) that [the decision considered] 'as settlement of all outstanding Kipsigis claims' in regard to the forest glades and Trans-Mara areas.[25]

The Colonial Secretary stressed that there was to be no 'bargaining on individual points.'[26] The Provincial Commissioner of the Nyanza province,[27] still attempting to convince the secretariat about the seriousness the Kipsigis attached to their land, cited at length the contents of a letter written to him by the LNC on behalf of the complainants. The letter in part stated as follows:

> We thank you for your communication, but we are disappointed. Respectively we point out that we have never suggested exchanging our land.... We wish to retain that land.... Our plea to Government has been the land at Kimalot should be returned to us, as we claim it to be part of our tribal land. We were driven from it some years ago and our houses were burnt.... We did not think that Government would give with one hand and take away with the other.[28]

In response to the letter, the provincial administration made three important observations to the higher authorities. First, the matter was solvable if an unbiased decision was to be made. Second, he re-emphasized the point about the loyalty of the community in question; and, third, this being a model agricultural community, they needed to be helped by the government to stay on course.[29] Consequently, the agricultural officials requested the government to re-examine the land questions as the matter was disrupting agrarian programs in the Kipsigis' areas.[30]

Unfortunately, those involved in discussions of the Kimalot land complaint (apart from the Kipsigis) continued to shift their position. The Provincial Commissioner's position was a case in point. He gave an ultimatum to the LNC to 'take it or leave it,' even warning them that if they entrenched their position, the government offer would be withdrawn. Accordingly, he wished to make it 'absolutely clear to the [LNC] that the decision was final and irrevocable. They had a choice, either to accept the government proposal "in toto",' or to reject it. Rejection would imply that the land would return to becoming Crown land. It would also mean that the Kipsigis would lose their other land complaints. If, however, they accepted the proposal, the government would increase their allocation from 6,500 to 7,500 acres. For some of the councilors on the LNC, the implications were grotesque. Agreement would seriously prejudice their case and the future of the tribe. Either way, the Kipsigis would be forced to abandon all outstanding land claims.[31]

What sustained their case, however, was ongoing indecision by the authorities—perhaps for lack of agreement on reclassification of the area that would shift some parts of the African land to the European highlands, while those parts that were to be exchanged would be shifted from the European highlands to the African reserves. For the government, it did not make sense for them to be preoccupied with solving complaints over land—sometimes bargaining and at other times having their offers rejected.[32] To pursue compliance, the government introduced the native land ordinances that specified actions to be taken if the people were not compliant.

The Native Lands Trust Ordinance

Following pressure from the government, the LNC agreed to the exchange of land, for which they were finally allocated 7,250 acres of the Kimalot block and a 10,000 ha ranch purchased by the government for use by the Kipsigis. It took a lot of convincing by provincial officials for the native council to accept this deal.[33] Another stringent condition was that the Kipsigis should clear the bush and undertake soil conservation measures. They were required to take a tribal oath to bind them to the agreement, pledging that they would not cut down trees on the steep slopes and their goats would be allowed into the forested areas only with the permission of the officials. Anyone who violated these rules would be expelled without the option to return.[34]

The terms were that the Kipsigis should immediately vacate the remaining land that was to be transferred to the European tea estates. Nevertheless, due to a lack of unanimity among the Kipsigis, the government removed them forcefully.[35] The Kipsigis took legal action to address their expulsion. Mr A. Ohanga, who served as a lawyer for the LNC, represented the group. His letter to the Provincial Commissioner of the Nyanza Province raised several interesting points. We cite excerpts from the document, below:

> I have in my office … a representative of the 86 Kipsigis families, 22 of which have been served with a removal order under the Native Authority Ordinance Section 13 (1).… The order which requires these people to remove themselves from the area in question … [are] the Kimalot

Administrative science for development 149

people, most of whom have occupied this area for no less than five years [this is a minimum legal limit for occupancy of land], have found it a bit difficult to cope with an order so drastic in three days' notice.... The [order] ... was bitterly opposed by every Kipsigis in the district.... It is true that the LNC members were drawn into accepting the [order]. But it is equally true that their action did not reflect the true opinion of the Kipsigis indigenous elders, whose opposition is so strong.[36]

Among the people removed by force and then arrested was one Kipsoi Arap Chemorore. He was convicted on two counts—first, he disobeyed the PC's orders under the Native Lands Trust Ordinance and, second, he masterminded the Kipsigis' land agitation. We now examine the court proceedings in this case more closely.

Kipsoi Arap Chemorore versus the Crown

For the British, justice was the epitome of a civilized society, and they were respectful of the rule of law in handling crimes and conflicts over land through formal court proceedings. In this case, the government found itself contending with a serious political problem, having removed people from their own land. The government had two options: either to use force, or to 'go very slowly,' considering that local opinion in the entire region had been muddied by this issue. The Kipsigis decided to show no cooperation with the government authorities, until the matter was 'settled to [their] satisfaction' in court.[37]

Before we analyze the court proceedings, it might be useful to know something about the accused man himself. He was a prominent member of the Kipsigis community and was viewed by the colonial officials as being progressive and an entrepreneur. Having lived on European farms and worked for Europeans, he had developed his own ideas about the injustices the African communities were suffering under colonial rule. Consequently, he believed that if the respected rule of the law was not arbitrary but would deliver justice to those whose rights were violated, he was prepared to appeal to the High Court against his conviction in the provincial court. His case raised an important legal question. According to the charge sheet, the accused—together with others not before the court—had unlawfully refused to vacate land 'in accordance with the Native Authorities Ordinance.' The ordinance under which he was accused states that 'Any African who without lawful excuse neglects to obey an order under this section shall be guilty of the offence' as charged.[38]

In his extensive ruling, the Crown Court judge re-interpreted what the ordinance implied. For purposes of brevity, we outline the essential parts of the rulings. An important point raised was whether by failing to obey the order of the Provincial Commissioner (PC), Kipsoi Arap Chemorore had committed a criminal offence. The accused and 60 others were claimed to have illegally occupied Crown land when they had been ordered to remove

150 *Ecological and social research*

themselves to the African reserve.[39] After hearing both sides, the sitting judge found that the accused had a 'lawful excuse' for his action. A question was whether the accused had any legal claims to the said land. Indeed, he had, and was able to produce a legal document in the form of receipts showing that he had paid the required fees in order to occupy the land. In summing up his ruling, the judge stated:

> when the question as to the legal rights of somebody to land arises, then the proper authority for determining that dispute ... is the Supreme Court' [and not the PC court]. [T]he question whether the accused ought to leave the land or not, was a question which he was entitled to hear a decision by a court, and I consider that it would be a grave injustice to force upon him the decision either to leave the land or to risk becoming an offender by not doing so. For these reasons, I consider the accused [to have had] a lawful excuse for not obeying the order of the PC.[40]

By resolving this land case, the court had, in effect, dismissed the administrative orders for removing the Kipsigis from the land. The administration therefore had to work out ways in which the land could be divided among the 60 families which had previously been removed by force. The Kipsigis families were allocated a parcel of land each for crop cultivation and grazing livestock, but subject to stringent rules in running the land allocation scheme. According to the Crown Land Ordinance, the residents in these schemes were given specific instructions, including demarcating their allotted pieces by live tree hedges, and avoiding any attempt to subdivide the land allocated to each family. The schemes were inspected to ensure that the farmers had fulfilled all these conditions, including building soil conservation infrastructure. By 1954, certain families had been identified by the officials as model farmers and were given government loans to develop their lands.[41]

By 1955, the main activity of the families was to clear large areas of the forest for planting crops and livestock grazing.[42] The Kipsigis hired tractors to plough their land—this was noted as 'progress,' for which they 'excelled' among other African farmers. By the end of 1955, 22 of the 60 farmers had paid their land loans.[43] Yet, even by 1956, they were still prevented from erecting permanent dwellings on their land holdings.[44] Similar to the Kimalot land case, the agriculture and soil conservation schemes were concerned with ordinances for compliance with project implementation. This is our second case study.

Case 2: Agricultural and soil conservation schemes, 1943–1954

In order to enforce compliance by the African peasants on soil conservation schemes, the government implemented rules that laid down guidelines on how the land plots should be managed by individual farmers. The Land and Water Preservation Ordinance of 1943 declares that: 'As soon as possible after any area has been declared "closed" the Director shall complete notification in the forms contained in the schedule'—a copy of this schedule was given to every farmer. Being illiterate, most of the African peasants did not understand the contents of the forms. Yet, they were expected to carry the documents around and produce them when the officials requested verification. The rules themselves were harsh and impractical. One forbidding regulation stated:

> [Farmers shall not] ... except with the permission of the Director [of the scheme] ... and subject to such conditions as the Director may impose, in any closed area cut down, remove or destroy, or cause to be cut down or destroy in any manner what so ever, any living vegetation, or depasture any livestock.[45]

Another rather absurd rule states: 'The Director may by order prohibit or limit the watering of stock at any stream or river except [under] such conditions as he may specify in such order.'[46] The most radical rule was the one in which a farmer might have planted crops that 'contravened' the order of the official. Officials were authorized to cut down and destroy such crops without fear of prosecution.[47] The agricultural officials were, however, under no illusion regarding the successes of the schemes, pointing out that the 'work of ... nature—represents capital expenditure' that often exceeds what individual farmers and the government could accomplish.[48] Soil conservation was a case in point.

Soil conservation

When dealing with problems of soil erosion on farmers' lands, other than verbal instructions, officials in the Department of Agriculture lacked both the financial and technical capacity to demonstrate actions that they recommended.[49] We may use an example here. The case concerns the Gem farmers in the Lake Basin. The Gem farmers in the lake region who planted monocultures of maize using cattle manure to fertilize their land enjoyed initial successes, until they were forced to remove their livestock. The agricultural officials realized that without access to cattle manure, and in the absence of soil conservation methods, crop production was declining. Indeed, the main challenge was how to recommend to the farmers to bring back the cattle, at the risk of destroying the crops[50]—this presented a serious setback to farming.[51]

According to the authorities, maintaining soil fertility would succeed only if the orders were reinforced by the rules of land ordinances. The rules specified the types of crops allowed and the seasons of planting. They also regulated the use of manure on family farms. One of the rules stated that: 'The authority may, after consultation with the indigenous elders, order all persons in possession of a livestock enclosure in any specified area to remove all the manure ... and apply to the land before each planting season.'[52] This is precisely what the farmers had previously done on their own—for which no rules had been required. Additionally, the by-law made it compulsory for all able-bodied persons to participate in soil conservation activities under instructions of local headmen.[53]

The agricultural officials admitted that the shortcomings of soil conservation activities arose from their own lack of familiarity with African systems of agriculture, especially in hilly areas. In a letter to the Director of Agriculture, an official stated:

> The trouble is that hillside cultivation is foreign to the British agriculturalist, whose usual attitude is that it ought to be suppressed. But the fact remains that it is a widespread form of African agriculture which cannot be got rid of and should not be ignored.[54]

Indeed, contrary to the agricultural officials' views, some African communities such as the Kipsigis had developed indigenous soil conservation methods on steep slopes, combining methods such as grass filters, trash of cut vegetation, and terraces, as well as methods of maintaining soil fertility and rotational cropping.[55] Nonetheless, in a written memorandum, agricultural officials admitted that it was challenging to apply soil conservation schemes on African peasant farms. The memorandum drew the following conclusions:

> It is impossible to lay down hard and fast rules with regard to the planning of arable holdings for African peasants, on account of the wide variations in ecological conditions which occur between relatively small areas.... For this reason, a policy for farm planning can seldom be applied on a district scale and is ... scarcely applicable to locations and even small recognizable political and administrative sections of the land.... In practice physical soil conservation work is unpopular with the African, because he does not appreciate that he is, to some extent, arresting further soil ... deterioration.[56]

Contrary to the above claim, we have already shown that indigenous methods of soil conservation existed. The inference one would draw from the above statement is that—despite the expansion of acres of land under soil conservation—its benefits had not been commensurate with financial investment by the authorities. What encouraged the colonial officials to persist was the perception that soil conservation was achievable, not forgetting its political imperative as a colonial policy. While accepting the failures of the past, the officials were determined to ensure success in the future. A provincial agricultural officer reported the following: 'I think it is logical reasoning to suppose that as ... the Africans progress in the direction they are going at the present ... we should base our programs on the future and not the past.'[57]

The opinion of the official was that the participation of African peasants in soil conservation efforts could be improved if there was a change in land tenure, from clan to individual land holdings. With individual holdings, the owners would be entirely responsible for the betterment of their land and would benefit from government extension programs by learning directly from demonstrations on their own farms. Another proposal was to lease land to farmers, subject to their performing soil control works.[58] An agricultural official appeared to be certain of this proposal, when he stated: 'Without control there can be no success and the present erosion will still carry on until the people are driven off the land.'[59]

The agricultural officials believed part of the failure of soil conservation efforts was due to African peasants using inappropriate technology for building terraces. The officials did not entertain the idea that it was enough to allow the African peasant to implement soil conservation practices on his own. The ordinance that was promulgated empowered the authorities to force farmers to carry out compulsory soil erosion control activities. If the farmers failed to carry out the necessary work, the officials were empowered to do so, and recover the costs from the farmers. To this effect, the District Commissioner of North Nyanza proposed a new bylaw, which required the peasants who failed in these activities to be taken before the African courts. According to the proposal, any fine charged to the culprit would compensate the headman for the time and trouble that he had expended in the court action.[60]

The Provincial Commissioner rejected this proposal, as it failed to take into account that no legal arguments could be conducted outside competent Crown courts.[61] The outcome was that the officials, despite their attempts to work on the challenge of soil conservation, had seldom been successful. This was partly because official guidelines of land use aggravated environmental problems—and unfairly blamed the African peasants for land degradation.[62] In the third case study, we examine how African societies were involved in agricultural schemes and bush clearing projects in the implementation of further controversial land ordinances. We will also examine the Kipsigis and the Maasai land conflicts linked to development of the schemes in case 3.

Case 3: Bush clearing projects, settlements and land conflict, 1938–1954

The participation of African peasants in settlement schemes and maintaining reclaimed areas was part of an elaborate policy framework. Conditions for their participation were prescribed by the official ordinances that laid down the rules on how the society should respond to the development schemes. For example, the Nyanza district authorities from the second case study presented a notice on the Native Lands Trust Ordinance of 1938, stating in part that:

> [n]o person shall, except with the permission of the headman, advice of a District Officer or Agricultural Officer [should] cultivate the land or pasture any livestock, or burn, cut down, or destroy in any manner whatsoever any tree, bush or other vegetation within a strip of such width as the headman may direct along any river, stream or lake shore.

This forbidding ordinance prohibited the communities from doing anything of their own accord, in contrast to the tsetse control programs, for which they were required to clear vegetation. We examine the reports more critically to elucidate the purpose of bush clearing projects, which included controlling the actions of local Africans.[63]

Bush clearing projects usually took longer than expected. In the Northern Nyanza and Kericho districts, the officials expected that mechanical bush clearing would be more efficacious and cheaper than hand clearing methods,[64] although heavy and continuous labor investment was still required. In his letter to the member of the Agriculture and Natural Resources, the District Commissioner of Kericho insisted that without bringing the Nandi and the Kipsigis into the picture, no success could be expected.[65] Nonetheless, developing agricultural schemes, combined with tsetse control programs, proved to be too costly—since all the labor used (except prison labor) had to be hired. In the opinion of the District Commissioner of Kisii, this was a poor policy, as it failed to oblige the African communities to become engaged. He stated:

> It is bad for the morale of the Africans at their present stage of development, to restrict their contribution to one of money only.... If they want their country to be cleared of *Glossina* ... they should be prepared to turn up and help to clear it by the sweat of their brows.[66]

There was, however, a different opinion about communal labor. The view of the Kavirondo District (Nyanza) Commissioner was that communal labor by itself was not as effective as skilled labor in maintaining the rehabilitated areas and keeping them free of tsetse flies. In his understanding, communal labor should be used only for unskilled labor services, such as maintaining land that had already been cleared. By comparison, skilled labor could establish patterns of clearings that would minimize the risk of re-infestation,[67] considering that the flies could be carried to cleared areas by wild game and the wind, thus re-infesting them.[68]

In the southern Kavirondo District (Nyanza) along the shores of Lake Victoria, different views were held by the Department of African Affairs responsible for settlement schemes and the provincial administration as to how development should be approached. According to the Department of

African Affairs, there needed to be agreement between the people and the government. In this official's view, local people would participate only if there was a definitive plan for their resettlement. The official concluded: 'I need hardly say that if agreement can be reached it will help you and us enormous[ly].... If it is forced there will be endless trouble.' The administrator in particular believed local investigations would assist in drawing up the settlement plans. The settlement officer on the other hand further warned: 'You do not need the development officer ... to formulate the scheme'[69]—this comment shows that the disagreements were not about the substance of the proposed schemes, but rather about the roles played by different officers. Another controversy was to do with the application of the native land ordinances, already mentioned.

Native land ordinances

According to the native land ordinances, the District Commissioner would expunge the names of people who had contravened the ordinance rules from the records of the registered members. Such persons would be required to remove their families and stock from the bush clearing scheme. The Provincial Commissioner of Nyanza, who had oversight responsibility for the bush clearing program, had wondered 'how the proposed rules could operate in a portion of land communally owned.' His reasoning was that it would be impossible to regulate livestock grazing outside the bush clearing scheme. His views are quite revealing:

> The only reason it seems to me these rules have been proposed is that it has taken someone some effort to clear, and cost someone money.... I should not like to confirm the suspicion now common in the minds of the less sophisticated Africans that cooperation with the government in getting something done means handing it to the government. If these rules were enforced against the wishes of the indigenous people, their suspicion would be that much established.... The only trouble is that these rules which I consider superfluous are overdoing the thing.[70]

It was perhaps for this reason that the Native Commissioner suggested a correction to the ordinance by inserting a clause which stated: 'The District Commissioner shall specify the number of stock which each registered person may keep on his land, and which shall be endorsed on his occupation permit.'[71] Where the local administrative authorities found technical advice difficult to implement, the guiding decision was to avoid any wasteful use of public funds.[72] One controversial idea that emerged was zoning of the riverine vegetation, which required different projects for different zones. Due to multiple land-use practices by the communities, it was therefore impossible to set aside some parts of the riverside for grazing and others for crop cultivation. If allowed, such zoning of the riverine areas would discourage the local communities from managing bush regeneration.

In the settlement schemes, individual farmers' responsibilities for maintenance of bush regeneration were unsuccessful, as the work exceeded the available labor. Furthermore, subdivision of the land made it impossible to claim rights of occupancy by the members of the clan that owned the area.[73] In other cases where land occupation by a different clan appeared to benefit land rehabilitation—which the officials supported—these claims became contentious and triggered land conflict.

The Kipsigis–Maasai land conflict

The densely populated Chepalungu highland was inhabited by the Kipsigis and the Trans-Mara area was grazed by livestock of the Maasai (Figure 7.1). In the forestlands of Chepalungu, considerable forest cover had been cleared by burning and the area had been settled under instructions of the agricultural department. Contrary to the Kipsigis' efforts, an estimated 966 km^2 of the Trans-Mara had been lost to the flies. Since the area of Chepalungu and the Trans-Mara were adjacent, the government officials allowed the Kipsigis to cross over the administrative boundaries to cultivate crops in Trans Mara.[74] From a political perspective, however, it had not been advisable to allow the Kipsigis to cross over into the territories of the Maasai. Consequently, the government had to manage a delicate balance, assuring the Maasai that the arrangement was temporary. Yet, this created a historical land-use conflict between the two communities, as it was not possible to remove the Kipsigis after they had settled in what used to be the ancestral land of the Maasai.[75]

In a short while, the Kipsigis farming community used burning and bush clearing, and the results of their work in halting the expansion of the tsetse and reclaiming vast areas of the bush lands impressed the administration.[76] Thus, the department encouraged the Kipsigis to take up residence in the areas from which the bush had been cleared. In addition, the Kipsigis were allowed to expand their cultivated areas by clearing more bushland on condition that 'they do not build huts or live on their land,' which made it impractical for them.[77] This was what was meant by the colonial officials giving with one hand and taking it with another. In Chapter 8, we will show that bush clearing alone did not completely succeed in controlling the spread of tsetse flies.

Notes

1 Woulfin, D.S., *Slaves, trains, and missionaries: British moral imperialism and the development of precolonial East Africa, 1873–1901*, Doctor of Philosophy in History, Stony Brook University, 2011.
2 Pearce, R.D., *The turning point in Africa: British colonial policy 1938–48* (London: Frank Cass, 1982), 8.

3 Sunman, H., *A very different land: Memories of empire from the farmlands of Kenya* (London: The Redcliffe Press, 2014), 193.
4 Wilder, G., 'Colonial ethnology and political rationality in French West Africa,' *History and Anthropology* 14.3 (2003): 219–252.
5 Pererira, H.C., 'Co-operation in research,' *East African Agricultural Journal* XXII.2 (1956): 57–59.
6 Leslie, B.L., 'Coercive development: Land shortage, forced labor, and colonial development in the Chiweshe Reserve, colonial Zimbabwe, 1938–1946,' *International Journal of African Historical Studies* 25.1 (1992): 39–65.
7 Chambers, Robert, *Settlement schemes in tropical Africa: A study of organizations and development* (London: Routledge & Kegan Paul, 1969), 51.
8 Harbeson, J.W., 'Land reforms and politics in Kenya, 1954–70,' *Journal of Modern African Studies* 9.2 (1971): 231–251.
9 PC/NZA/3/14/335, District Commissioner's Office, Kericho to the Honourable Provincial Commissioner, Nyanza Province, Kisumu, Crown Land – Kumulot, 13 July 1946.
10 PC/NZA/3/14/335, Kimulot location, Buret, complaints to HM Government, 2 April 1951.
11 PC/NZA/3/14/335, District Commissioner, Kericho to the Provincial Commissioner Nyanza, Kisumu, Kimulot petition of 2 April 1951.
12 PC/NZA/3/14/335, The Chief Secretary, the Secretariat, Nairobi to the Provincial Commissioner, Nyanza Province, Kisumu, Crown Land – Kimulot, 10 December 1946.
13 PC/NZA/3/14/335, The Provincial Commissioner, Nyanza to the Honourable Member for African Affairs, The Secretariat, Nairobi, Land Exchange Proposal, Kericho District, 21 April 1940.
14 PC/NZA/3/14/335, District Commissioner's Office, Kericho to the Honourable Provincial Commissioner, Nyanza Province, Kisumu, Crown Land-Kimulot, 18 February 1947.
15 PC/NZA/3/14/335, Burton, G., Settlement Officer, to the member for agriculture and natural resources, Native claims for land in Kericho-Sotik District, 3 December 1947.
16 PC/NZA/3/14/335, Agricultural Department, Kericho to the District Commissioner, Kericho, Kimulot land, 19 March 1948.
17 PC/NZA/3/14/335, The Secretariat, Nairobi to the Provincial Commissioner, Nyanza Province, Kisumu, Land exchange proposals, 4 January 1949.
18 PC/NZA/3/14/335, Gamble, G., Department of Agriculture, Kericho District to Major F.W. Cavendish-Bentick, Board for Agriculture and Natural Resources, Nairobi, Tea Land in Kericho, 15 May 1948.
19 PC/NZA/3/14/335, District Commissioner's Office, Kericho to the Provincial Commissioner, Nyanza Province, Land exchange proposals, 25 January 1948.
20 PC/NZA/3/14/335, Provincial Commissioner's Office, Nyanza Province, Kisumu to the Honourable Secretary, Nairobi, 28 January 1949.
21 PC/NZA/3/14/335, Member for Agriculture and Natural Resources to the Honourable Director Agriculture, Kimulot Crownland, Kericho, 22 February 1949. The sizes of land sections: A = 4,800 acres, B = 3,600acres, C = 3,100acres.
22 PC/NZA/3/14/335, The Secretariat, Nairobi to the Provincial Commissioner, Nyanza Province, Land exchange proposal, Kericho District, 5 April 1949.
23 PC/NZA/3/14/335, The Secretariat, Nairobi to the Provincial Commissioner, Nyanza Province, Land exchange proposal, Kericho District, 5 April 1949.
24 PC/NZA/3/14/335, District Commissioner's Office, Kericho to the Provincial Commissioner, Nyanza Province, Kisumu, Land exchange 20 April 1949.
25 PC/NZA/3/14/335, The Secretariat, Nairobi, to the Provincial Commissioner, Nyanza Province, Kisumu, Sotik-Kericho Land exchanges, 15 August 1949.

158 *Ecological and social research*

26 PC/NZA/3/14/335, The Secretariat, Nairobi, to the Provincial Commissioner, Nyanza Province, Kisumu, Sotik-Kericho Land exchanges, 15 August 1949.
27 PC/NZA/3/14/335, Provincial Commissioner Nyanza to the Chief Secretary, Sotik and Kericho land exchanges, 8 October 1949.
28 PC/NZA/3/14/335, Provincial Commissioner Nyanza to the Chief Secretary, Sotik and Kericho land exchanges, 8 October 1949.
29 Ibid.
30 PC/NZA/3/14/335, P.M. Gordon, member Agriculture and Natural Resources to the Honourable Director of Agriculture, Nairobi, Sotik and Kericho proposed land exchange, 18 October 1948.
31 PC/NZA/3/14/335, The Kimulot and Botik land proposals, n.d.
32 PC/NZA/3/14/335, Office of the Member of Agriculture and Natural Resources, to the Provincial Commissioner, Nyanza, Kisumu, 19 November 1949.
33 PC/NZA/3/14/335, A.C.C. Swann, District Commissioner Kericho to the Honourable B.A. Ohanga, NLC, Kisumu, 27 February 1950.
34 PC/NZA/3/14/335, Five-year District Agriculture, Schemes for organized settlement of the Kipsigis, 1951.
35 PC/NZA/3/14/247, Wilks, H.C.P., the District Officer's Office, Kericho to the Provincial Commissioner Nyanza Province, Kisumu, Kimulot demolitions Report for the period 2 March 1952.
36 PC/NZA/3/14/335, Ohanga, A., to the Provincial Commissioner, Nyanza, Kisumu on Kipsigis land claims: Kimulot, 30 October 1950.
37 PC/NZA/3/14/247, Department of Agriculture, Kericho to Executive Officer, African Land utilization and settlement, Nairobi, Kimulot Report, 2 November 1951.
38 PC/NZA/3/14/247, The Eldoret Magistrate's Court at Kericho, Criminal Case No. 196, Kipsoi Arap Chemorore vs. the State, Kisumu, March 1952.
39 PC/NZA/3/14/247, Opinions address by Learned Deputy Public Prosecutor, 1952.
40 PC/NZA/3/14/247, The Eldoret Magistrate's Court at Kericho, Criminal Case No. 196, Kipsoi Arap Chemorore vs. the State, Kisumu, March 1952.
41 PC/NZA/3/14/247, Department of Agriculture, Kericho to the Executive Officer, ALDEV, Nairobi, 2 November 1954.
42 PC/NZA/3/14/247, Department of Agriculture, Kericho, to Executive Officer African Lands Development (ALDEV), Nairobi, 1 April 1955.
43 PC/NZA/3/14/247, The Kimulot and Itember schemes to the Executive officer, African Lands Development (ALDEV), Nairobi, 3 June 1955.
44 PC/NZA/3/14/247, District Commissioner's Office, Kericho to C.H. Williams, Provincial Commissioner, Nyanza Province, Kisumu, Itember scheme.
45 AK/26/8, Director of Agriculture to the member for Agriculture and natural resources, Nairobi, 14 June 1946.
46 AK/26/8, Armitage, R.P., Clerk to the Executive Council, Government Notice no. 393, The land and water preservation (General) rules 1943.
47 Ibid.
48 AK/26/8, Director of Agriculture to the member for Agriculture and natural resources, Nairobi, 14 June 1946.
49 AK/26/8, Colchester, T.C., Department of local government, soil conservation measures, 15 November 1946.
50 AK/26/8, Allen, A.W., Provincial Agriculture to the Provincial Commissioner, Nyanza Province, soil conservation, 19 December 1948.
51 AK/26/8, Department of Agriculture, central Nyanza, to the Provincial Commissioner Nyanza Province, Kisumu, soil conservation question, 15 October 1949.
52 AK/26/8, Minutes of a meeting of the Meru African District Council held on 4–6 September 1950.

53 Ibid.
54 AK/26/8, Department of Agriculture to the District Agricultural Officer, African Affairs, 9 May 1951.
55 AK/26/11, Notes on soil conservation work, 24 and 25 April 1952.
56 AK/26/8, Memorandum: Planning of Arable holdings for peasant farmers in African areas, 1951.
57 AK/26/8, Provincial Agricultural Officer, Department of Agriculture to the Director of Agriculture, Nairobi, August 1951.
58 AK/26/11, Stein, G., soil conservation, Department of Agriculture to District Agriculture Officers, central Nyanza, Kisumu, 11 July 1953.
59 Ibid.
60 AK/26/11, Leslie, E.J.A., District Commissioner, North Nyanza to the Provincial Commissioner, Nyanza, soil conservation, 16 December 1953.
61 AK/26/11, Williams, C.H., Provincial Commissioner, Nyanza to the District Commissioner, South Nyanza, soil conservation, 28 December 1953.
62 PC/NZA/3/14/247, Provincial Offices, Department of Agriculture to the Provincial Commissioner Province, Kisumu, Hember settlement area, 7 August 1954.
63 PC/NZA/3/14/68, Nyanza local native council's resolutions 1936.
64 AGR/5/1/296, The African settlement and land utilization, to the Honourable Member for Agriculture and Natural Resources, 11 September 1946.
65 PC/NZA/3/14/335, Lewis, J.H., Acting District Commissioner, Kericho to the Member for Agriculture and Natural Resources, Nairobi, Kimulot Crown Land 11 September 1948; AG/4/1/1/76, Nandi bush clearing, Betterment of Agricultural land, 1948.
66 PC/NZA/2/14/28, Fox, D.S., The District Commissioner Kisii to the Honourable Director Medical Services, Nairobi, 15 November 1938.
67 PC/NZA/2/14/28, Provincial Commissioner Nyanza to the Honourable the Chief Secretary, Nairobi, 8 January 1941.
68 PC/NZA/2/14/28, District Commissioner's Office, South Kavirondo to the Honourable Provincial Commissioner, Nyanza, Kisumu, 1 April 1941.
69 AK/16/14, Kuja River Basin crossings and watering places–tsetse control for 1948; PC/NZA/3/14/68, Office of the Commissioner for African land utilization and settlement to Watt, W.L. Office of the Provincial Commissioner, Kisumu, 29 July 1948.
70 PC/NZA/3/14/68, Provincial Commissioner, Nyanza to the Commissioner for African Land Utilization and settlement, 21 April 1949.
71 PC/NZA/3/14/68, Native Courts Officer to the Commissioner for African land Utilization and settlement, native lands Rules, 1949.
72 DC/KISUM/1/29/13, Minutes of the meeting of the tsetse fly and trypanosomiasis, Kisumu, 10 April 1951.
73 DC/KISUM/1/29/16, Tsetse Survey and Control, Veterinary Services, Kabete to the Provincial Commissioner, Kisumu, 27 March 1951.
74 PC/NGO/1/7/29, District Commissioner's Office, Kericho to Provincial Commissioner Kisumu, 25 October 1955.
75 PC/NGO/1/7/29, Tsetse Survey and Control, Department of Veterinary Service; Kabate to the Chief Native Commissioner, Nairobi, 3 March 1952; BV/12/220, Minutes of the meeting of the tsetse fly and trypanosomiasis committee held at Kisumu, 12 September 1952.
76 PC/NGO/1/7/29, Tsetse Survey and Control Department of Veterinary Services to the Chief Field Zoologist, Kabete, 11 May 1951.
77 PC/NGO/1/7/29, Kenya National Farmers' Union to the Minister for Agriculture, 30 October 1955.

Part III

Vectors, pests and environmental change

8 Tsetse fly control in East Africa
Environmental and social impacts, 1880–1959

Nineteenth-century European travelers (see Chapter 2) had reported the prevalence of a disease-causing vector as a potential impediment to progress for European colonization of East Africa.[1] The travelers described a tiny grey fly (genus *Glossina*) that caused death when it bit cattle, horses, donkeys, mules and people.[2] By the time of colonial establishment in East Africa, large areas were devoid of human habitation due to the tsetse fly— the vector of sleeping sickness in people and *trypanosomiasis* in cattle. The fly had been around for a much longer period, considering its co-evolution with its wildlife hosts, and by the mid-nineteenth and early twentieth centuries it had spread over vast areas of East Africa.[3] To the African peoples, the vector is a familiar nemesis.[4] African societies had learnt to modify their environments by bush clearing around settlements and fumigating cattle with the smoke of cattle manure (to repel the flies), among other traditional remedies.[5] Local communities also responded by grazing livestock in the infested areas during the dry season, and driving livestock through the areas during the night when the flies are inactive. Historically, the communities inhabiting the fly belt bordering Rwanda and Burundi raised a trypanosome-tolerant breed of cattle called Sanga.[6] Another local adaptation was to manage sheep and goats that are not vulnerable to the fly.[7] The infection occurs when the fly transmits the trypanosome parasite in its salivary glands into the blood stream of the host and the victim.[8]

We are interested in understanding, first, impacts of the sleeping sickness pandemic of the late nineteenth and early twentieth centuries on human and livestock demography in the Lake Victoria Basin in East Africa (Figure 8.1). Second, we investigate progress in tsetse research during the depression years of the 1930s. Third, we examine progress made in tsetse control during the Second World War, and, fourth, during the post-war years.

Tsetse fly and *trypanosomiasis* research and control in East Africa

The late nineteenth and early twentieth century evidenced a pandemic of sleeping sickness, with the epicenter around the Lake Victoria basin shared

164 *Vectors, pests and environmental change*

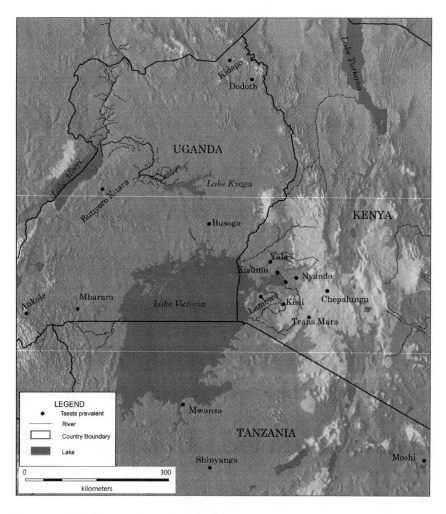

Figure 8.1 Lake Victoria Basin in East Africa.

by the three East African colonies (Figure 8.1). The progressive encroachment by tsetse flies on human inhabited areas forced people out of vast grazing lands and fertile farming areas.[9] The geographical distribution of the tsetse fly and its impacts on the pastoral and agricultural economy attracted imperial scientific research interest and control in East Africa.[10] During this early period, breaking the host–vector cycle—by killing wildlife on the one hand and destroying the fly's habitats on the other—were perceived to control the spread of the tsetse and the infectious trypanosome parasite.

The colonists had faith in imperial science to control the trypanosome to save people and stock.[11] This is reflected in the attitudes of European settlers and officials, a fact they communicated to African populations. In his communication with the African Chief B. Nyambole in the Nyanza province in Kenya, a European mining entrepreneur stated: 'We are enjoying the privileges of the British Empire, and we are grateful to be under this western civilization, with its highly [developed technologies] in the prevention of diseases and curing.'[12] This discussion arose around the subject of tsetse flies that had caused sleeping sickness and claimed the lives of many subjects of Chief Nyambole. The view of the European entrepreneur demonstrates the importance of preventive and curative medical treatments against one of the most debilitating diseases in tropical Africa.

Indeed, John Ford's study[13] on the tsetse fly and *trypanosomiasis* described the ecological complexity that characterizes transmission of the disease. In stressing the importance of ecological interactions between the fly, its habitats and mammalian hosts, he concluded that there are no simple strategies for fighting the vector, given the complex chain relations between these contributing factors. Ford was of the opinion that those involved in its 'control are likely to experience many disappointments.'[14] The colonial officials by comparison perceived that manipulating the vegetation by breaking up the fly's habitats would disrupt its expansion into settled areas. Additionally, from these earlier times, there was a hypothesis that the destruction of wildlife would break the fly–host cycle by denying the flies regular blood meals.[15]

British medical practitioners, according to E.B. Worthington,[16] were interested in investigating the disease epidemics from three perspectives. The first type of research concerned the physical environment and the biological complexities in relation to the hosts, plant communities, seasonality, parasitism and host–fly life cycles. The second type of research was experimental. Its aim was to alter the physical environments of the flies using fire, chemical control, quantitative changes in host populations and habitat manipulation. The third type of research focused on biological control (e.g., sterilization of the female flies) and was the least reported.[17]

As readers might appreciate, because of the complexity of the circumstances, the outcomes and the narratives, as opposed to progressing towards the desired solution, tsetse controls may be likened to a metaphor of fire fighters putting out oil fires. When the fires appear to have been contained, more fuels rekindle new fires, forcing the fire fighters to repeat the process *ad infinitum*. In the case of the tsetse, whether to control the fly caused a dilemma—abandonment of this pursuit would risk far greater damage, while perpetual trials offered no permanent solutions. Indeed, Paul Richard[18] argues that where tsetse control trials were reported a success, 'they were too expensive to maintain.' The motivation for tsetse research and control in East Africa, was the sleeping sickness pandemic.

Sleeping sickness pandemics, 1880–1929

The history of tsetse control reflects the history of tropical medicine in East Africa.[19] During the late nineteenth and early twentieth century, the epidemic of sleeping sickness killed an estimated 300,000 to 500,000 people in the Congo Basin, in Busoga in Uganda, and in Kenya.[20] The epicenter of the disease was the kingdom of Bunyoro Kitara (in Uganda), from where the pandemic spread to neighboring regions. Bunyoro Kitara became empty of human habitation and became a wilderness.[21] According to Endfield and colleagues,[22] the colonial disruptions of populations, tribal warfare and the earlier slave trade had prepared the ground for such outbreaks of sleeping sickness. Moreover, the culmination of the rinderpest cattle epidemics in the late nineteenth century had concentrated populations in smaller areas and exposed them to tsetse flies.

By the 1890s, when environmental management had collapsed, farming communities lost the ability to control the tsetse flies.[23] The abandoned grazing and agricultural lands became bushlands—further ideal habitats for tsetse flies.[24] The British Royal Society appointed a committee in 1896 to assist the colonial governments with scientific investigations. Lord Lister, the President of the Royal Society requested the Tsetse Committee for information on the distribution of the fly in the British East African colonies.[25] The survey showed that in the Protectorate of Uganda, more than 25 percent of the total population had died of sleeping sickness; and in the region of central Tanganyika bordering the Lake Victoria Basin, huge numbers of the population had either died or been infected by sleeping sickness.[26]

The focus was on the regions bordering the Lake Basin, where sleeping sickness pandemics resulted in high human fatalities in 1900.[27] The most severe outbreaks were in 1902, when the Royal Society Commission sent a medical team to investigate the pandemic.[28] By 1903, the infestation across East Africa had worsened with an estimated 90,000 deaths in Uganda alone.[29] By 1904, the Royal African Society had estimated that an additional 40,000 people had died in Uganda. Consequently, Sir Michael Foster, the Secretary of the Royal Society, recommended medical research on a large scale to keep the British government well-informed about the pandemic in the East African colonies[30] (discussed in the following subsection).

Between 1900 and 1904, along the Lake Victoria littoral, over 200,000 people had died of the disease, which was 90 percent of the total human population.[31] The areas abandoned by human populations became subject to bush encroachment, thus expanding the habitats of the tsetse flies. An estimated 90 percent of the grazing lands were infested, rendering large areas uninhabitable.[32] From local sources, such as Chief Elija Bonyo living on the Kenyan side of the lake, the sleeping sickness pandemics had reduced the human populations along the lakeshore, forcing survivors to flee to Tanganyika.[33] From the Ugandan side of the lake, the flies had been transported by boats and infested the islands in the lake that experienced epidemics of sleeping sickness in 1903 and 1904. Busoga Island was depopulated by sleeping sickness, and populations were displaced from other islands.[34] From the islands, the tsetse spread to the marshes along the lake shores and then on to the adjoining dry lands on the Kenyan side of Lake Victoria, extending further inland.[35]

By 1905 there were reports of deaths of cattle,[36] and by 1907 the cattle population in the infested areas in Uganda along the shores of Lake Victoria had been removed.[37] In southern Ankole, cattle died in large numbers in 1909 from a variant of the trypanosome (*Trypanosomea congolese*), with mortalities reaching 75 to 80 percent by 1910. On the Kenyan side of the lake, the epidemics had terminated by 1911 when the Provincial Commissioner reported the problem as 'slight.'[38] In Uganda, the cattle populations in Ankole and the southwestern districts were on the path of recovery from 1912, before collapsing again. The disease had by 1913 forced the population into the German East African territory.[39] The demographic collapse caused environmental ripple effects, favoring further expansion of tsetse fly.[40]

Following the British military invasion of the German East African territory in 1914–1915, Ankole was re-infested by tsetse flies which were introduced along with the military and civilian traffic. Vast herds of the ration cattle and horses died of the *trypanosomiasis*.[41] In other regions of East Africa, the tsetse fly threat to cattle and people remained widespread. By 1916, the fly was reported in the Kedipo Valley bordering South Sudan, and in the Dodoth country in northeastern Uganda. The expansion of the flies changed the grazing patterns of the Dodoth herds by concentrating people and livestock in the remaining tsetse-free areas.[42] The period was quickly followed by the complete collapse of the cattle population between 1919 and 1920 that forced the Ugandan colonial government to again seek measures to halt the expansion of the tsetse fly.[43]

In the Sukumaland in Tanganyika, rapid expansion of the tsetse was responsible for the deaths of some 20,000 people between 1912 and 1921. Populations were again displaced[44] and by 1918, the fly was expanding in central and East Africa at the rate of 1,609 km^2 per annum, thus overrunning the region.[45] By 1920 and 1921, sleeping sickness resurgence was reported on the islands on the Kenyan side of the lake and along the Lake Victoria coastal littoral. However, it was not until 1924 that a survey was conducted on the Kenyan side of the lake to provide a better overview of the distribution of tsetse flies. The survey found very low human populations in the region. The survivors reported that prior to the earlier pandemic, the areas had been densely settled by farming communities.[46] Clearly, tsetse fly research and control had become urgent.[47]

Tsetse research and control

Initial large-scale initiatives to control the tsetse flies began in 1910. Over time, more radical methods were used, including the destruction of tsetse habitats through bush clearing and extermination of wildlife. Due to limited labor capacity, bush clearing was not a permanent solution—the vegetation regenerated and the flies returned.[48] In the German East African territory of Tanganyika, the demographic changes were followed by major transformation of the natural vegetation—the open grasslands were transformed into bushlands[49] that were utilized by the flies which increased their geographical distribution.[50] Although the threats to people and cattle required emergency action in which time was of the essence, ecological studies that linked the distribution of tsetse with wild ungulates required complex experiments.[51] Methods of control that might have worked for one species did not necessarily work for others. This may be partly explained by the different species of tsetse that required different ecological conditions and types of hosts. It had become clear that different species of tsetse flies were responsible for different strains of *trypanosomiasis*. In the Speke Gulf of Mwanza on the Tanganyika side of Lake Victoria, the sleeping sickness outbreak was linked to the prevalence of *Glossina rhodesience*. Thus, decimation of elephant populations in central Uganda were aimed at controlling the spread of the fly.[52] In 1925, the spread of *Glossina morsitans* in Uganda was attributed to the recovery of wildlife after the earlier destruction attempts.[53]

Nevertheless, the main failing of imperial science research was to seek solutions before investigating the problems. In this regard, experimental trials were not distinguished from practical land reclamations.[54] Scientific research approaches showed a preference for regional research centers and subsidiary research stations across the three colonies. The first regional research center was established at Shinyanga in Tanganyika in about 1918. It coordinated the activities of an interdisciplinary research team.[55] Medical research on the epidemiology of the trypanosome did not begin until 1919, due to a lack of funds and specialized research personnel. By 1922, attempts were being made to secure more funds for large-scale experimental attacks on the tsetse.[56] Consequently, in 1923, a labor force of 10,000 was organized to clear a barrier 'in front of the fly advance,' in order to separate the tsetse-infested areas from the settled areas.[57] Species prevalence, the types of vegetation cover and climatic conditions were investigated.[58]

During early ecological research activities, land reclamation was marked by both optimism and inadequate practices. The optimism was due to the fact that ecological research in Africa was a new field of investigation, offering experienced researchers, opportunities to test new scientific theories and methods. However, inadequacy was evident in that the researchers were not trained in tropical ecology, which forced them to rely on methods developed in Europe to solve African medical and environmental problems.[59] One imaginative method attempted was conducting a census of the flies by using 'fly boys'—mainly local African men trained to catch the flies (by attracting them to themselves). Later, the human objects were replaced by dark clothes.[60] However, according to the first director of the Tsetse Fly

Research Center (C.F.M. Swynnerton, after whom G. *swynnertoni* was named), tsetse control is complex, involving a vicious cycle of attack and retreat. In his opinion, bush clearing alone, without determining how the people and livestock would be isolated from the fly, would not produce the desired results.[61] In other words, no method was sufficiently robust to stop the expansion of the flies.

The tsetse research and control efforts had raised two questions that needed to be examined. First, is it possible for experimental treatment alone to wipe out tsetse flies and consequently sleeping sickness, or could medical treatment control the disease (if not future infection)? Second, would land reclamation and resettlement solve the problem of tsetse expansion?[62] The emphasis of further action was on the practical application of research findings. In 1928, the Tsetse Committee of Civil Research embarked on the first ever systematic experimental work in the field, stimulating scientific research interests on the questions of human health and the economic impacts of tsetse fly control. There was, however, a major shift in tsetse research and control activities when the Department of Tsetse Research was established in 1929 by means of a five-year research grant from the East African Loan Scheme.[63] The tsetse research combined ecological and entomological investigations with bush clearing. It was still apparent that tsetse flies would be difficult to eliminate unless their contact with wildlife and domesticated stocks was broken.[64] By the 1930s, the dilemma for the colonial officials was balancing tsetse fly research with other development initiatives—in particular, soil erosion control.[65]

The depression years of the 1930s

The 1930s was climatically and economically a difficult period for the East African colonies, as mentioned earlier. During this time, tsetse research and control continued to be particularly worrisome. The challenge was how to sustainably put down the repeated tsetse outbreaks. Emergency programs for reducing the immediate adverse impacts of sleeping sickness did not allow for long-term investigations. Instead, tsetse research at this time focused on two issues: first, on the populations of the different species of tsetse flies and, second, on their biology. However, since the focus of the research was still on elimination of the flies, little attention was given to understanding the relationship between the fly and its various hosts.[66] There were no comparative studies on the selection of habitats and hosts. Contrary to what had been expected, the destruction of large mammalian hosts did not deny the flies blood meals or starve them out of existence—other sources of blood were small mammals, reptiles and birds. Further, nearly all the mammalian hosts were mobile—as opposed to having fixed habitats, which made them an unreliable source of food for the flies.[67] We now examine attempts at ecological control of the tsetse.

Until the 1930s, tsetse research and control had focused on two areas of action: research on the population dynamic of the fly; and bush clearing.[68] Denying the tsetse a suitable habitat was claimed to reduce expansion of the fly populations. However, as we mentioned earlier, this was never accomplished. Additionally, two new methods of manipulating bush growth were tested in research experiments by the Shinyanga regional research center.

The first new method was to divide an area into blocks separated by cleared barriers. Each block was subdivided into squares of 1,829 m on all sides, and all the vegetation was removed in the border areas using hand hoes. The second method involved fire treatment, which varied according to seasons—fires were more effective in the hotter, dry season than the cool season.[69] Repeated fires at four- to five-year intervals transformed the vegetation into grasslands. This was then followed by short-term fire intervals. The direct impact was that the fire either drove out or killed the tsetse, reducing fly populations in the experimental areas by 70 percent. However, the fly population in general increased by 300 percent—the flies from the treated blocks might have taken refuge in the adjacent grasslands that were protected from burning.[70] The finding was that, in the long term, the tsetse fly population recovered after fire.[71]

In 1931 in Sukumaland in Tanganyika, community labor and mechanical methods were used to clear some 1,347 km² of bushland. In the same area, some ten years before the sleeping sickness outbreak, Goodenough and co-workers[72] reported that the advancing tsetse front had driven out about 30,000 people. The peasants were 'greatly worried over this progressive loss of their country.' In the Ugandan section of the Lake Victoria Basin that had earlier experienced the sleeping sickness pandemic, the methods of tsetse control again involved the use of fire which proved to be successful in eliminating the flies, albeit temporarily. Bush thinning and the periodic use of fires provided temporary respite from fly infestations.[73] Between 1936 and 1938, the fly populations increased in the area of Mbarara in Uganda, to which fire had been applied. On the advice of the researchers, the rehabilitated areas were allocated to settlement schemes.[74]

The methods of settling African peasants described by Ford[75] involved four steps over four years: 'no anti-tsetse measures were needed before people could occupy the bush.' In the first year, settlers would mark out their plots and fell enough bush to cultivate crops and build a house. In the second year, they extended their cultivation and brought in their sheep and goats. In the third year, the family brought in their calves and in the fourth year, the whole family joined the settlement, with their adult cattle. It is uncertain if the effectiveness of these proposed methods were tested. What was however clear was that efforts aimed at tsetse control had not produced sustainable success, despite repeated attacks using a variety of methods.[76] Methods such as the mechanical trapping of the flies, the destruction of wildlife, bush clearing and the application of fire provided temporary reductions in fly population densities.[77] In particular, experimental control of tsetse flies through deforestation caused the same outcome of environmental destruction for which the African peasants had been blamed by officials. The paradox of environmental destruction on the one hand, and tsetse fly control on the other, caused some experts to question the effectiveness of bush clearing.[78] Perhaps, the most controversial subject was whether to control soil erosion or tsetse as a priority.

Tsetse or soil erosion control

A complicating challenge arose because the various institutions involved in tsetse control did not agree on the methods used.[79] This sparked discussions over institutional responsibilities—in terms of those that supported research and development schemes, and those that advocated soil erosion control above investment in tsetse control. Other researchers preferred to focus on the medical aspects of sleeping sickness (*trypanosomiasis*). Medical researchers from the London School of Hygiene and Tropical Medicine, headed by Professor P.A. Buxton, investigated preventative and curative control of *trypanosomiasis*[80] in both cattle and humans.[81] By putting their work into geographical and regional contexts, the medical researchers soon realized that the tsetse problems would not be solved piecemeal, and that integrated action was required—with ecological science running side by side with social science research and development. This implied that research activities should comprehensively address questions related to land reclamations, resettlements, soil erosion control and the consequences of tsetse resurgence.[82]

Goodenough and colleagues[83] described the contesting viewpoints between those who supported soil erosion control on the one hand, and tsetse control on the other—in the 1930s, both problems demanded equal research urgency. The paradox of the debate was whether the tsetse was a curse, or a possible boon for soil conservation. In other words, the tsetse flies had indirectly contributed to environmental conservation by returning the countryside to bushlands, while the relocation of human and livestock populations into the cleared areas had aggravated soil erosion. In avoiding the tsetse flies, people had been concentrated into smaller areas that inevitably became over-utilized resulting in soil erosion (as claimed by some). Consequently, from the soil erosion perspective, the debate considered the presence of tsetse fly as a boon, while on the other hand it was a bane for cattle keeping. The argument contended that 'tsetse [is] a blessing in disguise, as it can be regarded as acting as the trustee of the land for future generations.'[84] Conversely, the clearing of bushes increased grass production on rehabilitated land, and in absence of the tsetse, attracted grazing and crop cultivation.[85] Those concerned with public health advocated the safety of future human settlements, arguing that bush clearing and the application of fire would reduce tree regeneration and free the land from the flies.[86] We move on now to consider the Second World War period which experienced various impacts on the progress of tsetse research and control.

The Second World War years, 1939–1945

The outbreak of the Second World War led to the closing down of the research stations and environmental development schemes. Experiments in culling game was halted.[87] Consequently, during this time, the areas that had previously been rehabilitated from the tsetse regenerated into bushlands. This was followed by an upsurge in the flies, which posed a threat to neighboring areas.[88] Later, researchers repeated the same methods that had failed earlier, somehow expecting different outcomes—thus making the findings less reliable for purposes of development.

Some of the land reclamation projects were too large and the impact on tsetse flies was disproportionate, given the amount of time and money expended. For example, in central Tanganyika around Moshi, following outbreaks of sleeping sickness, the government cleared some 804 km^2 of all woody vegetation with the aim of stopping the spread of the disease. While research reported effective control of the flies, the outcomes were unsustainable due to the resurgence of the fly.[89] Research projects had demonstrated that the tsetse species *Glossina pallidipes* is the most resilient—in terms of recovery after treatments.

Tsetse research and development

During the 1940s, on the Kenyan side of the Lake Victoria Basin, tsetse research was conducted along the many marshes, streams and rivers that discharged into the lake.[90] These areas had shown evidence of a resurgence in sleeping sickness. In the Kavirondo (Kisumu) District, for example, 500 cases of sleeping sickness were reported between 1942 and 1944. The people were visiting the rivers and marshes to water their livestock and, in the process, encountered the flies. One solution suggested was sterilization of female flies[91]—on which no progress was reported.

There were disagreements among administrative officials and the technical departments on ways to manage the rehabilitated areas. For example, the District Commissioner of Kisii in Kenya expressed his disappointment that the agricultural schemes were established with the narrow objective of tsetse fly control. He was particularly disappointed that bush clearing was limited to corridors of land a short distance from the rivers and marshes, while larger tracts of land infested by the tsetse were ignored. He considered such limited aims as 'nibbling' at larger problems such as soil erosion control, grazing schemes and agricultural development.[92]

By 1945, an estimated 90 km of land in the lake Basin on the Kenyan side of the political border has been rehabilitated from bush encroachment. The experimental clearings, rather than removing all vegetation, left open corridors between blocks of bush, which from a land-use perspective was considered inadequate by the administration for resettlement.[93] According to the District Commissioner of central Kavirondo, it would be preferable to clear large blocks of vegetation to plan settlements. From a practical point of view, the cleared blocks might be subdivided into grazing units that could be allocated to individual families. The agricultural department would then undertake the protection of settled land from returning to bushlands.[94] The provincial team was convinced that the best use of the tsetse-rehabilitated areas was livestock grazing. By contrast, the experimental clearings along the rivers and marshes adjoining the lake—where the object was to build barriers between the river and the adjacent dry lands—would serve as research plots.[95] One might however question some of the proposed methods—such as grass planting.[96] In the tropical environment, which has a high potential for regenerating grass, the planting of grass was unnecessary.

By 1945, the discussion by the various authorities turned to the logistics for planning agricultural schemes. It was important therefore that the technical departments and administration officials should become familiar with the research activities. At the research sites, the authorities received full briefings from the technical teams on the planned cycles of experimentation and project implementation.[97] However, the agricultural department was dissatisfied with various activities, for example, bush clearing in central Kavirondo. Over the years, the department had conducted bush clearing work along the river, with the object of preventing the tsetse flies from spreading into the rehabilitated areas. The challenge was the rapid recovery of the bushlands.[98]

Another concern of the department was that with limited technical personnel, they were unable to conduct the required surveys, while at the same time being expected to supervise the reclamation works. The Trans-Mara area in Kenya is a case in point. About 1,931 km² of grazing lands that were free of tsetse flies had been divided into grazing blocks. However, in the Isuria highlands (still in the Trans-Mara), some blocks were infested by the tsetse species G. *swynnertoni*, the dispersal of which was considered a serious threat to livestock. The large game populations indicated a high reservoir for *trypanosomiasis* in the tsetse-free areas. Similarly, in the Chapalungu forest in the western Rift Valley bordering the Lake Basin, the high human population was under threat from the expanding tsetse fly belt. The conclusion of the agricultural team was that in the future, the development of agriculture would continue to be hindered by the twin problems of tsetse and soil erosion.[99] Yet, despite the previous disappointing outcomes, researchers viewed that bush clearing and game shooting would solve the tsetse fly problem.[100] Would it? Let us examine the events of the post-war years.

The post-war years, 1946–1959

As with elsewhere in the world, the post-war years were a period of economic reconstruction. Through the Colonial Development and Welfare

Act of 1940, an amount of £500,000 was allocated to tsetse research in East Africa.[101] With this funding, many thousands of square kilometers of land previously infested by tsetse flies had been cleared of vegetation in Uganda, Tanganyika and Kenya. The advancing fly belt was halted, and the populations of flies reduced to very low levels in some of the experimental sites.[102] However, as before, extensive game culling, trapping, and application of fire and bush clearing did not produce long-term solutions to the tsetse fly problem. This was the case particularly in the Ankole region of Uganda, where cattle continued to die from *trypanosomiasis* during the 1940s.[103] By 1945, the flies had re-infested much of the countries, pushing the human populations into areas too marginal for crop cultivation.[104] The Director of Veterinary Services in Uganda during the same period planned large-scale clearing of vegetation. The methods involved removing herbaceous vegetation and then applying fire. Additionally, the buffalo—the main host of the tsetse—were exterminated.[105] Elsewhere in East Africa, tsetse surveys were conducted to estimate the distribution of tsetse populations. We use a Kenyan example.

Tsetse surveys in Kenya

In their progress report of 1947, researchers described the prevalence of tsetse flies across varied ecological and climatic regions in Kenya. The large-scale surveys mapped the distribution of the flies that posed threats to people in different areas. The findings were expected to guide land reclamation programs at district levels. In the coastal province of Kenya, for example, an estimated 10,315 km^2 were surveyed—the species of tsetse flies were identified, their habitats described, and the risks they posed to people and livestock appraised. It was noticed that the flies were being concentrated in a small number of areas. Based on their distribution, large-scale clearing of vegetation using mechanical methods was proposed. The focus was on the riverine vegetation that was heavily infested with tsetse flies.[106]

The survey teams interviewed local communities about the past history of the tsetse and *trypanosomiasis* problems, as well as their knowledge of animals which showed resistance to the trypanosome parasite.[107] In Makueni, in the Akamba District, in Kenya, where a settlement scheme was planned, large-scale clearing of natural vegetation was expected to achieve multiple development goals. First, the clearing would disrupt the mobility of the flies and reduce infection by *trypanosomiasis*, while regenerating grass would be used for grazing schemes. By opening the bush along the riverine forest, the risks of new infestations from those landscapes were expected to be reduced. Previous experience of land clearing in the same areas in 1944 had shown that the incidence of *trypanosomiasis* had declined following treatments. A further advantage was that once the areas had been cleared and individual farmers allocated their plots of land, they would be responsible for the maintenance work to keep the flies away from people and livestock.[108] A major challenge, however, was the lack of investigation into the social implications of tsetse research and control.

Social implications of tsetse research and control

The administration was hesitant to allow the societies to solve their own problems; thus, officials placed limitations on the numbers of people and livestock in the rehabilitated areas. However, controlling the influx of African settlers for fear they would aggravate the problem of soil erosion was not based on facts.[109] By implementing such a policy, the colonial state created multiple problems. The contradictory government policy was to control threats posed by the tsetse fly, but at the same time it restricted settlement by African peasants on rehabilitated lands.[110] Indeed, the land accessible to African communities was shrinking,[111] while the colonial administration enacted rules that made it compulsory for people to return to the rehabilitated land to espouse soil conservation.[112] The multiple demands on African people only caused confusion in the implementation of the government's own programs.[113]

Consequently, although the colonial administration had planned to involve African communities in development schemes, they were 'convinced that there was neither the time nor the trained personnel necessary to persuade the majority of the measures and so relied on enforcement of regulations.'[114] Among other issues, this did not solve the labor problem. The Veterinary Director in Kenya, in a letter to the Provincial Commissioner of Kisumu, explained his views on the question of labor. In his opinion, replacement of hired with communal labor was likely to alter the spirit of establishing agricultural schemes.[115] According to the provincial commissioner, if the experiments were to be abandoned in favor of a more extensive scheme, it would be like throwing 'away expenditure of the last four years,' or repeating the experiments all over again.[116]

Five concluding remarks were made at the time, as follows (notes in verbatim):

- No satisfactory method of dealing with G. *pallisides* has been found.
- The attempt to compel or persuade immigrants to clear thickets for cultivation, without pay, has not worked.
- It is impractical and undesirable to conduct tsetse eradication programs in areas opened up for settlement. In any such area, the method of tsetse eradication should be decided on in advance and put into effect as vigorously as possible.
- Tsetse funds should be flexible to deal with new situations created by unavoidable changes in settlement plans.
- Elimination of tsetse will not necessarily mean concurrent elimination of *trypanosomiasis*. Infection rates in cattle in neighboring fly-free areas are high and suggest that much mechanical transmission occurs.[117]

176 *Vectors, pests and environmental change*

We now examine the impacts of bushland clearing on settlement schemes.

The success of settlement schemes depended on the capacity of the officials and the tsetse research teams to clear more bushland. However, the supply of local labor continued to be inadequate. For example, in 1951, in the Nyando area of the Lake Basin in Kenya, a labor team of 200 took some three years to deforest an 11 km riverine area. In 1953, about 450 Mau Mau convicts were sent down to the lake shore to clear the vegetation and by 1953/1954, there was evidence of a reduction in the tsetse fly infestations. Between 1954 and 1955, using more prison labor, a total area of 200 acres of the Lake Victoria littoral vegetation had been cleared. Yet, the officials of the technical departments showed no interest in ongoing maintenance work. The lack of willingness by the officials to repeat bush clearing activities undermined the success in freeing the Nyando area from tsetse fly. Provincial officials argued that disinfestation of the fly prior to settlement should be legally regulated under the native land ordinances.[118]

These preventive methods were costly and the departments charged with the responsibilities had limited funds to devote to tsetse control.[119] After many years, the research teams and the officials were still debating possible long-term solutions.[120] The communities who were settled in the rehabilitated areas raised their opposition to breaches of customary land tenure rights. When areas were rehabilitated, the clans claimed the rights over immigrants. To distinguish these rights, the officials used confusing terminology, such as 'resettlement' (referring to settling the people previously displaced), and 'dispersal settlement' (referring to the immigrants displaced from elsewhere but settled on a different clan's land).[121] A factor that remained little understood was impact of the extermination of wildlife on sustained population of tsetse flies.[122]

Extermination of wildlife

From 1951, tsetse control in the area of Bunyoro-Kitara in Uganda adopted radical methods, which instead of focusing on the flies, sought extermination of their mammalian hosts. The experiments initially involved shooting only large hoofed animals, while sparing smaller ones such as antelopes and pigs. Robertson and Bernacca[123] report that along a narrow strip of land between the Nile and Sezibwa in Uganda, the wild game killed included 293 buffalo, 69 hippopotami and 2,178 other animals. In Acholi in Uganda, the host of *G. morsitans* is the rhino. Although shooting of these animals was initially resisted by the authorities, when eventually allowed, it was claimed that fly populations had dropped. Before this destruction of game in Acholi, the concentration of *G. moristans* had extended for about 48 km from Gulu in northern Uganda; by 1945, the species had been eliminated from that part of the country at the cost of killing 855 buffalo and 10,128 smaller animals. The systematic destruction of the game resulted in the disappearance of G. *morsitans* which had displaced human settlement from 305,775 of the 333,134 km^2 of country in Tanganyika, and approximately 38,624 km^2 in Uganda. Following further destruction of game in Shinyanga in Tanganyika, the adjoining Narok area of Kenya, and from Uganda, G. *swynnertoni* and G. *morsitans* were eradicated at least in the short term.[124]

From 1954, the *Trypanosomiasis* Research Committee was firm that there were no alternative methods to the destruction of game if the tsetse was to be controlled effectively. The systematic extermination of the game (large and small) had been completed by 1956.[125] The report of the Commission was empathic that 'the destruction of game should continue for at least a few years,' and should be combined with greater control of development programs in the tsetse-infested areas.[126] Yet, what was being reported as 'successes' were short-term outcomes and, in the majority of cases, the situations were reverted with the return of the flies and the game to the areas from where they had reportedly been eliminated. Furthermore, tsetse control continued to frustrate the authorities. In January 1955, an official of the tsetse survey and control program reported his desperation as follows: 'I fear that we will not achieve much by clearing.'[127] The reasons given were the vastness of the areas, lack of funds, lack of staff, and the extensiveness of tsetse infestations beyond the riverine forests. Researchers and technical departments disappointed by the repeated bush clearing and game destruction, then placed their hopes in the application of pesticides for tsetse control.

The application of pesticides

In the area of Fort Victoria on the Kenyan side of the lake, the vegetation was subdivided into blocks to concentrate the flies; some blocks were sprayed with insecticide and the control areas were left without treatment. The costs of pesticide spraying between 1933 and 1943[128] are shown in Figure 8.2. The spraying experiments were followed by tsetse fly catching by the 'fly boys.' The plots were repeatedly sprayed with DDT, which reduced the fly density and the catches then dropped in numbers.[129] Increasing the dosage by 80 percent eliminated the flies. The implication was that in the short term, the use of insecticides was effective.[130] However, considering that the pesticides entered the environment and passed along the food chain, their persistence in the ecology of the area and effects on biotic systems remained unknown.

Elsewhere in Africa, experiments with DDT had also been successful in controlling tsetse flies in the short term,[131] by reducing their numbers considerably.[132] In the Lake Victorian Basin, G. *palpalis* was reduced by 99 percent. The spraying methods were costly, however, varying from £500 to £1,000 per km^2. The costs of aerial spraying worked out at £200 to £300 per river kilometer in 1952.[133] In Uganda, the Colonial Pesticide Unit sprayed the islands of Lake Victoria with DDT and benzene hexachloride, reducing the population densities of the tsetse. Aerial and ground spraying

178 *Vectors, pests and environmental change*

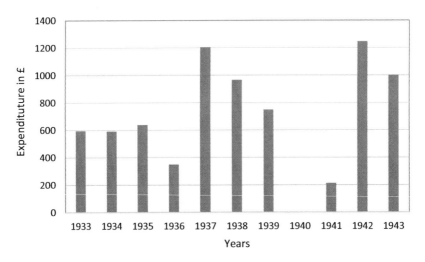

Figure 8.2 Annual costs of aerial sprays of DDT for tsetse fly control.

of insecticides was used widely in sections of the Nyando River from 1952 to 1955. The sprays reduced the fly density but did not eliminate them.[134] Meanwhile, the areas along the lake shore and the Yala River continued to experience tsetse infestations. Consequently, about 120 km of the vegetation in these areas was sprayed. About 454 liters per km of Dieldrex was applied at a total cost of £2,430 for spraying only one-third of the planned area.[135] In spite of all the efforts to eradicate it, the tsetse fly continued to have dire impacts on the pastoral economy.

Impacts on the pastoral economy

Considering that substantial funds had been spent on disease surveillance and land reclamation, the Director of Veterinary Services in Kenya recommended that farmers might be 'compensated for deaths [of their cattle] from *trypanosomiasis* and to treat all cases free of charge, at about £50 per annum,' as a substitute to expending more funds on programs for controlling the flies. In Makueni, 56 percent of the herds (3,127 head of cattle) received treatment, with deaths estimated at 4.2 percent of the total cattle population.[136] Based on the figures available, about 50 percent of the cattle presented for veterinary diagnosis tested positive for *trypanosomiasis* (Figure 8.3). Positive infections were reported during the wet season and the fewest were reported during the dry season. Consequently, this reservoir (cattle) was treated with prophylactic drugs such as ethidium and prothidium that required continuous disease surveillance.[137]

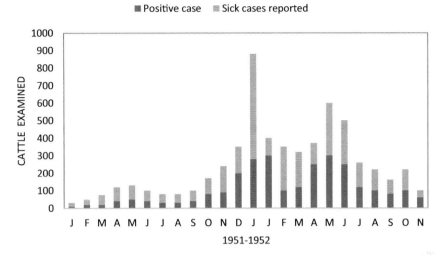

Figure 8.3 Number of cattle reported sick and those diagnosed positive for trypanosome parasites in their blood.

Data source: Kenya National Archives (KNA).

In Ankole, Uganda, by 1944 the tsetse had re-invaded areas from which the pandemic had previously wiped out all the cattle.[138] The agriculture policy at the time prohibited the use of grass fires, allowing bush to re-invade the areas.[139] In response to the ecological changes, the cattle populations in this area showed fluctuations over a period of 16 years, perhaps reflecting periods between the tsetse upsurges (Figure 8.4). Between 1951 and 1955, the increase in cattle numbers was associated with successful control of *G. morsitans*.[140] In Uganda, the northward retreat of the tsetse fly freed the area for cattle grazing. It was claimed that the combined effects of bush clearing, and the destruction of game had a negative effect on the tsetse fly populations.[141] However, what was rarely emphasized was the reversal of these gains, resulting in further expansion of tsetse flies. Without drug treatments, cattle eventually disappeared from areas that experienced a resurgence of the flies. Such was the case in the country east of Ankole where by 1959 cattle had almost completely disappeared. The few surviving herds were sustained only by drug treatments against the trypanosome variant caused by *G. morsitans*.[142]

By the 1940s, in central and northern Uganda, an estimated 12,874 km² of cattle country had been lost to *G. mortisans* and *G. pallidipes*. Additionally, in the region of Busoga, also in Uganda, there was a new outbreak of sleeping sickness. The tsetse control team was overstretched and due to the limited number of qualified staff, the tsetse flies advanced into new areas. In a few places where control of the flies was targeted, a combination of methods

180 *Vectors, pests and environmental change*

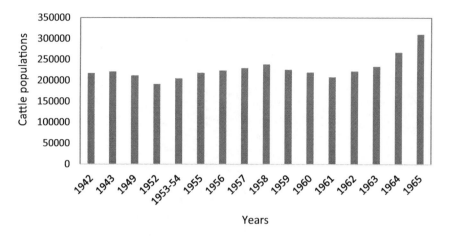

Figure 8.4 Cattle census in Ankole, Uganda, 1942–1965.

including game elimination and intensive pig hunting, as well as the application of late season hot fires showed some promising results.

By the end of the 1950s—nearly 70 years after tsetse control had first been attempted—research efforts had still not succeeded in the war against the vector.[143] In ending this chapter, three factors have become clear. First, tsetse research and control were responsible for vast destruction of the vegetation in East Africa. Second, imperial science—despite the overwhelming evidence—did not admit that tsetse research and control had contributed to the so-called environmental crisis. Third, the fly had displaced human populations from vast areas. In Chapter 9 we will investigate the history of locust plagues—a pest that caused much damage to the economies of the East African colonies.

Notes

1 Hartwig, G.W., 'Economic consequences of long-distance trade in East Africa: The disease factor,' *African Studies Review* 18.2 (1975): 63–73.
2 Anderson, R., *The forgotten front: The East African campaign* (Stroud, Gloucestershire: Tempus, 2004).
3 McCracken, J., 'Experts and expertise in colonial Malawi,' *African Affairs* 81.322 (1982): 101–116, 102; Waller, R.D. 'Tsetse fly in western Narok, Kenya,' *Journal of African History* 31.1 (1990): 81–101.
4 Ormerod, W.E., 'Ecological effect of control of African trypanosomiasis,' *Science* 191.4229 (1976): 815–821.
5 Giblin, J., 'Trypanosomiasis control in African history: An evaded issue?' *Journal of African History* 31.1 (1990): 59–80.
6 Epstein, H., 'The Sanga cattle of East Africa,' *East African Agricultural Journal* XXII.3 (1957): 149–164.

7 Oba, G., *Herder warfare in East Africa: A social and spatial history* (Winwick: White Horse Press, 2017).
8 DC/KISUM/1/29/12, Tsetse survey and control, Nyanza Province, 1950.
9 Ormby-Gore, W.G.A., 'The work of the East Africa commission,' *Journal of the Royal African Society* 24.95 (1925): 165–177.
10 These are two types of protozoan trypanosome; *gambiense* and trypanosome *rhodesiense*, see White, L., 'Tsetse visions: Narratives of blood and bugs in colonial Northern Rhodesia, 1931–9,' *Journal of African History* 36.2 (1995): 219–245.
11 Ford, J., 'The natural history of tsetse flies,' *East African Agricultural Journal* XXI.2 (1955): 137.
12 DC/KISUM/1/29/15, From Nandi, P.N, Galley and Rocherts Ltd, to the Chief B. Nyabole, Kisumu, 8 October 1954.
13 Ford, J., *The role of the trypanosomiases in African ecology. A study of the tsetse fly problem* (London: Clarendon Press, Oxford University Press, 1971).
14 Church, A., *East Africa a new dominion: A crucial experiment in tropical development and its significance to the British Empire* (Connecticut: Negro Universities Press Westport. 1927), 99.
15 Ford, 'The natural history of tsetse flies,' 137.
16 Worthington, E.B., *Science in Africa: A review of scientific research relating to tropical and southern Africa* (Oxford: Oxford University Press, 1938), 271.
17 MacLeod, R.M. and Andrews, E.K., 'The Committee of Civil Research: Scientific advice for economic development 1925–30,' *Minerva* 7.4 (1969): 680–705.
18 Richards, P., 'Ecological change and the politics of African land use,' *African Studies Review* 26.2 (1983): 1–72.
19 Darling, F.F., 'An ecological reconnaissance of the Mara Plains in Kenya Colony,' *Wildlife Monographs* 5 (1960): 3–41.
20 See Steverding, D., 'The history of African trypanosomiasis,' *Parasites and Vectors* 1.3 (2008): 3.
21 Baker, R., 'Stages in the development of a dairy industry in Bunyoro, Western Uganda,' *Transactions of the Institute of British Geographers* 53 (1971): 43–54.
22 Endfield, G.H., Ryves, D.B., Mills, K. and Berrang-Ford, L., 'The gloomy forebodings of this dread disease, climate, famine and sleeping sleekness in East Africa,' *Geographical Journal* 175.3 (2009): 181–195.
23 Ibid., 70
24 Endfield, Ryves, Mills and Berrang-Ford, 'The gloomy forebodings of this dread disease,' 192.
25 Keay, R., 'Scientific cooperation in Africa,' *African Affairs* 75.298 (1976): 86–97.
26 Malowany, M., Geissler, P.W. and Lwoba, A., '"Go back to the land!": Negotiating space, framing governmentality in Lambwe Valley, Kenya,' *Canadian Journal of African Studies* 45.3 (2011): 440–479.
27 Good, C.M., 'Salt, trade, and disease: Aspects of development in Africa's Northern Great Lakes Region,' *International Journal of African Historical Studies* 5.4 (1972): 543–586.
28 Endfield, Ryves, Mills and Berrang-Ford, 'The gloomy forebodings of this dread disease,' 190.
29 Soff, H.G., 'Sleeping sickness in the Lake Victoria Region of British East Africa, 1900–1915,' *African Historical Studies* 2.2 (1969): 255–268.

30 Beck, A., *A history of the British medical administration of East Africa, 1900–1950* (Cambridge, Mass.: Harvard University Press, 1970), 35.
31 Soff, 'Sleeping Sickness in the Lake Victoria Region,' 255–268.
32 Huxley, J., 'Travel and politics in East Africa,' *Journal of the Royal African Society* 30.120 (1931): 245–261.
33 DC/KISUM/1/29/15, Office of the District Officer, Kisumu, 1958.
34 DC/KISUM/1/29/15, Ashcroft M.T. Medical Research Officer, East African trypanosomiasis Research Organization (East Africa High Commission), Uganda, June 1958.
35 DC/KISUM/1/29/15, District Officer Bondo, Kisumu, Tsetse fly in Sakwa location, August 1958.
36 Vail, L., 'Ecology and history: The example of Eastern Zambia,' *Journal of Southern African Studies* 3.2 (1977): 129–155, 138.
37 Endfield, Ryves, Mills and Berrang-Ford, 'The gloomy forebodings of this dread disease,' 190.
38 DC/KISUM/1/29/15, Ashcroft, M.T., Medical Research Officer, East African trypanosomiasis Research Organization (East Africa High Commission), Uganda, June 1958.
39 Ford, J. and Clifford, H.R., 'Changes in the distribution of cattle and of Bovine Trypanosomiasis associated with the spread of Tsetse-flies (*Glossina*) in southwest Uganda,' *Journal of Applied Ecology* 5.2 (1968): 301–337.
40 Doyle, S., 'Population decline and delayed recovery in Bunyoro 1860–1960,' *Journal of African History* 41.3 (2000): 429–458.
41 Anderson, *Forgotten front*.
42 Deshler, W., 'Livestock trypanosomiasis and human settlement in northeastern Uganda,' *Geographical Review* 50.4 (1960): 541–554.
43 Ford and Clifford, 'Changes in the distribution of cattle and bovine trypanosomiasis.'
44 Ford, *The role of the trypanosomiases in African ecology*, 196.
45 Worthington, *Science in Africa*, 271.
46 DC/KISUM/1/29/15, District Officer Bondo, Kisumu, Tsetse fly in Sakwa location, August 1958.
47 Whiteside, F.F., 'The control of cattle *trypanosomiasis* with drugs in Kenya: Methods and costs,' *East African Agricultural and Forestry Journal* XXVIII.1 (1962): 67–73.
48 de Vos, A., 'Specific environmental problems,' in De Vos, A., *Africa, the Devastated Continent? Man's impact on the ecology of Africa. Vol. 26.* (Dordrecht: Springer Science & Business Media, 1975), 149.
49 Bates, M.L., 'Tanganyika: The development of a Trust territory,' *International Organization* 9.1 (1955): 32–51.
50 Ford, J., Whiteside, E.F. and Culwick, A.T., 'The trypanosomiasis problem,' *East African Agricultural Journal* XIII.4 (1948): 187–194.
51 Buxton, P.A., *The natural history of tsetse flies: An account of the biology of the genus Glossina (Diptera)*, London School of Hygiene and Tropical Medicine (London: H.K. Lewis & Co., 1955).
52 'Sleeping sickness: Some new observations on nits transmission and prevention,' *British Medical Journal* (BMJ) 1.3244 (1923): 384–385.
53 Ford and Clifford, 'Changes in the distribution of cattle and of Bovine Trypanosomiasis,' 304–5.

54 Bates, M., 'The natural history of tsetse flies [Review],' *Ecology* 37.1 (1956): 207.
55 Worthington, E.B., *A survey of research and scientific services in East Africa, 1947–56* (Nairobi, 1952), 41.
56 Cited in Glasgow, J.P., 'Shinyanga: A review of the work of the Tsetse Research Laboratory,' *East African Agricultural and Forestry Journal* 26.1 (1960): 22–31.
57 Ibid.
58 Phillips, J., 'Some important vegetation in the central Province of Tanganyika territory (formerly German East Africa): A preliminary account,' *Journal of Ecology* 18.2 (1930): 193–234.
59 Phillips, J., *Agriculture and ecology in Africa: A study of actual and potential development south of the Sahara* (London: Faber and Faber, 1959), 27.
60 White, 'Tsetse visions.'
61 Beck, A., *A history of the British medical administration of East Africa, 1900–1950* (Cambridge, Mass.: Harvard University Press, 1970), 118, 119.
62 PC/NYAZ/2/14/52, Director of Medical Services to Chief Secretary, 14 April 1945.
63 Tilley, H., 'Ecologies of complexity: Tropical environments, African trypanosomiasis, and the science of disease control in British Colonial East Africa, 1900–1940,' *Osiris* 19 (2004): 21–38.
64 Worthington, E.B., 'Geography and the development of East Africa,' *Geographical Journal* 116.1/3 (1950): 29–43.
65 Macleod and Andrews, 'The Committee of Civil Research.'
66 Ford, *The role of the trypanosomiases in African ecology*, 6, 13.
67 Glasgow, 'Shinyanga,' 26.
68 Shao, J., 'The villagization program and the disruption of the ecological balance in Tanzania,' *Canadian Journal of African Studies* 20.2 (1986): 219–239.
69 Glasgow, 'Shinyanga,' 23, 32.
70 Worthington, *Science in Africa*, 270.
71 Swynnerton, C.F.M., 'Appendix, Game circular No. 734/96,' *East African Agricultural and Forestry Journal* XXVI.1 (1960): 32–34; Phillips, J., 'Some important vegetation in the central province of Tanganyika territory (formerly German East Africa): A preliminary account,' *Journal of Ecology* 18.2 (1930a): 193–234.
72 Goodenough, W., Grantthan, D.R., Swynnerton, C.F.M., Laws, J.B. and Dixey, F., 'Soil erosion: A problem in human geography [Discussion],' *Geographical Journal* 82.2 (1933): 146–150.
73 Ford and Clifford, 'Changes in the distribution of cattle and of Bovine Trypanosomiasis,' 305.
74 Worthington, *Science in Africa*, 277.
75 Ford, *The role of the trypanosomiases in African ecology*, 198.
76 Ford and Clifford, 'Changes in the distribution of cattle and of Bovine Trypanosomiasis,' 304–5.
77 Beinart, W., Brown, K. and Gilfoyle, D., 'Expert and expertise in colonial Africa reconsidered: Science and interpretation of knowledge,' *African Affairs* 108.432 (2009): 413–433.
78 Deshler, W., 'Livestock trypanosomiasis and human settlement in northeastern Uganda,' *Geographical Review* 50.4 (1960): 541–554.
79 PC/NYAZ/2/14/52, Hunter, K., Provincial Commissioner's Office to the Honorable Chief Secretary, Nairobi, 3 April 1945.

80 PC/NYAZ/2/14/52, Colonial Office, 9 March 1946.
81 AK/16/14, Moon, J.T., Department of Agriculture, Nyanza Province to the Director of Agriculture, Nairobi, 16 September 1944.
82 DC/KISUM/1/29/13, Office of District Commissioner, Central Nyanza to the Assistant Director (Zoology) Veterinary Laboratories, Kabete, Nairobi, 8 December 1955.
83 Goodenough, Granthan, Swynnerton, Laws and Dixey, 'Soil erosion.'
84 Jacks, G.V. and Whyte, R.O., *The rape of the earth: A world survey of soil erosion* (London: Faber & Faber, 1939), 69.
85 Goodenough, Granthan, Swynnerton, Laws and Dixey, 'Soil erosion.'
86 'Medical problems of East Africa,' *British Medical Journal* 2.3949 (1936): 554–555.
87 BV/12/223, Conference on coordination of tsetse and Trypanosomiasis Research and Control in East Africa, held in Nairobi on 25 to 26 June 1943, Government Printers.
88 PC/NZA/2/14/28, Box, D.S., The District Commissioner Kisii to the Honourable Director Medical Services, Nairobi, 1 September 1939.
89 BV/12/223, Davies, M.J., Colonial Office, Church House, London, 31 December 1947.
90 PC/NZA/2/14/52, Meeting held with Provincial Commissioner in Kisumu, 20 December 1942.
91 PC/NZA/2/14/52, The Acting Director of Tsetse Research Shinyanga, Tanganyika, 4 August 1944; PC/NZA/2/14/52, Provincial Commissioner Nyanza to the Honourable Chief Secretary, Nairobi, 25 March 1944.
92 PC/NZA/2/14/52, The District Commissioner, Kisii to the Director of Veterinary Services, Kabate, 18 August 1945.
93 Ibid.
94 PC/NZA/2/14/52, The District Commissioner's Office Central Kavirondo to the Provincial Commissioner, Nyanza, 22 November 1945.
95 PC/NZA/2/14/52, Anderson, G.W., Department of Agriculture to the District Commissioner, North Kavirondo, 28 November 1945.
96 DC/KISUM/1/29/13, Minutes of meeting held in the District Commissioner's Office, Kisumu, 12 September 1951.
97 PC/NZA/2/14/52, Department of Veterinary Services to the Provincial Commissioner of Nyanza, Kisumu, 6 November 1945.
98 AK/16/14, Department of Agriculture, Nyanza Province to the Honourable Director of Agriculture, Nairobi, 14 September 1945.
99 AK/16/14, Tsetse fly and Trypanosomiasis survey and controls in Kenya colony: Second Progress Report, 27 June 1947.
100 DC/KISUM/1/29/13, Hornby, H.E., Tsetse problems in relation to those of soil conservation, 1948.
101 Osborne, M., 'Controlling development: "Martial race" and empire in Kenya, 1945–59,' *Journal of Imperial and Commonwealth History*, 42.3 (2014): 464–485.
102 Ford, *The role of the trypanosomiases in African ecology*, 146.
103 Ford, and Clifford, 'Changes in the distribution of cattle and of bovine trypanosomiasis.'
104 Beinart, Brown and Gilfoyle, 'Experts and expertise in colonial Africa reconsidered.'
105 Deshler, 'Livestock trypanosomiasis and human settlement in northeastern Uganda'; Pereira, H.C., Riney, T., Dasgupta, B. and Rains, A.B., 'Land-use in

semi-arid southern Africa [and discussion],' *Philosophical Transactions of the Royal Society of London* (Series B) 278.962 (1977): 555–563.
106 PC/NGO/1/7/30, Jarret, T., Field Assistant, Fly survey in Migwani location, Kitui, 1954.
107 AK/16/14, Lewis, E.A., Chief Field Zoologist, Tsetse fly and Trypanosomiasis Survey and controls in Kenya colony, Second Progress Report, 27 June 1947.
108 Ibid.
109 Goodenough, Grantthan, Swynnerton, Laws and Dixey, 'Soil erosion,' 149.
110 BV/12/223, Conference on coordination of tsetse and Trypanosomiasis Research and control in East Africa held in Nairobi from 25 to 27 June 1943, Government Printers, Nairobi.
111 Ford, *The role of the trypanosomiases in African ecology*, 196.
112 Hailey, W.M. (Baron), *An African survey, revised 1956: A study of problems arising in Africa south of the Sahara* (Oxford: Oxford University Press, 1957).
113 Giblin, 'Trypanosomiasis control in African history,' 77.
114 Brown, K., 'From Ubombo to Mkhuzi: Disease, colonial social science, and the control of Nagana (livestock trypanosomiasis) in Zululand, South Africa, c.1894–1955,' *Journal of History of Medicine and Allied Sciences* 63.3 (2008): 285–322.
115 PC/NZA/2/13/28, Director of Veterinary Services, Department of Veterinary Services, Kabate to the Honourable Provincial Commissioner Kisumu, 6 December 1939.
116 BV/12/223, Provincial Commissioner's Office Nyanza Province, Kisumu to the Secretary, Tsetse fly and Trypanosomiasis Committee, 19 July 1940.
117 BV/12/239, Lambwe Valley, Kenya, 1940.
118 DC/KISUM/1/29/13, Minutes of meeting held in the District Commissioner's Office, Kisumu, 12 September 1951.
119 DC/KISUM/1/29/12, Tsetse survey and control, Nyanza, 1950.
120 DC/KISUM 1/29/15, From Whiteside, E., Field Zoologists to the Veterinary Officier Nyanza Province, 13 September 1955.
121 AK/16/14, Atkins, C.F., District Commissioner's Office Central Kavirondo to the Provincial Commissioner Nyanza, 22 November 1948; PC/NZA/2/14/63, District Commissioner's Office, Kericho to Provincial Commissioner Kisumu, 14 October 1948.
122 Swynnerton, C.F.M., 'Appendix, game circular No. 734/96,' *East African Agricultural and Forestry Journal* XXVI.1 (1960): 32–34.
123 Robertson, A.G. and Bernacca, J.P., 'Game elimination as a tsetse control measure in Uganda,' *East African Agricultural Journal* XXIII.4 (1958): 254–261.
124 Ibid.
125 Prins, H.H.T. and Doughlas-Hamilton, I., 'Stability in a multi-species assemblage of large herbivores in East Africa,' *Oecologia* 83.3 (1990): 392–400.
126 Hailey, *An African survey, revised 1956*, 879.
127 DC/1/29/16, Tsetse Survey and Control to the District Commissioner Central Nyanza, 6 June 1955; PC/NGO/1/7/29, Minutes of the meeting held at Kibosek on fly barrier in Trans-Mara, 25 March 1955.
128 DC/KISUM/1/29/15, Office of the District Commissioner, central Nyanza, to the Acting Director (Zoology) Veterinary Research Laboratory, 8 December 1955.
129 The chemical name of the insecticide is *dichlorodiphenyltrichloroethane*.
130 BV/12/109, Colonial insecticide research, Progress Report No. 2, 31 July 1946.

131 Brown, 'From Ubombo to Mkhuzi.'
132 Fairclough, R. and Thomson, W.E.F., 'The effect of insecticidal spraying against *Glossina palpalis fascipes*, Newstead in the Nyando River Basin of Kenya,' *East African Agricultural Journal* XXIII.3 (1958): 186–189.
133 Ibid.
134 Ibid.
135 Ibid.
136 BV/12/220, Minutes of the meeting of the tsetse fly and trypanosomiasis Committee held in Nairobi, March 1952; BV/12/220, Minutes of the meeting of the tsetse fly and trypanosomiasis Committee held in Nairobi, 12 September 1952.
137 Ford, J., Whiteside, E.F. and Culwick, A.T., 'The trypanosomiasis problem,' *East African Agricultural Journal* XIII.4 (1948): 187–194.
138 Ford, and Clifford, 'Changes in the distribution of cattle and bovine trypanosomiasis.'
139 Van Rensburg, H.J., 'Land usage in semi-arid parts of Tanganyika,' *East African Agricultural Journal*, 20.4 (1955): 247–253.
140 Robertson and Bernacca, 'Game elimination as a tsetse control measure in Uganda,' 259.
141 Ibid., 255.
142 Ford and Clifford, 'Changes in the distribution of cattle and bovine trypanosomiasis.'
143 Robertson and Bernacca, 'Game elimination as a tsetse control measure in Uganda.'

9 Locust invasion and control in East Africa

Economic and environmental impacts, 1890–1960s

In the late nineteenth century, European travelers and explorers witnessed the devastation caused by locust swarms to the agricultural and pastoral economies in the East and the Horn of Africa.[1] We refer to eyewitness accounts. In 1883, crossing the Maasai savanna steppes, the caravan of the explorer Joseph Thomson[2] witnessed how locust swarms ruined the grazing lands. He stated: 'A cloud of locust settled in the land and left not a blade of grass.' In 1892, William Astor Chanler[3], journeying through the semi-desert of northern Kenya, watched vast swarms of locusts in disbelief. He reported: 'For hours the locusts had swept by us in millions, and it seemed that there was no end to them.' Similarly, in 1895 in northern Somalia, the large caravan of Arthur Donaldson Smith[4] witnessed how desert locust swarms, after stripping the land of its green vegetation, caused starvation for the inhabitants and their livestock. Traveling from the city of Harar on his way to Addis Ababa, Herbert Vivian[5] described scenes of desert locust swarms thus: 'I looked up and beheld a driving rain of locusts whirling at a terrific rate high in the air against the white clouds.... I could scarcely see a yard in front for many minutes.' Such invasions by locusts had been going on since ancient times. For the pastoralists and farmers in East Africa, every visit by swarms of locusts inevitably resulted in economic ruin and hunger.

This chapter analyzes historical outbreaks and control of two types of locusts: the most widespread desert locust (*Schistocerca gregaria* Forsk) and the red locust (*Nomacris septerfasciata* Serville)—the latter has restricted breeding grounds in East Africa.[6] Due to their nomadic habits, the locust swarms posed regional and international challenges, thus making collaboration by several countries obligatory. Due to the frequent upsurge of new generations of swarms, systematic research has been mainly of an experimental nature and short-term.[7] This investigation was conducted in the context of African environmental crisis hypothesis often associated with indigenous land use. We will encourage readers to bear in their mind extent to which the locust swarms contributed to environmental crisis, though the fact was not acknowledged directly by researchers.

The discussions are structured as follows: (1) the ecology of locust swarms; (2) outbreak areas of locust plagues; (3) economic impacts on the agricultural and rangelands; (4) locust control programs, including application of poisoned arsenic bait and aerial sprays using pesticides; (5) experimental research; and (6) monitoring of locust swarms.

The ecology of locust swarms

Modern surveillance methods (1920–1960s) have established that the desert locust used convectional air currents in the north to south of the intertropical convergence zone (ITCZ) to aid their migrations. Taking advantage of the movements of the ITCZ, the swarms moved from outbreak areas into other regions rich in food supplies.[8] The most significant biological behavior of locusts is their ability to respond to changes in their populations and climatic conditions. When not swarming, the populations become scattered, with locusts existing as solitary individuals.[9]

Periods of heavy rainfall and abundant growth of vegetation trigger the synchronic breeding and swarming phases, while during dry years, the swarms are in recession. This implies that during the remission phase, gregarious populations are completely absent—until environmental conditions become favorable again.[10] The conditions that trigger swarming include suitable soil moisture that is required for laying eggs.[11]

There are no accurate records of locust numbers involved in swarming, although biologists have made some reasonable estimates, based on the amount of land covered by the swarms and the numbers of locusts observed per small land units.[12] In one estimate, about 150 million locusts per km^2 had been recorded. Extrapolating this means that a swarm covering 1,600 km^2 (which was common) would contain at least 150,000 million locusts, weighing a total of approximately 300,000 tons. Each kilometer of the infested area would have 100–1,000 tons of locusts.[13] A locust plague occurs when many countries are infested by generations of locusts from the area of outbreak to the destination of the swarms.[14]

Outbreak areas of locust plagues

Both the desert and red locusts complete different phases of population growth, ranging from solitary to gregarious and transient phases, before the swarms take flight during the mobile phase.[15] During a single season, the swarms spread and reach many thousands of kilometers from their breeding grounds. Originating in West Africa, some swarms pass through Sudan into the Red Sea region and the Ethiopian highlands; or from the deserts of India and Pakistan, others move across Iran, the Middle East and cross the Red Sea into Somaliland and Ethiopia[16]—from there they cross into East Africa (Figure 9.1). Desert locusts and red locusts disclose different patterns of swarming.[17] We begin by analyzing the desert locust breeding patterns and swarms, before going on to discuss those of the red locust.

Locust invasion and control in East Africa 189

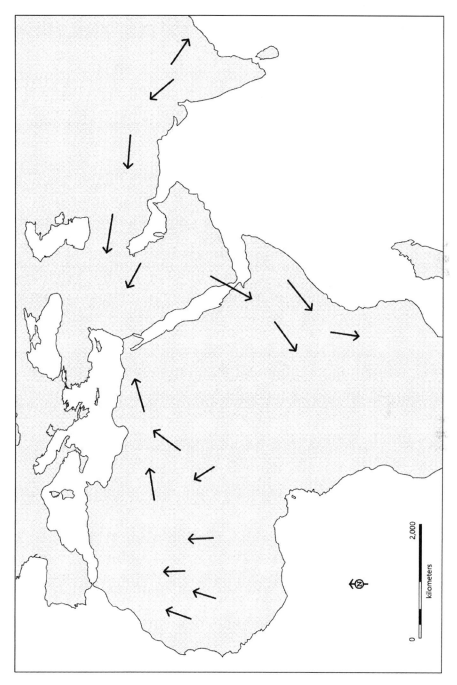

Figure 9.1 Desert locusts' migration routes from the outbreak areas in Indo-Pakistan and Arabia to the regions of East Africa.

Outbreaks of desert locusts

The population dynamics of the desert locust sometimes created a puzzle for researchers and analysts. Population outbreaks occurred during some years but were followed by recession. For example, the desert locust plagues that commenced in the 1940s came at a time when countries outside East Africa and the Middle East were considered free from immediate danger.[18] During the period 1941–1947, swarms of desert locusts arrived on the coast of Somaliland after crossing the Red Sea. By 1944, numerous swarms were reported in western Somaliland and the adjacent Ogaden region of Ethiopia where they began breeding. In 1946, some of the swarms crossed the Gulf of Aden from Somaliland and eastern Ethiopia to breed in the Arabian Desert during the monsoon season.[19] In 1948, excessive rainfall in the Arabian Desert—and deserts in Pakistan and Indian—created favorable breeding conditions. The large swarms then crossed into British Somaliland in 1949 and in the early part of 1950. From there, they spread into Sudan, eastern Ethiopia and northern Kenya.[20] From December 1949 to April 1950, breeding took place on the coast of Saudi Arabia and in the Somali Protectorate.[21]

Then after the short rains in 1951, the swarms arrived on the borders of East Africa. Following successful breeding in winter and spring in the east, by the end of that year, a new plague was crossing into Somaliland and eastern Ethiopia on the heels of the earlier swarms.[22] Heavy short rains throughout East Africa in late 1951 produced another event that puzzled observers, in that the swarms were spreading against prevailing northerly and north-easterly winds.[23] By 1952, the center of locust activities had shifted from Indo-Pakistan to the Red Sea coast, the Ethiopian highlands, Somaliland, and the northern region of Kenya. In Eritrea, heavy locust infestation posed a serious threat to agriculture.[24] Once again, the region that caused the greatest concern was the Somali Peninsula and the Somali region in eastern Ethiopia. From there, the swarms crossed into East Africa in plague proportions like those of the preceding year (1951).[25]

A series of swarms arrived simultaneously in the Horn of Africa in 1952, through 1953, scattering in various directions into the Sudan, Eritrea and East Africa.[26] By 1953 it was becoming clear to the Desert Locust Survey Organization based in Nairobi that protecting the croplands in East Africa would require control of locusts in the more remote regions of the Horn of Africa—Ethiopia and Somaliland and the Arabian Peninsula, the Aden Protectorate and Indo-Pakistan.[27] The island of Socotra (south of the Arabian Peninsula) was heavily infested, from where new generations of swarms crossed into Somalia.[28] During the short and long rains in 1954, following successful breeding of the locusts in Arabia, another large swarm crossed the Red Sea and the Gulf of Aden into Eritrea, the Ethiopian highlands and the Somali Peninsula. This swarm was augmented by those that bred in the Danakil Desert (the Afar region of Ethiopia) and others that had successfully laid eggs in the Somali Peninsula during the short rains.[29] This invasion by an estimated 50 different swarms of locusts spread into Kenya and overwhelmed preventive measures.[30]

The successful breeding of the desert locust in Eritrea, the Danakil and the Somali Peninsula resulted in large-scale, severe infestations (reported by some observers as 'unprecedented'). The hopper bands varied in size from tens of thousands to two to three million insects.[31] The apprehension of government officials and the desert locust survey team is therefore understandable. Later, these swarms moved into drier regions such as Turkana and the Maasailand in East Africa where they continued to breed.[32] Meanwhile, after the short rains of 1955, new locust generations invaded Kenya, Tanganyika and Uganda. Some of these locusts remained in the Somali Peninsula and produced a new generation during the long rains. In the short term, new generations of locusts invaded eastern Ethiopia and the Red Sea coast of Eritrea where they bred to re-invade the Somali Peninsula and finally Kenya and the rest of East Africa, thus repeating the cycle. The populations remained unstable, shifting across the region with different generations of swarms spreading as far as northwest Africa, and eastwards to India, where breeding followed successful monsoon rains. Thus, the Arabian Peninsula served as a crossroads for different swarms that originated from different regions.[33] Within East Africa, the red locusts caused great concern.

Outbreaks of red locusts

The red locust had its outbreak areas in the marshes of Lake Rukwa in Tanzania (Figure 9.2) and Lake Mwenu in Northern Rhodesia (present-day Zambia). Lake Rukwa lies in the southern East African Rift Valley. The lake is about 129 km long and covers an area of 402 km^2 when not in flood. During wet years the area expands to 804 km^2.[34] The alternating floods and droughts had a marked influence on the ecology of the edaphic grasslands, creating ideal conditions for breeding by the red locust.[35] The species had attracted research interest, partly because of its restricted habitat, and partly because of their periodic swarms. Their populations periodically expanded into huge swarms, alternating with disappearance at other times—only to reappear again.[36] The cyclic events of the red locust swarms were related to the dynamics of the floods in the marshes. The shallow alkaline lakes fluctuated in size from one season to another. During the solitary phase, individual locusts existed in the marshes. After the water receded, breeding ensued in the soft mud—with the grass growth providing food for the hoppers and adults.[37] The breeding did not occur in landscapes covered by trees,[38] or in flooded marshes.[39]

The red locust swarms of 1927 spread over an area of 482 km^2 and continued to threaten the region until 1945, bringing about huge financial losses in terms of agricultural production in Tanganyika.[40] During the period 1935–1936, various generations of red locusts spread across Tanganyika.[41] By 1951, experiments were conducted to estimate the population, using scouting

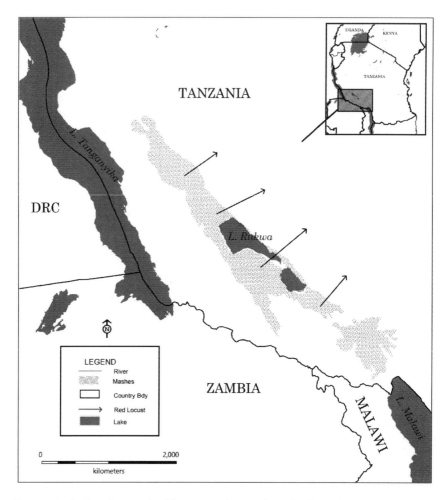

Figure 9.2 Outbreak area of red locusts in the marshes of Lake Rukwa in Tanganyika.

by land rovers and foot methods.[42] During the period 1953–1956, scouts monitored the marshes for the flights of the non-swarming populations, in order to identify the sites which could become outbreak areas.[43] Thirteen years of continued outbreaks were suddenly followed in 1956 by no record of any swarms at all. This period coincided with flooding of the marshes.[44] Both the desert and the red locusts caused huge economic impacts.

Economic impacts

The bands of wingless hoppers and adult locusts have insatiable appetites, consuming some 100 million tons of green vegetation in a single year.[45]

Following several years of successful locust breeding, the damage to agricultural production had become phenomenal.[46] Late nineteenth-century European travelers reported that locust damage to crops and vegetation was responsible for causing famine.[47] From the 1890s, reports of the pest devastations of food production meant that both the Germans and the British considered locust swarms to be a serious economic impediment to agricultural and rangeland development.[48] From the frequencies of the outbreaks and sizes of the swarms, it was possible to use probabilities to estimate the potential damage to agricultural and rangelands.[49] The damage to crops was expressed according to whether or not control of the swarms had been attempted, and whether or not it had been successful. The damage was expressed as a function of vegetation/crops consumed by individual locust swarms.[50] Knowledge of the amount consumed was then used to estimate the extent of economic damage.[51]

An average sized swarm covering a space of 182 square meters would consume green vegetation equivalent to a cow weighing 250 kg. A typical swarm covering 16 km^2 and with a density of 30 locusts per m^2, at a mean body weight of 1.7 g, would consume not less than 157 tons of green vegetation in a single day, while ten swarms covering 160 km^2 would consume ten times as much of green food per day which is an equivalent of 150,000 mature cattle.[52] The level of damage caused depends upon the development stage of the crops. For example, if maize is attacked and eaten when the seedlings are 7 to 14 cm high, the loss of the crop would be total.[53] Locust invasion at the time of flowering of crops would result in major loss of the season's crops, while infestations at the time of grain ripening would ruin the expected harvest. A locust attack at harvest time would result in the loss of a substantial proportion of the produce and if the problem was widespread, famine would be inescapable.[54] A 100 percent loss of crop production every ten years would be disastrous to local economies.[55] This situation was common before the colonial period.[56]

The 1920s in East Africa coincided with periods of severe infestations by the desert and red locust. Losses to agricultural production in the three East African colonies attributable to locust swarms were estimated at 150,000 tons of grain in Kenya (worth £2 million) and in both Tanganyika and Uganda at 50,000 tons of grain (valued at about £700,000) annually.[57] In Kenya alone, from 1928 to 1929, crop losses due to locusts amounted to £300,000 annually. The damage was equally severe in all the countries along the locust migration routes.[58] Between 1926 and 1931, the damage to crops in Africa was estimated at £7 million.[59] From 1928 to 1934, the estimated agricultural loss in Kenya was put at £800,000 and if control was lacking, the loss valued at £3 million would have occurred annually.[60] Considering that agriculture was being promoted at the time, and the land under crop production was expanding, the costs could even have exceeded these estimates.[61] The 1930s was a period of great destructions by desert locusts throughout East Africa. The swarms that arrived in 1930 wiped out 75 percent of the crops that had been ready to harvest. Mervyn Hill[62] reported an event in January 1930 as follows:

> In the afternoon, all may be well, the crops ripening to harvest and the cattle grazing contentedly. Then the sky darkens, as a vast swarm of locusts, miles across and miles deep, threatens from the horizon. At first it looks like a dirty smudge, like the drifting smoke of a forest fire or the gloomy murk of a sandstorm. Soon the locusts fill the air and man is virtually powerless to prevent their landfall if they so wish. If a large swarm settles for the night, there is little worth harvesting on the morrow and little for cattle to eat—they lay the earth bare to excessive erosion by wind and rain.

Like the case with agricultural lands, the damage done by locust invasions in grazing lands was enormous.[63] In the 1930s, the locust swarms consumed vegetation and wasted 9,600 km^2 of rangelands in Lemek-Mara in Maasailand. The combined effects of locusts and drought resulted in hunger that killed large cattle herds of the Maasai.[64]

The locust invasions accelerated during the period from 1931 to 1935. We have, however, better estimates of the damage for the later periods. Based on data from the Anti-locust Research Centre in Nairobi, Kenya, the desert locust swarms during 1942–1954 cost individual countries millions of British pounds.[65] In the Somaliland Protectorate in 1953, the cost of desert locust damage was estimated at £250,000, while in the following year (1954), the destruction cost £600,000. Over the same period, Morocco lost crop exports worth £4 million.[66] In Ethiopia, damage to crops in 1958 was estimated at $4 million. In the northern and eastern regions of Ethiopia during the same period, locust infestation resulted in losses of several thousand tons of grain harvest, plunging the region into famine.[67] On the Red Sea coast of Eritrea, F.T. Bullen[68] reported the loss of 43,000 tons of grain in a single year—risking hunger for many people. In September 1958, swarms caused heavy damage to crops, with economic losses estimated at £600,000. Along the migratory routes from the outbreak areas (from the Middle East to East Africa) over 300 million people were adversely affected.[69] The damage by locusts to crops and grazing lands required effective control methods.[70]

Locust control programs

Research on desert and red locusts did not start until the 1920s,[71] although outbreaks were reported as early as 1916. Finding immediate and long-term solutions required proper understanding of the cycles of swarming and possible methods of control. One strategy was to attack and destroy isolated locust populations, to stop them from breaking out of the source regions. This required timely interventions during the recession phase, before the locusts laid eggs to start the next swarming generations. Another strategy was to destroy hoppers, which required regular monitoring by mapping the breeding grounds and mobilizing logistics to attack the swarms before they became mobile.[72] However, locust control was not a one-off event, considering that invasions from the outbreak areas were an ongoing—and sometimes unpredictable—occurrence.[73] We now consider regional and international efforts to halt the swarms before they reached further agricultural regions in East Africa.

Regional control

The control methods were either 'reactive' or 'preventive'—the former being an emergency response to swarms that suddenly invaded a region.[74] The reactive method has been compared to attempting to stop hurricanes; one could only minimize the damage, but it would be impossible to stop hurricanes.[75] Even if locusts could not be stopped by attacking them, the damage they caused might be reduced. The most preferred method is preventive—that is, to stop the swarms in their breeding and hopper stages, since after they have taken flight, control becomes much more costly.[76] After the 1940s, on the recommendations of Sir Boris Uvarov, the scientific advisor to the locust control in Britain, the preventive strategy was used to attack swarms in the outbreak areas, before they had an opportunity to invade other countries.[77] Preventive methods required various monitoring systems (see later section). The challenge was the scale of control, across many countries simultaneously, and during successive generations of locust populations.[78]

Due to their fast-moving habits, one might imagine that locusts are unstoppable. However, there are weak points in their population cycles, at which the swarms might be attacked and destroyed, particularly during solitary and hopper phases when they are the most vulnerable.[79] The methods included physical attacks during the hopper stage, such as digging trenches in their paths, using tree branches to kill as many hoppers as possible, and use of fire and poisoned bait. For mature locust swarms, pesticides were applied (see later section). However, as mentioned before, such surveillance and control methods provided emergency responses as opposed to long-term solutions. Consequently, a policy of a limited number of campaigns was proposed, but this was criticized by both the administration and the affected communities. Halting the locust invasions usually involved political dimensions and decisions. For the African farmers, the idea that scientists were determined to estimate the losses, but did not do much to stop the swarms, caused much apprehension. Their preferred solution was to take immediate control of the swarms, regardless of the consequences.[80] If not stopped before they reached their destinations, severe damage to agricultural production would be inevitable.[81] During the Second World War, the authorities' methods of controlling locust plagues were not effective due to a lack of capacity to coordinate the control of the pests over large areas. This meant that each event became a crisis until later in the 1950s, when institutional capacities had improved.[82] Owing to the multiple invasion threats, locust control required vigilance and continuous campaigns, stretching planned preventive surveys into operations against new threats, which inevitably required extensive and well-funded organization.[83] Control methods needed to take into consideration the sporadic outbreaks that were difficult to predict. This required the coordination of locust campaigns over several outbreak regions simultaneously.[84] If not stopped, these swarms would pose a direct threat to agricultural regions in East Africa.[85] In the Somali Peninsula, in the 1950s, a major initiative was launched in the fight against this huge desert locust plague—squads were recruited from local communities (comprising a total of 4,367 men) and a strong team of 100 officers with supplies ferried to the affected areas by some 250 vehicles. The campaign destroyed more than 1 million hopper bands. However, setbacks were suffered due to inaccessible countryside, thus giving the locusts the opportunity to escape and continue to form large swarms.[86] When successful, locust control was attributable to various forms of international collaborations.[87]

International collaboration

Internationally, the leading force behind the study of locust ecology and control was Sir Boris P. Uvarov, who established the Anti-Locust Centre in London and became the world's authority on the pest.[88] The Desert Locust Information Service, operated by the Anti-Locust Centre, recognized that locusts are much more difficult to control than first anticipated. International collaboration was becoming increasingly necessary in order to minimize the damage caused by locusts to agricultural production.[89] The internationalization of locust control was enabled through the support of various United Nations (UN) organizations. Understanding the seasonal cycles of locust outbreaks required the use of meteorological services to forecast rainfall patterns and distribution that had direct influence on the migrations of locust swarms.[90] During the first international conference held in Rome in 1920 and the second international conference in the 1930s, two key goals were achieved. The first was to invite the governments of countries affected by locust problems and request them to cooperate in 'sending regular reports to the Anti-Locust Research Centre in London.' The second was to use the reports to analyze the seasonal breeding cycles of migratory locusts, map their breeding grounds and mark the trajectories of the swarms.[91]

Four types of institutions were needed in decentralizing anti-locust activities. The first was a scientific institution responsible for understanding the ecology and behavior of the locust. For this purpose, the Imperial Institute of London was selected to play an advisory role.[92] The second type of institution coordinated international collaboration to support scientific work and mobilize finances. The third type of institution was regional to deal with locusts in the outbreak areas. The fourth type was at the local level, where local communities needed to be mobilized.

This decentralized approach to locust control required establishing both scientific and emergency organizations that could respond to imminent locust invasions.[93] Considering the wide ranging threat to several regions simultaneously, Locust Survey Committees were organized to deal with regional control.[94] Additionally, financial commitments by international organizations such as the Food and Agriculture Organization (FAO) of the United Nations increased capacity in conducting anti-locust activities.[95] International locust control services organized research on locust ecology to understand conditions that triggered swarming.[96] The 1938 international conference held in Brussels reported on established swarm control in the Sahelian region of Africa.[97] In East Africa, the three countries (Kenya, Tanganyika and Uganda) spent £750,000 annually on organizations to control the desert locust.[98] Yet it was not until the 1940s that sustained attacks on the locusts began to bear fruit.[99]

In January 1949 the British Government approved a five-year budget of £470,000 to support field campaigns in Eritrea, British Somaliland, western Saudi Arabia and the breeding areas in Indo-Pakistan. The aim was to attack the different swarms simultaneously in their breeding grounds. In total, the campaigns involved 124 officers (and many thousands of local people) and 140 vehicles to support the anti-locust activities.[100] By 1950, the budget for anti-locust campaigns in the region was increased to £1.22 million per annum, with Kenya alone expected to contribute £244,400 of the total budget.[101]

The success of the campaigns was nonetheless limited by several factors. The first was that staff in local locust control organizations were on short-term contracts, which implied that after they had subdued the swarms, many of them would be dismissed—thus recruitment proved difficult. Second, considering that the Desert Locust Control Organization had established a number of stations in different countries, the lack of permanent staff and the high staff turnover adversely affected locust control efforts.[102] The successes of desert locust control in the 1950s were partially attributable to the assistance of the military authorities who—after the Second World War—provided vast numbers of vehicles and other supplies to support activities of the organization. In particular, the use of aerial surveillance and aerial spraying became possible, using refitted military planes (see later section).[103]

Using these additional assets, a close watch on the outbreak areas was maintained in attempting to save the countries of East Africa from the swarms. The British Government decided with the Italian Government in Somalia to coordinate anti-locust activities, at a cost of £20,850 per annum. Funding made available through the Colonial Development and Welfare

198 *Vectors, pests and environmental change*

Scheme provided 24 percent of this sum. The collaborating countries were expected to provide an additional sum of £200,000 necessary to sustain the fight against locust infestations. The colonial governments in East Africa needed to make urgent decisions as to whether the 1950s campaigns would be mounted, in which case an estimated total of £500,000 to £1 million would be needed.[104]

The challenge was that, while funding was being negotiated, the incipient swarms were already arriving in Eritrea and British Somaliland. Part of the reason for the delay was bureaucratic. A condition in granting the funds was that the East African High Commission should request authorization from the British Government to begin the anti-locust campaign and start spending the money. Another condition was that the colonies should not embark on any exercises without knowledge of the extent of the threats and potential consequences, after which they would be permitted to spend the money. For the British Government, attention should be focused on areas of higher economic returns and less on other areas—by doing so, it would be possible to control the plague at reduced costs. The British Government justified its decisions on the grounds that the high cost of locust control campaigns across the neighboring countries would be an unfair economic burden on the governments of the East African colonies notwithstanding the additional funding that had been made available.[105] Thus, delays in funding created a dangerous situation that served to undermine the effectiveness of locust control in the region.

Simultaneously, there were extensive infestations of hoppers in the Tigre Province of Ethiopia. Due to the difficult topography, a considerable number of the swarms escaped and dispersed. The year 1951 was among the worst in recent history, with the locust plague threatening large expanses of countries extending from Ethiopia, Somaliland and into East Africa. The locusts coalesced into series of swarms which—with the equipment at hand (comprising 35 Land Rovers and a tribal labor force)—were impossible to put out of action. Were it not for the coordination of international efforts, East Africa would not have been spared. With greater technical coordination by the FAO, the reconnaissance unit was able to map areas where the outbreaks occurred.[106]

Nevertheless, the heavy rains in the region had produced successive generations of locusts that were proving difficult to contain.[107] This caused policy changes on locust control. The strategy of protecting crop-producing areas while neglecting remote regions as being not so important for immediate economic development was opposed by the Desert Locust Survey Committee. Such a selective approach to controlling locusts would not reduce invasions in the long term. Not only would it undermine the confidence of the cooperating countries, but it would allow the locusts to reach plague levels that would be impossible to stop before they invaded East Africa.[108]

Agreeing with this analysis, the East Africa Commission suggested that more investment was needed for research in the outbreak areas and to apply the findings in the farming areas where crops were at risk of locust invasion.[109] The challenge was that until 1951, there was weak cooperation between the British Government and the FAO.[110] The extent of frustration induced by desert locust control attempts is demonstrated by the large amount of archival material that repeats similar messages every month during the years 1953 and 1954, when swarms of various sizes threatened agricultural lands in East Africa—this had been occurring without a break since 1947. New danger was posed by swarms breeding in the remote arid regions of Kenya—such as Turkana—from where it was only a short flight to the agricultural lands in Uganda and western Kenya. From the assessments available, the 1954 invasion covered more than 1600 km^2 into Kenya.[111] The campaigns might have succeeded in reducing the effects of swarms but were never able to halt them entirely. Political problems in the outbreak regions such as Saudi Arabia had left large parts of the countries inaccessible. In other areas, the campaigns had arrived too late, after the swarms had begun migration, spreading to the East African countries.[112]

By 1955, the swarms had subsided, following successful containment in Somalia. However, following successful breeding in Arabia and Aden, new generations of swarms entered Somaliland during July and August in 1955, posing another threat to East Africa. Reports predicted that if not stopped, these swarms would cause damage to agriculture to the tune of £3 million. As before, the first objective of this control initiative was to prevent the swarms from reaching East Africa, and the second objective was to prevent damage to crops.[113]

Despite the international organizations spending between £4 million and £8 million annually to control desert locusts, successful breeding in Arabia and the incipient swarms in the Horn of Africa continued to threaten East Africa.[114] It was very clear to the Desert Locust Survey Commission that temporary institutions would not be able to sustain defense against the swarms. This led to the formation of the Desert Locust Control Organization of East Africa (DLCOEA)[115] with an annual budget that varied between £900,000 in 1955–1956 and £450,000 in 1958–1959, to experiment with aerial spays of pesticides, among a myriad of other methods.[116]

Application of poisoned arsenic bait

We examine experiences of applying pellets of arsenic-coated wheat bran and pesticide sprays. The arsenic bran was applied by ground crews, while the pesticides were delivered both on the ground and from the air. The high costs involved and persistence of the pesticides in the environment were some of the disadvantages that have seldom been discussed. First, the baits were applied by hand over large areas where the swarms had landed or bands of hoppers were present, which made it extremely labor intensive. Second, the materials were too bulky to transport in countries without established road infrastructure. Third, the locusts were not always attracted to the wheat brans, and therefore those that survived were able to form future generations. Fourth, the method is expensive compared to aerial spraying of swarms (see below). Fifth, the arsenic baits posed dangers to livestock in the local areas.[117]

In inaccessible areas, the anti-locust teams were often forced to use camels to haul the sacks containing the baits.[118] In both Somaliland and the Reserved Area of Ogaden in Ethiopia, the Somalis were opposed to the use of arsenic baits against locusts. This became a political issue when the Somali nomads accused the government of poisoning the environment with the intention of killing their livestock. According to Jama Mohamed,[119] resistance by the Somali pastoralists intensified in 1945 when poisoned bait killed their livestock, which the Somalis used 'as incontrovertible evidence of government policy to reduce livestock by any means necessary.' For fear of violent reaction by the nomads, the anti-locust teams were given military escorts, and even so, anti-locust activities in several districts were stopped.[120] In other areas, despite the opposition, the anti-locust teams continued to lay wet bran against mature locusts and dry wheat bran against hoppers, with some success. In the Red Sea Hills campaigns,[121] 3,000 tons of bait were used during the summer and winter campaigns in 1950. The baiting was applied in the morning before the hoppers began marching. We now present aerial application of spray methods for locust control.

Application of aerial sprays

The 1940s and 1950s were periods of experimentation, using the donated military vehicles and planes. The aircrafts were medium to heavy Second World War bombers that had been converted into transport planes and fitted with pesticide sprays. This availability of former military planes increased the capacity for surveillance of locusts over wide areas. A search belt of about 300 km was covered to locate the locusts in flight, while the locations of those that had landed were communicated by radio to the ground teams. The airborne insect radar could pick up even low densities of locusts in flight, and their 'volume-density [was] measured and variations in density with height.'[122]

The ability to synchronize surveillance between countries was essential to the success of the anti-locust campaigns. Most importantly, using military planes for spraying the swarms while in the air and on the ground, the organizations involved in desert locust control developed the capacity to work across international borders. This method was designed to kill large populations of locusts before they landed and damaged crops and grazing lands. The method was least constrained by the rugged topography that was inaccessible to ground crews. In addition, aerial surveillance provided a bird's eye view of the behavior of the swarms in flight in relation to wind direction, thus allowing the sprays to be applied with greater precision.[123] Due to the promising results, the British Government organized a coordinated series of attacks between 1942 and 1947, while the locusts were still in Indo-Pakistan, Arabia and Somaliland. The operations were coordinated with military precision and cost £1 million per annum.[124]

The method of aerial spraying also contributed to scientific experimentation, in terms of appropriate concentrations of pesticides, patterns and frequencies of applications, and killing rates. The choice of pesticides was based on their effectiveness and safety.[125] Three types of pesticides were used: a 20 percent concentration of DNC (dinitrocresol) in oil, against adults (either settled or in flight) and dieldrin emulsion against hoppers.[126] Application of dieldrin[127] at an average of 2.5 gallons ha^{-1} produced a kill rate of 100 percent; and the application of 50 gallons of 11 percent gamma BHC (benzene hexachloride) in oil killed about 60 to 80 tons of locusts.[128]

Aerial sprays allowed coverage of topographies that would otherwise be difficult to reach.[129] About 50,000 gallons of pesticide would spray roughly 50,000 acres.[130] The insecticide is persistent in the environment and would continue to kill any hoppers that eventually began to feed on the vegetation.[131] Regardless of the effectiveness of these pesticides, opinions on their use were divided. On one hand, there were those who demanded that the pesticides should be banned, and stocks destroyed; while on the other hand, there were those who advocated continuing application thereof in remote areas, under supervision. Moreover, researching and producing alternative pesticides was not conducted, due to the costs involved.[132]

The results of the spraying campaigns were reported to the Anti-Locust Research Centre in London to evaluate the reliability of the insecticides. D.L. Gunn[133] listed a number of factors to be considered when assessing the effectiveness of insecticides, including dosage, persistence in the environment under field conditions and, most importantly, safety for those applying the insecticides. Contrary to claims of the insecticides being 'safe,' their long-term impact on other biological organisms, as well as on livestock and wildlife, was not evaluated. The pesticide residues are known to be present in milk and meat products.[134] Indeed, Gunn[135] even claims that the safety of popular insecticides such as dieldrin was exaggerated as part of the propaganda used by the Desert Locust Control Units.[136]

There were also other problems with aerial sprays. The first was transportation of large quantities of BHC dust on poor roads over long distances, to places where the chemicals were loaded into the aerial spray tanks of Beaver fixed-wing aircraft. A further problem was the long time it took to load the chemicals into the spray tanks. Such delays often allowed the swarms to escape. The most serious setbacks to the aerial spray method was that convectional air currents could suddenly change course, causing the 'clouds of the insecticides' to be carried away from the target; this could be avoided if the sprays were applied a few hours after sunrise.[137] Considering that the swarms could travel at more than 50 km per hour, a Beaver aircraft had to load up from a single base and spray the airborne swarms in four sorties before sunset.[138] The effectiveness of aerial spraying and the types of pesticides continued to be investigated as part of experimental research on locust control.

Experimental research

New insecticides were developed, and mass-produced (after field trials) for the purpose of locust control.[139] The success of these insecticides was limited unless they were dissolved in certain oils to increase their potency for killing locusts. However, the resultant compound was found to be more persistent in the environment—a factor that indicates the disadvantage when applied to vegetation.[140] The delays in experimenting with new insecticides and the continued use of harmful ones continued to raise uncertainties. In particular, the application of aerial sprays in remote regions that also served as dispersal areas for migratory birds highlighted the possibility that the insecticides might have undesirable effects on other creatures.[141]

Between 1952 and 1960, more efficient and safer control methods were developed under coordination of the FAO.[142] This included rotary atomizer sprays that were more economical than other methods (such as the baiting method already mentioned, which was labor intensive). The rotary atomizer could spray swarms of locusts while in flight below the plane, thus enabling locust control over large areas within a short period of time.[143] However, the application of pesticides over wider areas required the cooperation of local communities.[144] The common practice was to send information about the pesticides and spraying campaigns to officials in order to warn local communities.[145]

Nonetheless, the Desert Locust Control Advisory Committee in East Africa was worried that an essential aspect of research was lacking, since the application of pesticides was based mostly on what was practical. Hence, in 1951 the committee requested the High Commission to approach the Colonial Office for research funds from the Development and the Welfare Grant in order to conduct more focused small-scale trials of the pesticides.

The new experiments were applied over an area of 300–400 acres in Kenya that was densely settled by locust swarms—estimated at 10 to 100 million individuals. After applying 340 gallons of dieldrin, an estimated 100,000 to one million locusts dropped dead within an hour, destroying one swarm. In June 1952 alone, 890 gallons of pesticides were used against four swarms in 21 sorties of aerial dusting. Between 31 December 1952 and 31 January 1953, about 14 swarms, each about 2 km long, were heavily dosed with 3,045 gallons of concentrated pesticides during 93 sorties across Kenya, covering a total of 644 km.[146] Any locusts that had escaped from other areas, on entering Kenya were attacked using 45,425 liters of DNC poison in aerial sprays.[147] The technique of applying the sprays from above the swarms in flight caused the pesticides to be 'filtered out by the flying swarms of locusts during spraying' with insignificant amounts of pesticides reaching the ground.[148]

Like the desert locust, control of the red locust presented challenges, despite their restricted outbreak areas. The two factors that supported the control of red locusts were their highly fluctuating populations and restricted geography. In 1954, areas in northern Rukwa had become heavily infested by red locust hoppers. Tests had shown that high dosages of gamma BHC powder would destroy the hoppers more economically than other methods. The hoppers were dusted with a 40-ton 6 percent gamma BHC concentration, which destroyed nearly 433 million of them over 28,000 acres.[149]

In the same area in 1955, Gunn[150] used experimental plots of about 20 acres. The use of puffer dusters (by hand, at night) and aerial spraying effectively controlled the adult population. Aerial spraying was most appropriate where many swarms were on the move. In 1955, there were a total of 429 air-to-ground spraying sorties. By the end of 1955, the residual breeding population in Tanganyika was estimated at between 50 and 100 million individuals. However, after the marshes flooded between 1956 and 1957, no more locusts were reported.[151]

Unfortunately, scientific data on the efficacy of aerial spraying was seriously defective. Although the technique had been carefully developed and field tested in Britain, some adjustments were required in the field for it to be operational in East Africa. It was impossible to extinguish large swarms often covering greater than covering 160 km². The remnants of targeted swarms spread out and were joined by new swarms, thus posing a continued threat to East Africa.[152] Between 1954 and 1955, aerial attacks on individual bands of hoppers were abandoned with the introduction of dieldrin spray lines that were quite effective in killing hoppers.[153] It was considered essential to combine control campaigns with careful monitoring, if long-term success was to be achieved in ending locust threats.

Monitoring locust swarms

The success of locust control was dependent on the capacity of international organizations to develop effective technologies to make regular surveys in order to monitor fluctuations in locust populations. Regular surveys and careful monitoring of breeding grounds allowed the organizations and researchers to closely observe hopper bands before they reached the gregarious phase and formed massive migratory swarms.[154] By focusing on preferred breeding habitats and monitoring rainfall distribution, potential breeding and swarming patterns could be identified. Aerial surveys assisted in spotting early stages of swarm formations, or scattered swarms, and were able to warn ground teams in the countries facing imminent invasion. Aerial surveillance by a single plane could cover 8,000 km² per day. This allowed surveillance teams to estimate the sizes of swarms and their direction of movement, which were then plotted on maps and grids in order to identify potential target areas.[155]

Monitoring was also essential in order to support experimental research.[156] Experiments were conducted to determine the activities of locusts in relation to changes in humidity, wind speed and upward convectional air currents.[157] Different landscapes that the swarms crossed were also examined. In the case of the red locust, the special hydraulic conditions of the flood plain and grasslands of Lake Rukwa in Tanganyika were closely watched.[158] Regarding desert locusts, their breeding patterns and synchrony with the onset of the rains were closely monitored.[159] In particular, the monitoring unit paid attention to different generations of locusts that had reached high plague densities.[160] Ecologists examined changes in the behavior of locusts in relation to changes in population densities, which varied between the solitary phase (during recession) and the swarming phase.[161]

The monitoring that operated simultaneously with research and control activities had an obvious constraint in terms of the huge budgets required, including the necessity for countries to be members of the DLCOEA. The DLCOEA used aircraft facilities and various stations linked through radio communications to respond to distress information. Using aerial photographic methods to estimate swarm sizes and other variables, fairly reliable information could be relayed in a timely fashion to the ground teams.[162] Monitoring continued in order to manage temporary emergencies caused by new outbreaks and avoid diverting attention from producing vital results that would contribute to future planning.[163] The reports of 1936 indicate that locust swarms were not being sighted in the northern part of Kenya—a vast arid environment occupied mostly by nomadic communities.[164] In 1940, there was a false report that the threats by swarms had ended and that the countries of East Africa were no longer in immediate danger. Even so, the Desert Locust Control survey unit maintained vigilance to be able to act against incipient swarm threats. In 1948 information emerged that swarms had successfully bred in the Aden Protectorate (present-day southern Yemen). By this date, technical advice was being sought from the Anti-Locust Centre in London on appropriate actions to be taken.[165] However, delays in communication enabled the swarms to spread from the breeding grounds and cross into the Horn of Africa.[166]

The 1940s and 1950s were crisis periods, when series of locust swarms arrived in East Africa one after the other. The 1960s were a major turning point in experimental research, which included regular monitoring and control of the desert and red locusts. While the early 1960s experienced patterns of re-invasion—as had been reported during the previous decades—the late 1960s experienced the lowest infestation rates ever reported. It is difficult to attribute any single factor to the near extermination of the annual swarms in the 1960s[167]—was it a natural cycle of subsidence in the locust populations, or the cumulative effects of campaigns during earlier decades? In Chapter 10, by way of a synthesis and epilog, we bring the investigations to a close.

Notes

1 Lecoq, M., 'Recent progress in desert and migratory locust management in Africa: Are preventive actions possible?' *Journal of Orthoptera Research* 10.2 (2001): 277–291.
2 Thomson, J., *Through the Masai land: A journey of exploration, among the snow-clad volcanic mountains and strange tribes of eastern equatorial Africa* (London: Sampson Low, 1885), 414.
3 Chanler, W.A., *Through jungle and desert: Travels in East Africa* (London: Macmillan & Co., 1896), 439.
4 Smith, A.D., *Through unknown African countries: The first expedition from Somaliland to Lake Lamu* (New York: Edward Arnold, 1897).
5 Vivian, H., *Abyssinia: Through the lion-land to the court of the lion of Judah* (London: C.A. Pearson, 1901), 151.
6 Lecoq, M., 'Desert locust management: From ecology to anthropology,' *Journal of Orthoptera Research* 14 (2005): 179–186.
7 Enserink, M., 'Can the war on locusts be won?' *Science* 306.5703 (2004): 1880–1882; Greathead, D.J., 'A brief survey of the effects of biotic factors on populations of the Desert Locust,' *Journal of Applied Ecology* 3.2 (1966): 239–250.
8 Smith, Dorothy, 'Scientific research centres in Africa,' *African Studies Bulletin* 10.3 (1967): 20–47.
9 Van Huis, A., Woldewahid, G., Toleubayev, K. and Van der Werf, W., 'Relationships between food quality and fitness in the desert locust, *Schistocerca gregaria*, and its distribution over habitats on the Red Sea coastal plain of Sudan,' *Entomologia Experimentalis et Applicata* 127 (2008): 144–156.
10 Hemming, C.F., Popov, G.B., Roffey, J., Waloff, Z. and Rainey, R.C., 'Characteristics of desert locust plague upsurges,' *Philosophical Transactions of the Royal Society London B*, 287.1022 (1979): 375.
11 Van der Werf, W., Woldewahid, G., Van Huis, A., Butrous, M. and Sykora, K., 'Plant communities can predict the distribution of solitarious desert locust *schistocerca gregaria*,' *Journal of Applied Ecology* 42.5 (2005): 989–997.
12 BV/29/9, Gunn D.L., International Red Locust control service, Annual Report of the Director for 1956, Abercorn Northern Rhodesia, 1957, 5.
13 Joyce, R.J.V. and Reginald, C.R., 'The evolution of an aerial application system for the control of Desert Locusts,' *Philosophical Transactions of the Royal Society of London Series B, Biological Sciences* 287.1022 (1979): 305–314.
14 Hemming, Popov, Roffey, Waloff and Rainey, 'Characteristics of desert locust plague upsurges,' 375.
15 Sánchez-Zapata, J.A., Donázar, J.A., Delgado, A., Forero, M.G., Cebullos, O. and Hiraldo, F., 'Desert Locust outbreaks in the Sahel: Resource competition, predation and ecological effects of pest control,' *Journal of Applied Ecology* 44.2 (2007): 323–329.
16 BV/29/25, Colonial Office, Desert Locust Control Commission Draft Report (Nairobi, 1955).
17 McKay, A.D., 'Range management research at E.A.A.F.R.O.,' *East African Agricultural and Forestry Journal* XXXV.4 (1970): 346–349.
18 BV/29/25, Thornley, C.H. Chief Secretary to the Government of Uganda. Recommendations of the meeting the Desert Locust Survey Advisor Advisory Committee held in Nairobi from 19 to 21 January 1954 (Appendix A).

19 Rainy, R.C. and Waloff, Z., 'Desert Locust migrations and synoptic meteorology in the Gulf of Aden area,' *Journal of Animal Ecology* 17.2 (1948): 101–112.
20 BV/29/19, Minutes of a meeting of the Board of Agriculture held in the Council Room Chamber of Commerce Ported House, Nairobi, Wednesday 27 September 1950.
21 BV/29/25, Colonial Office, Desert Locust Commission, Draft Report, Nairobi, 1955.
22 BV/29/19, Uvarov, B.P., 'Campaign to beat the locusts,' *East African Standard*, 15 July 1950; BV/29/19, Minutes of Annual Meeting of the Desert Locust Survey Advisory Committee, Nairobi, 23 to 26 June 1952.
23 BV/29/9, Rainey, R.C., Notes on the movements of swarms across Arabia from East Africa during January–March 1952, Minutes of Annual Meeting of the Desert Locust Survey Advisory Committee, Nairobi, 23 to 26 June 1952.
24 BV/29/9, Desert locust survey and control, Desert Locust Survey Advisory Committee, Minutes of meeting held in Nairobi, 23 to 26 June 1952.
25 BV/29/9, Recommendations of the Advisory Committee meeting held at Bishoftu, Addis Ababa, Ethiopia, 10 to 13 June 1953.
26 BV/29/9, Recommendations of the meeting of the Desert Locust Survey Advisory Committee held at Bishoftu, Addis Ababa, Ethiopia, 10 to 13 June 1953.
27 BV/29/9, Recommendations of the meeting of the Desert Survey Advising Committee held in Bishoftu, Addis Ababa, Ethiopia, 10–13 June 1953.
28 Popov, G., 'The Desert Locust (*Schistocerca gregaria* Forsk.) in the Island of Socotra,' *Journal of Animal Ecology* 28.1 (1959): 89–95.
29 BV/29/25, Recommendations of the meeting of the Desert Locust Survey Advisory Committee, Confidential conclusions, Entebbe, Uganda, 19 to 21 January 1954.
30 BV/29/25, Ashall, C., Report for Research Project No. 7 for period July 1953 to December 1953. Recommendations of the meeting of the Desert Locust Survey Advisory Committee held on 19 to 21 January 1954 (Appendix G).
31 BV/29/25, Meeting of the Desert Locust Survey Advisory Committee held in Nairobi on 19 to 21 January 1954.
32 BV/29/25, Hewitt J.S., Chief Field Officer, 'Locust campaign: long rains breeding,' 1954.
33 BV/29/22, Secretary of State for the Colonies to the Officer Administering the Government of Kenya, 21 September 1954.
34 Robertson, I.A.D., 'The reproduction of the red locust, *Nomadacris septemfasciata* (Serv.) (Orthoptera, Acrididae), in an outbreak area,' *Bulletin of Entomological Research* 49.3 (1958): 479–496.
35 Vesey-Fitzgerald, D.F., 'The origin and distribution of valley grasslands in East Africa,' *Journal of Ecology* 58.1 (1970): 51–75.
36 Woodrow, D.F., 'Observations on the Red Locust (*Nomadacrisi septtemfasciata* Serv.) in the Rukwa Valley, Tanganyika, during its breeding season,' *Journal of Animal Ecology* 34.1 (1965): 187–200.
37 Chapman, R.F., 'Observations on the flight activity of the Red Locust, *Nomadacris septemfasciata* (Serville),' *Behaviour* 14.4 (1959): 300–334.
38 Robertson I.A.D., 'Tree-planting trials for the control of the red locust (*nomadacris septemfasciata*) in the Rurkwa valley, Tanganyika,' *East African Agricultural Journal* XXIII.3 (1958): 172–178.

39 Brown, H.D., and. Gunn, D.L., 'The development of aircraft attack on locust swarms in Africa since 1945 and the start of operational research on control systems: Discussion,' *Philosophical Transactions of the Royal Society of London Series B* 287 (1979): 261–263.
40 Hailey, W.M. (Lord), *An African survey, revised 1956: A study of problems arising in Africa south of the Sahara* (Oxford: Oxford University Press, 1957).
41 Backlund, H.O., 'Small patches with permanent red locust population in Northern Tanganyika territory,' *East African Agricultural Journal* XX.3 (1955): 202–214.
42 BV/29/9, Gunn, D.L., International Red Locust Control Service, Annual Report of the Director 1953, Abercorn Northern Rhodesia, 1946.
43 Chapman, R.F., *Field observations of the behaviour of hoppers of the Red Locust (Nomadacris Septemfasciata Serville)* (London: Anti-Locust Research Centre, 1959).
44 BV/29/9, Gunn, D.L., International Red Locust Control Service, Annual Report of the Director for 1956, Abercorn Northern Rhodesia, 1957, 5.
45 BV/29/25, Colonial Office, Desert Locust Control Commission (Nairobi: Draft Report 1955), 7; Weiss, H., *Locust invasions in colonial northern Ghana*, WOPAG Working Paper on Ghana: Historical and Contemporary Studies 3 (2004), 6, 7.
46 Hemming, Popov, Roffey, Waloff and Rainey, 'Characteristics of desert locust plague upsurges,' 375; Bullen, F.T., 'Locusts and grasshoppers as pests of crops and pasture: A preliminary economic approach,' *Journal of Applied Ecology* 3.1 (1966): 147–168.
47 Little, M., 'Colonial policy and subsistence in Tanganyika 1925–1945,' *Geographical Review* (1991): 375–388.
48 Brooke, C., 'Types of food shortages in Tanzania,' *Geographical Review* (1967): 333–357.
49 BV/29/25, Colonial Office, Desert Locust Control Commission, Draft Report, 1955; BV/29/25, Minutes of a territorial meeting at Ministerial level to discuss the report of the Commission of the Desert Locust Control Organization held in Nairobi, 1956.
50 Weiss, *Locust invasions in colonial northern Ghana*, 7.
51 BV/29/25, Colonial Office, Desert Locust Control Commission, Draft Report, Nairobi, 1955.
52 BV/29/24, Fearon, S.P., Office of the East Africa High Commission, to the Honourable Minister for Agriculture, Animal Husbandry and Water Resource, Nairobi, 22 July 1957; Bullen, 'Locusts and grasshoppers as pests of crops and pasture.'
53 BV/29/25, Note on desert locust in Kenya: Distribution of agriculture in the Territory, Nairobi, 1955.
54 Ibid.
55 Bullen, 'Locusts and grasshoppers as pests of crops and pasture.'
56 Sunman, H., *A very different land: Memories of empire the farmlands of Kenya* (London: The Redcliffe Press, 2014), 40.
57 BV/29/25, Colonial Office, Desert Locust Control Commission, Draft Report, Nairobi, 1955.
58 Ibid.
59 MacLeod, R.M. and Andrews, E.K., 'The Committee of Civil Research: Scientific advice for economic development 1925–30,' *Minerva* 7.4 (1969): 680–705.

208 *Vectors, pests and environmental change*

60 BV/29/9, Desert Locust Survey Advisory Committee, Recommendations at the meeting held in Nairobi on 19 to 21 July 1951.
61 Hailey, *An African survey*.
62 Hill, M.F., *Permanent way: The story of the Kenya and Uganda Railway* (Nairobi: East African Railways and Harbours, 1961).
63 Bullen, 'Locusts and grasshoppers as pests of crops and pasture.'
64 Waller, R.D., 'Tsetse fly in western Narok, Kenya,' *Journal of African History* 31.1 (1990): 81–101.
65 BV/29/25, Colonial Office, Desert Locust Control Commission, Draft Report, 1955.
66 Uvarov, B.P, 'Efforts to control locusts in Africa described,' *Science* 30.3388 (1959): 1564–1565.
67 Bellehu, A. and Reginald, C.R., 'The Desert Locust Control Organization for Eastern Africa (DLCOEA) and its background,' *Philosophical Transactions of the Royal Society of London. B, Biological Sciences* 287.1022 (1979): 265–268.
68 Bullen, 'Locusts and grasshoppers as pests of crops and pasture.'
69 Gartrell, B., 'Searching for "The roots of famine": The case of Karamoja,' *Review of African Political Economy* 33 (1985): 102–110.
70 Gunn, D.L. and Brown, H.D., 'Setting the scene: The development of aircraft attack on locust swarms in Africa since 1945 and the start of operational research on control systems,' *Philosophical Transactions of the Royal Society of London, Series B*, 287.1022 (1979): 251–263.
71 Nevo, D., 'The Desert Locust, *Schistocerca gregaria* and its control in the land of Israel and the Near East in antiquity, with some reflections on its appearance in Israel in modern times,' *Phytoparasitica* 24.1 (1996): 7–32.
72 Hemming, Popov, RoffeyWaloff and Rainey, 'Characteristics of desert locust plague upsurges,' 384.
73 Enserink, 'Can the war on locusts be won?'; Hemming, Popov, Roffey, Waloff and Rainey, 'Characteristics of desert locust plague upsurges.'
74 Lecoq, M., 'Recent progress in Desert and Migratory Locust management in Africa: Are preventative actions possible?' *Journal of Orthoptera Research* 10.2 (2001): 277–292.
75 Enserink, 'Can the war on locusts be won?'
76 Lecoq, 'Desert locust management.'
77 Roy, J., 'Decisive steps towards control of the desert locust, 1952–62,' *Philosophical Transactions of the Royal Society of London: Series B. Biological Sciences*, 287.1022 (1979): 301–304.
78 Rainey, R.C., Betts, E., Lumley, A., Lamb, H.H., Gunn, D.L., Hemming, C.F., Zena Waloff, Joyce R.J.V. and Yeo, D., 'The decline of the Desert locust plague in the 1960s: Control operations or natural causes? [and Discussions],' *Philosophical Transactions of the Royal Society of London* 287.1022 (1979): 315–344.
79 Lecoq, 'Recent progress in desert and migratory locust management in Africa.'
80 Peveling, R., 'We believe what we see and vice versa: Evidence versus perception in locust control,' *Journal of Orthoptera* 14.2 (2005): 207–212.
81 BV/29/19, From Chairman, Desert Locust Survey Advisory Committee to the East African High Commission, Nairobi, 2 February 1950.
82 Lecoq, 'Recent progress in desert and migratory locust management in Africa,' 288.
83 Hailey, *An African survey*, 901–902.

84 Hemming, Popov, Roffey, Waloff and Rainey, 'Characteristics of desert locust plague upsurges,' 384.
85 BV/29/9, McDonald, J., 'Threatened locust invasion,' 1953.
86 BV/29/25, The meeting of the Desert Locust Survey Advisory Committee held in Nairobi on 19 to 21 January 1954.
87 Haskell, P.T., 'Locust control: Ecological problems and international pests,' in Farvar, M.T. and Milton, J.P. (eds), *The careless technology: Ecology and international development* (Tom Stacey, 1973), 499.
88 Walsh, J., 'Return of the locust: A cloud over Africa,' *Science* 234.4772 (1986): 17–19.
89 Uvarov, 'Efforts to control locusts in Africa described.'
90 Walsh, J., 'Locusts in Africa: A plague is possible,' *Science* 242.4886 (1988): 1627–1628; Kellou, R., Mahjoub, N., Benabdi, A. and Boulahya, M.S., 'Algerian case study and the need for permanent Desert Locust monitoring,' *Philosophical Transactions of the Royal Society of London Series B*, 328.1251 (1990): 573–583.
91 Bellehu, A., Pringle, J.W.S., Brown, H.D. and Rainey, R.C., 'The Desert Locust Control Organization for Eastern Africa (DLCOEA) and its background,' *Philosophical Transactions of the Royal Society of London, Series B* 287.1022 (1979): 265–268.
92 Hailey, *An African Survey*.
93 Lecoq, M., 'Recent progress in desert and migratory locust management in Africa.'
94 Bellehu, A., Pringle, J.W.S., Brown, H.D. and Rainey, R.C., A Report: 'The Desert Locust Control Organization for Eastern Africa (DLCOEA) and its background' (Ms).
95 Bullen, 'Locusts and grasshoppers as pests of crops and pasture.'
96 Haskell, 'Locust control,' 507.
97 Hailey, *An African survey*, 898.
98 Uvarov, 'Efforts to control locusts in Africa described.'
99 Walsh, J., 'Return of the locust: A cloud over Africa,' *Science*, 234.4772 (1986): 17–19.
100 BV/29/19, Recommendations made at a meeting of the Desert Locust Survey Advisory Committee held in Nairobi on 19 to 21 July 1951.
101 BV/29/11, The Secretariat to members of standing finance committee on Desert Locust campaign, 7 September 1950.
102 BV/29/25, Colonial Office to Desert Locust Control Commission, Draft Report, Nairobi, 1955.
103 Ibid., 16.
104 BV/29/19, From the Secretary of the State for the Colonies to the Chairman, East African High Commission, Nairobi, 1950.
105 BV/29/19, Minutes of a meeting of the Desert Locust Survey Advisory Committee held in Nairobi on 5 May 1950; BV/29/19, Recommendations made at a meeting of the Desert Locust Advisory Committee held in Nairobi on 17 July 1950.
106 BV/29/9, Recommendations and minutes of the annual meeting of the Desert Locust Survey Advisory Committee, Nairobi, 23 to 26 June 1952; Popov, G., 'The Desert Locust (*Schistocerca gregaria* Forsk) in the Island of Scotra,' *Journal of Animal Ecology* 28.1 (1959): 89–95.
107 BV/29/9, Recommendations and minutes of annual meeting of the Desert Locust Survey Advisory Committee Nairobi, 23 to 26 June 1952.

210 Vectors, pests and environmental change

108 BV/29/19, From Chairman, Desert Locust Survey Advisory Committee to East Africa High Commission, Nairobi, 2 February 1950.
109 BV/29/19, Office of the East Africa High Commission to the Under-Secretary of State for the Colonies, Nairobi, 10 February 1950.
110 BV/29/22, From the Secretary of State for the Colonies to the officer administering the Government of Kenya, Brief for the UK representative to the meeting of the FAO working part on Desert Locust Control, 9 September 1954
111 BV/29/25, Stower W.J., Report for the Research project no. 7 for period July–December 1954; BV/29/25, Colonial Office, Desert Locust Control Commission Draft Report, Nairobi, 1955.
112 BV/29/25, Recommendations of the Meeting of the Desert Locust Survey Advisory Committee held on 19 to 21 January 1954; Colonial Office Desert Locust Control Commission, Draft Report, Nairobi, 1955.
113 BV/29/25, Minutes of an inter-territorial meeting at ministerial level to discuss the report of the Commission of the Desert Locust Control Organization, held in Nairobi, 1956.
114 BV/29/24, Fearon S.P., Office of the East Africa High Commission to the Honourable Minister Agriculture, Animal Husbandry and Water Resources, Nairobi, 22 July 1957.
115 BV/29/25, Colonial Office to Desert Locust Control Commission, Draft Report, Nairobi, 1955.
116 Joyce and Reginald, 'The evolution of an aerial application system for the control of Desert Locusts.'
117 BV/29/19, Karachi Desert Locust Conference, Pakistan, 22 to 27 October 1949.
118 Gunn and Reginald, 'Setting the scene.'
119 Mohamed, J., '"The evils of locust bait": Popular nationalism during the 1945 anti-locust control rebellion in colonial Somaliland,' *Past and Present* 174 (2002): 184–216.
120 BV/29/9, Desert Locust Survey and Control, Desert Locust Survey Advisory Committee, Nairobi, 23 to 26 June 1952.
121 BV/29/9, Recommendations made at a meeting of the outbreak Desert Locust Survey Advisory Committee held in Nairobi on 19 to 21 July 1951; Uvarov, 'Efforts to control locusts in Africa described.'
122 Rainey, R.C., Joyce, R.J.V., Haggis, M.J., Riley, J.R., Pedley, D.E., Dickson, R.B.B. and Jonas, P.R., 'An airborne radar system for desert locust control,' *Philosophical Transactions of the Royal Society of London*, Series B 328.1251 (1990): 585–606.
123 Joyce and Reginald, 'The evolution of an aerial application system for the control of Desert Locusts.'
124 Hailey, *An African survey*, 901.
125 MacCauig R.D., Le Berre R., Thomson, A.T. and Castel, J.M., 'Pesticides for locust control,' *Philosophical Transactions of the Royal Society of London*, Series B 287.1022 (1979): 447–455.
126 Haskell, 'Locust control,' 510.
127 Dieldrin and organochloride pesticides might be effective against locust but have also been known to be long-persistent in the environment posing a great danger to humans and wildlife and domesticated stock, e.g., Walsh, 'Locusts in Africa.'
128 BV/29/25, Note on Air spray operations against flying swarms May–October 1953 (Appendix B).

129 Wiktelius, S., Ardö, J. and Fransson, T., 'Desert Locust control in ecologically sensitive areas: Need for guidelines,' *Ambio* 32.7 (2003): 463–468.
130 Lloyd, J.H., 'Locust control by aircraft in Central and East Africa,' *East African Agricultural Journal* 24.1 (1958): 26–32.
131 Roy, J., and Rainey, R.C., 'Recent developments in locust control: Decisive steps towards control of the Desert Locust 1952–62,' *Philosophical Transactions of the Royal Society of London, B* 287.1022 (1979): 301–304.
132 Skaf, R., Popov, G.B. and Roffey, J., 'The Desert Locust: An international challenge,' *Philosophical Transactions of the Royal Society of London, B. Biological Sciences* 328.1251 (1990): 525–538.
133 Gunn, D.L., 'Systems and management: Strategies, systems, value judgements and dieldrin in control of locust hoppers,' *Philosophical Transactions of the Royal Society of London, B* 287 (1979): 420–445.
134 Peveling, R., 'We believe what we see: and vice versa: Evidence versus perception in locust control,' *Journal of Orthoptera Research* 14.2 (2005): 207–212.
135 Gunn, 'Systems and management.'
136 Walsh, 'Return of the locust.'
137 BV/29/9, Minutes of annual meeting of the Desert Locust Survey Advisory Committee, Nairobi, on 23 to 26 June 1952.
138 Joyce and Reginald, 'The evolution of an aerial application system for the control of Desert Locusts.'
139 Tufty, B., 'Man fights swarming insects,' *The Science Newsletter* (1965): 90–91; Walsh, 'Return of the locust.'
140 BV/29/19, Minutes of a meeting of the Desert Locust Survey Advisory Committee, held in Nairobi on 3 October 1949.
141 Sánchez-Zapata, Donáza, Delgado, Forero, Cebullos, and Hiraldo, 'Desert locust outbreaks in the Sahel.'
142 Roy, and Rainey, 'Recent developments in locust control.'
143 Rainey, Joyce, Haggis, Riley, Pedley, Dickson and Jonas, 'An airborne radar system for desert locust control.'
144 Ibid.
145 BV/29/19, From Chief Secretary to East Africa High Commission, Nairobi, 15 September 1950; BV/29/19, Interdepartmental Committee on locust control aerial curtain experiments against flying locust, 1950.
146 BV/29/9, Rainey, R.C. and Sayer, H.J., 'Summary of results of small-scale aerial spraying trials against flying swarms,' Minutes of annual meeting of the Desert Locust Survey Advisory Committee, Nairobi, on 23 to 26 June 1952.
147 BV/29/25, The meeting of the Desert Locust Survey Advisory Committee held in Nairobi on 19 to 21 January 1954.
148 BV/29/9, Roddan, G.M., Director of Agriculture to Windley, E.H. Acting Chief Native Commissioner, Nairobi, 1953.
149 BV/29/9, Gunn, D.L., International Red Locust Control Service, Annual Report of 1954, by the Director Abercorn, Northern Rhodesia, 1955.
150 BV/29/9, Gunn, D.L., International Red Locust Control Service, Annual Report of the Director, Abercorn, Northern Rhodesia, 1956.
151 BV/29/9, Gunn, D.L., International Red Locust Control Service, Annual Report of the Director, Abercorn Northern Rhodesia 1957, 5, 7, 8, 9.

212 *Vectors, pests and environmental change*

152 BV/29/25, Stephenson, P.R., Director, Desert Locust Control to the Administrator East Africa High Commission, Minutes of the sixty-eighth meeting of Desert Locust Control Executive Committee held in Nairobi, Friday 21 May 1954.
153 Gunn, 'Systems and management.'
154 Schaefer, G.W., and Rainey, R.C., 'An airborne radar technique for the investigation and control of migrating pest insects,' *Philosophical Transactions of the Royal Society of London. B, Biological Sciences* 287.1022 (1979): 459–465.
155 Joyce, R.J.V., 'The evolution of an aerial application system for the control of Desert Locusts'; Van der Werf, Woldewahid, Van Huis, Butrous and Sykora, 'Plant communities can predict the distribution of solitarious desert locust *Schistocerca gregaria*.'
156 Riley, J.R. and Reynolds, D.R., 'Radar-based studies of the migratory flight of grasshoppers in the middle Niger area of Mali,' *Proceedings of the Royal Society of London. Series B* 204.1154 (1979): 67–82.
157 Weis-Fogh,T., 'Biology and physics of locust flight: II. Flight performance of the Desert Locust (*Schistocerca gregaria*),' *Philosophical Transactions of the Royal Society of London. Series B* 239.667 (1956): 459–510.
158 Chapman, R.F., *Field observations of the behaviour of hoppers of the red locust (Nomadacris Septemfasciata Serville)* (Anti-Locust Research Centre: London, 1959), 327.
159 Skaf, Popov, Roffey, Scorer and Hewitt, 'The Desert Locust: An international challenge.'
160 Pedgley, D.E., 'Weather during Desert Locust plague upsurges,' *Philosophical Transactions of the Royal Society of London. Series B* 287.1022 (1979): 387–391.
161 Farrow, R.A. and Longstaff, B.C., 'Comparison of the annual rates of increase of locusts in relation to the incidence of plagues,' *Oikos* 46.2 (1986): 207–222.
162 Rainey, Betts, Lumley, Lamb, Gunn, Hemming Waloff, Joyce and Yeo, 'The decline of the locust plague in the 1960s.'
163 BV/29/9, Recommendations made at a meeting of the Desert Locust Survey Advisory Committee held in Nairobi on the 19 to 21 July 1951; GRA/10, Mr. Chenevix Trench C.P. to Mr. Mills R.C., Handing over Report, Garissa District, October 1951.
164 GRA/9, Mr. Norman C.B. to Darroch R.G., Handing over Report of Garissa District, 1936.
165 BV/29/19, East Africa High Commission, Memorandum by the Director, Desert Locust Survey on the re-appearance of swarms in S.W. Arabia, June 1949.
166 BV/29/9, Recommendations made at a meeting of the Desert Locust Survey Advisory Committee held in Nairobi on 19 to 21 July 1951.
167 BV/29/25, Stower, W.J., Report for the Research project no. 7 for period July–December 1954; BV/29/25, Colonial Office, Desert Locust Control Commission Draft Report, Nairobi, 1955.

10 A synthesis
Conclusions and epilog

Whilst acknowledging the important scientific contributions made by colonial scientists, their successors have since expanded their thinking by providing alternative explanations for environmental crisis.[1] Our focus will be on research on pastoralism and the grazing lands. We have grouped the discussions into seven subsections: (1) Conclusions from the chapters. Under the epilog, we will consider: (2) Trends in scientific research and institutions responsible for producing development ideas during the post-independence period; (3) The era of 'big science' that characterized the 1970s and 1980s. Under 'big science' we examine the roles played by the UNESCO-MAB (Man and the Biosphere) ecosystem programs; and (4) the long-term ecological research (LTER) project which began in Europe and the USA and comprises networks of ecosystem research at the global level. The UNESCO-MAB and LTER networks were also based on the ideas of the International Biological Program (IBP). (5) Following the idea of 'big science' the notion of systems analysis for decision making based on dynamic ecological models also emerged—developed by leading scientists in the USA.[2] The systems analysis approach attempts to integrate aspects of ecological and social sciences for the purposes of solving development problems. (6) We briefly consider a 'new ecology,' based on ideas laid down by earlier programs, but given a major impetus as a result of scientific research conducted by international scientific communities working in arid and semi-arid regions in Africa in the 1990s.[3] We discuss why the 'new ecology' might have offered a better approach to solving development problems in East Africa. (7) Finally, we briefly examine emerging issues of science for development. We summarize each part in turn.

Conclusions from the chapters

The African environmental crisis

In Chapter 1, we raised the question of the African environmental crisis. The chapter briefly highlights key findings presented in more detail elsewhere in the book. We asked how and why development processes were influenced by the African environmental crisis hypothesis. This hypothesis argued that alternative methods of resource use—using new technologies and imperial scientific knowledge—would expand economic growth and reverse environmental degradation. Using political and ecological event histories, we described how the proponents of the hypothesis neglected the environmental causes in decision making for development. We examined the links between imperial science and development initiatives across time—thereby scrutinizing historical changes in development and research trends.

We strove to understand why the hypothesis became the working tool for imperial scientific investigations of African agrarian and husbandry production systems. By dissecting the performance of imperial science theories and methods, we showed that the hypothesis provided a powerful tool at the time, for arguing in favor of colonial land-use and development policies. However, the hypothesis failed to consider the socio-ecological factors unique to the African environments that stimulated environmental changes. The widespread lack of knowledge of the ecology of the African rangelands, African peasant agrarian systems and the nature of African soils resulted in a misreading of development needs and aims. Large-scale development projects designed to solve perceived environmental problems and promote an economy of scale failed to achieve the intended goals. The chapter concludes that the evidence analyzed shows a lack of support for the African environmental crisis hypothesis.

Empire, science and development

In Chapter 2 we used pre-colonial East Africa as a benchmark on which to re-appraise the environmental crisis hypothesis. We conducted a textual analysis of narratives written by European travelers who reported their observations of environmental conditions in the mid- and late nineteenth centuries. Some observers in Europe claimed that the observations and the texts were not scientific and therefore do not supply reliable information on pre-colonial environments in Africa. Others, however, were of the opinion that these textual narratives provide accurate representations, since the European travelers, missionaries and explorers were well educated in geographical sciences.

The texts provide a spatial analysis of the socio-ecological systems in Africa that comprised a diversity of cultural landscapes. Human settlement patterns not only portrayed the potential of the land for economic production, but also revealed limitations caused by disease vectors in humans and livestock. Based on their spatial analyses, some of the European travelers proposed environmental desiccation hypotheses, suggesting that the African environments were drying up. They cited evidence such as drying lakes, dry river courses that once carried water, African traditions of rainmakers and frequent droughts. However, such propositions ignored the fact that the climate in Africa is highly variable and characterized by cycles of droughts, famine and periods of heavy rainfall. Our textual analysis in Chapter 2 provides no evidence of environmental desiccation: later reconstruction of the events from missionary archives found no support for the hypothesis. On the contrary, the European textural narratives described diverse landscapes, including some with high soil fertility. In most cases, the African-managed landscapes were described using symbols and examples of European best-managed landscapes that would have been known to the travelers.

The narratives present evidence of sophisticated indigenous agricultural practices, in which soil conservation played an integral part. Various cultural landscapes were allocated to crop cultivation and animal husbandry. However, in the late nineteenth century, a train of disasters collapsed African systems of production.

In Chapter 3, we examined imperial scientific infrastructure from development perspectives. In a deterministic manner, the imperial scientific research infrastructure had promoted the African environmental crisis hypothesis, which influenced the thinking about agricultural and husbandry production and land use, as well as environmental conservation programs. In examining the 'architecture' of imperial science, we organized our review chronologically to provide a sense of time and events in the field of scientific research in East Africa. The pioneer years were crucial for planting the 'seeds of science,' and it was from this earlier period that the hypothesis of African environmental crisis emerged. The writings of the time placed the responsibility for reversing environmental problems with colonial scientists.

Scientific research during the pioneer years took the form of establishing research stations and research networks. Nevertheless, political, climatic and global economic events influenced investment in scientific research. The First World War years resulted in discontinuing many research programs, while the period of regional and global economic depression (the 1930s) was accompanied by further decline in investment in research activities. The scale of development had also shifted to large-scale schemes. Thus far, despite attempts to accelerate research on a variety of development problems, success had been limited. Rather than diminishing in influence, the African environmental crisis hypothesis gained popularity among colonial officials, who exaggerated the extent and rates of damage to the environment that they believed was caused by indigenous land use. Research was therefore considered as a tool for 'testing' various ideas, meaning that failures, too, would be part of the testing. During this period, the colonies had continued to rely on professionals from the metropole.

The Second World War and post-war years (1935–1950s) coincided with the application of social science research to development imperatives which merely investigated the behavioral responses of African peasants to development changes. A contradiction arose between social science researchers and colonial officials in that the researchers wished to proceed with empirical work, while the administrators preferred technical advice. It was not until the internationalization of research that better coherence between development and scientific research evolved—although, by that time, the focus had shifted from a local to a global development agenda. This required major changes in the relation between scientific application and the development agenda—for instance, it involved removing African peasants from their traditional lands, and using the land to establish large-scale agricultural schemes. By the time of independence in the 1960s, new problems had emerged. The expatriate scientific staff were leaving the colonies. Due to the lack of sufficiently trained indigenous scientists, the colonies were forced to rely on international organizations and the former colonial empire for financial and technical support.

In Chapter 4, we examined the global and local origins of the environmental crisis narratives. The colonial land-use policies that had associated indigenous land use with environmental degradation had themselves directly contributed to environmental problems. However, the officials did not report or acknowledge this fact. For example, the official policy of land alienation and displacement of populations created conditions that increased the risks of an environmental crisis. We presented case examples to show that the development projects that focused on soil conservation, agricultural and grazing schemes not only failed to reverse the conditions described as representing an 'environmental crisis' but triggered the very problems the officials had hoped to address. The colonial development policy was to shift from small-scale indigenous production systems to large-scale commercial ones, in order to capitalize on economies of scale.

Chapter 4 went on to show how the lack of scientific information for development planning contributed to project failures. Of the large-scale schemes into which much investment was sunk, none was successful, almost all for similar reasons—either neglect of indigenous systems of resource use or misreading of the African ecology. The groundnut scheme is a case in point—it resulted in removing the natural vegetation from many millions of hectares of African savannas and ploughing up the land; this accelerated soil erosion, thus producing a technical and ecological disaster.

Ecological and social science research

In Chapter 5, we developed a schematic framework to describe the responses of proxy environmental indicators to intensification of land use, in terms of either the equilibrium or disequilibrium hypothesis. Among the agronomic experiments we investigated were those concerned with loss of soil sediments, and river and storm discharges that invariably related to soil loss from the watershed. The experiments—mostly at plot scale, and a few at landscape scale—showed the importance of vegetation cover in soil conservation. However, considering that none of the experiments were conducted on farmers' lands, it is impossible to relate the findings directly to indigenous land use.

In addition to land use, rainfall variability is a critical factor that determines the amount of soil lost from a watershed. Rainfall (as described by the disequilibrium hypothesis) plays a crucial role in soil moisture, in that the number of soil moisture days has a direct impact on crop yields. Many of the experiments conducted at the time ignored this important ecological variable and explained changes only in terms of land use. It was also part of the hypothesis that indigenous systems of land use were linked to a decline in soil fertility. Although the application of commercial fertilizers and cattle mature caused temporary improvements in soil fertility, the lower soil fertility was attributable to the environmental factors as opposed to intensifications of land use. In terms of soil conservation and fertility, we found that the evidence does not support the environmental crisis hypothesis, while the alternative hypothesis is applicable.

In grazing experiments, without exception, all the experiments demonstrated superiority of the indigenous methods of grazing over the rest and rotational systems. In all the grazing systems, rainfall variability, and not grazing, was decisive in influencing rangeland productivity and range restoration. Environmental restoration was possible only when rainfall was plentiful. Other trials, such as reseeding experiments, also showed the critical role played by variable rainfall in restoring degraded lands. We were able to finally show that none of the experiments supported the environmental crisis hypothesis.

The outcomes of social science research (Chapter 6) show interesting trends in relation to the African peoples' behavior in terms of whether they accepted or rejected development programs. The colonial authorities made several suppositions. First, their opinion was that social responses to development are predetermined by groups' socio-ecological and economic specializations. Second, anthropologists had predicted that, according to their social behavior, communities might be arranged on a continuum, ranging from those who were quick to accept changes, to those who resisted. Along the continuum, it was supposed that agro-pastoralists were more adaptable to change than pastoralist herders who were predicted to be more resistant to change. These assumptions caricatured African social behavior towards development initiatives. On the contrary, the African societies showed flexibility in their responses, readily accepting those projects that benefited them and rejecting those that undermined their indigenous economic production systems.

The main obstacle was colonial policies that fixated on the intensification of economic production, without adequate knowledge of prevailing ecological and social conditions. Our comparative analyses have shown that African societies responded positively to development changes, although acceptance varied across space and time. Acceptance was much greater when development plans incorporated social cultural institutions and indigenous knowledge. Such transformations enabled the communities to participate in the market economy, by changing their systems of animal husbandry and crop cultivation in acceptable ways.

We get glimpses of these changes and responses from the case studies presented in Chapter 7, which investigates the implementation of administrative science. The case studies illustrate the preference of colonial authorities, particularly administrators, for expert knowledge in planning and implementing development projects, as opposed to scientific research-based findings. We investigated dialogues between officials in technical departments and provincial administration on matters that influenced the welfare of African societies, the security of indigenous land tenure and African communities' participation in development projects.

The administrative authorities, who were responsible for implementing government policies, also worked and supported the Africans whom they administered—some of the time. But—depending on pressure from the colonial government—they often relaxed their support to local communities and acted decisively to implement government policies. The local communities, who did not participate in the dialogue, often used representatives or hired lawyers to intervene on their behalf. An interesting aspect of the dialogue is the role played by the Crown Courts in settling land disputes. As the first case study shows, if the officials had violated the statutes, the courts—in the true spirit of British justice—overturned the decisions of the lower courts and returned the land to the Africans.

The second and third case studies are concerned with agricultural and soil conservation and settlement schemes. The colonial officials used ordinances with strict requirements to force compliance by the African peasants, even though some of the ordinances were impossible to comply with. Evidence shows that the Europeans running technical departments did not themselves understand the rationale of African indigenous methods of soil conservation and soil fertility. They continued to blame African peasants for the erosion of hillsides and loss of soil fertility. This is despite—as acknowledged by some colonial officials—the communities having excelled in the practice of their indigenous conservation methods. Yet, the policies promoted clearing of large areas of natural vegetation to control tsetse flies, while at the same time blaming the African peasants for their 'unwise' use of the land. There was no evidence that the ordinances succeeded, and soil conservation along the lines recommended by the officials took a long time to work—and when it did work, it was only when the peasants did what they knew best in terms of working their land.

Disease vectors and pest control programs

Chapter 8 analyzed the tsetse fly (*Glossina* species) which was responsible for displacing populations from vast areas that in turn resulted in underdevelopment of the affected regions in East Africa. The flies' natural hosts that supply them with blood meals are small mammals, birds, reptiles, large mammals, cattle and people. From ancient times, the African peoples have known about the vector and practiced some indigenous control methods. This did not, however, stop the outbreak of the pandemic.

For five decades, starting in the early twentieth century, the East African colonial governments embarked on large-scale control of, and research on, tsetse flies. Several methods were applied. The most drastic were extensive destruction of the tsetse habitats through bush clearing and extermination of wild game, in the hope of breaking the trypanosome parasite life cycle. There were disagreements between researchers who conducted small-scale experimental trials and administrators who preferred large-scale clearing of bushy vegetation to be replaced by agricultural and grazing schemes. The challenge was that none of the methods provided a long-term solution. Tsetse control, more than any other imperial scientific research method, was therefore responsible for the destruction of vegetation from vast areas of East Africa.

Chapter 9 examines six aspects of locust research and controls: ecology of locusts, outbreak areas, economic impacts, international collaboration, regional controls, control methods and monitoring. The pest's life cycle varies from solitary to gregarious, with breeding phases significantly influencing control methods. Locust swarms demonstrate behavioral changes, which also reflect morphological changes in relation to climatic conditions and food supplies. Knowledge of rainfall and seasonality are crucial in gleaning information on the breeding success of locusts.

From the outbreak areas swarms of various generations of desert locusts were arriving head-to-tail in destinations in East Africa. In some years, as many as 50 separate swarms might arrive, requiring prompt responses before they devoured all agricultural produce in their path.

The economic impact of locust invasions has few comparisons—they were more frequent than other natural disasters, and the damage to agricultural production was in millions of British pounds. From the few available estimates, the impacts on grazing lands, though least investigated, were equally serious. In order to combat locusts, regional control campaigns were organized on a massive scale, year after year. The story was always the same—when one series of swarms was extinguished, other swarms were arriving. Were it not for international participation in the locust swarm controls, no single country would have had the resources to meet the massive challenges.

During the post-war years, the British donated military vehicles and aircraft for locust control work. The vehicles and planes were refitted with sprays. Until the late 1960s, research and monitoring were combined to deal with the locust plagues; however, despite the huge amounts of funding expended, the methods met with little success. Although laboratory experiments for producing and testing pesticides made important contributions to locust control, the fast-moving events did not allow for long-term field research. Finally, and most importantly, in the context of the African environmental crisis hypothesis, the damage to the environment by locusts exceeded what humans had accomplished. This conclusion is significant considering that the originators of the hypothesis only considered human agencies as the causal factor.

Our work would be incomplete without attempting to understand the trajectory of science for development during the first three decades of post-independence which is discussed in the epilog.

Epilog
Trends in scientific research

By the end of the 1960s and beginning of the 1970s, scientific research in Africa had attracted global attention, partly because of adverse environmental disasters that resulted in mass mortality of livestock, huge human populations dying from starvation and increasing international focus on environmental degradation—referred to as 'desertification.'[4] This post-independence period experienced increased international donor participation in scientific research and project financing. International assistance was necessary to support rapid training of local scientific researchers and technicians, particularly under programs funded by bilateral international organizations.[5] A peak in investments in large-scale development programs was evident—focusing mainly on environmental conservation and livestock development.[6] The challenge again was that, in general, donor agencies had poor understanding of the social dynamics of the communities benefiting from development programs.

Concurrently, scientific research focused on consultancy services—short-term result-based information gathering to guide donor agencies in supporting development and emergency humanitarian programs. There were also other changes in the application of scientific research. Following greater focus by international donor agencies on the Sahelian region of Africa, national priorities shifted to emergency programs. Development agencies and researchers found themselves grappling with seeking solutions to long-term development problems.

The decade 1970 to 1980 witnessed integration of ecological and social science research in the form of two approaches. The first approach involved social science research that made more concrete proposals on what the futures of pastoral peoples would look like. The International Union of Anthropological and Ethnological Sciences (IUSES) formed the Commission on Nomadic Peoples, which championed these ideas. The second approach was social science research conducted by anthropologists considered that researchers were morally obliged to save pastoral peoples and integrate their subsistence economies into national and global economies by focusing on practical solutions to development problems.[7]

During the 1980s (20 years later), interdisciplinary research was becoming popular with development agencies, in addressing development problems. Unlike the past, when ecological research had been isolated from social science research, the merging of the two disciplines created hybrid methods that were applied in implementing development programs.[8] Most importantly, there was growing interest in improving the scale of conventional experimental research to the level of ecosystems, in an attempt to understand better the drivers of ecosystem changes (from ecological and social perspectives). The shift—particularly in development aid agendas—was from local to regional programs, with greater participation by private researchers from western academic institutions.[9]

By the 1990s, the large-scale rangeland and pastoral developments of the previous decades had ended.[10] Donor fatigue and disappointment from investments in large-scale programs seem to have been the cause. Consequently, large-scale pastoral development initiatives were on the decline, while scientific research was growing. This mismatch created wide gaps between research and development that had not been experienced since the colonial period (Figure 1.2). Nonetheless, growing interest in the internationalization of scientific research in Africa had created what came to be called an era of 'big science.'

The era of 'big science'

The 'big science' has three characteristics. First, it is scale-dependent. Second, it involves collaborations by large international interdisciplinary teams of researchers comprising natural and social scientists. Third, it includes diversities of ecosystems and cultures across the world. The concept of 'big science' emerged from work of the International Biological Program (IBP) launched in the USA in the 1964.[11] This network provided rapid methods of sharing research information among its members via peer-reviewed publications. Before it ended in 1974, the IBP provided an international forum for natural scientists on a variety of ecological research topics; however, it made less of a contribution to social and economic research for development programs.[12] An important contribution of the IBP was to challenge ecologists to coordinate their research for 'a common cause' for humanity around the world[13]—a philosophical approach that was adopted by UNESCO's Man and the Biosphere (MAB) program.

The UNESCO-MAB program

The enthusiasm generated by the IBP motivated UNESCO to launch the 'Man and the Biosphere' (MAB) program in 1971 to support interdisciplinary research and collaboration with individual countries. These country-based programs created international research networks focusing on various ecosystems around the world.[14] The MAB studies were significant for four reasons. First, the programs extended investigations into ecosystem studies that had been neglected under the IBP. Second, MAB radically improved the work started by IBP in terms of interdisciplinary research. Third, under MAB, ecosystem studies were expanded to include all natural systems on which societies depend.[15] The scale of research was unprecedented, compared to the experimental investigations during the colonial period.[16] Fourth, UNESCO-MAB recognized that the work of IBP (despite its high scientific value) had limitations in terms of developing methods needed to produce practical solutions.[17] The hypothesis of UNESCO-MAB is that ecological problems are interconnected with socio-environmental and economic problems. MAB's research also focused on production systems that integrated the work of social and ecological sciences with administrative decision making. The merger of scientific and administrative science was part of the vision of Francesco di Castri, General Secretary of UNESCO-MAB (1971–1984), who advocated the application of ecological sciences to solve socio-environmental problems.[18] The aim was to organize international research projects through training personnel required in country programs.[19] Among the MAB field projects, some served as pilot projects focusing on research of international significance, attempting to test scientific ideas,[20] for example on understanding the processes driving 'desertification.'

We use an example here. Between 1976 and 1986, UNESCO-MAB conducted an integrated research project on arid lands (IPAL) in northern Kenya. This project was concerned with understanding ecological and social factors that triggered desertification. The study region represented two ideal conditions associated with desertification processes. The first was that it was an arid ecosystem where the processes of desertification were believed to be active. The second was land use by indigenous pastoralists often blamed as causative agents of environmental problem. The participants were interdisciplinary teams of researchers who used a 36,000 km^2 area of the Rendille nomads' grazing lands for experimental research. The grazing territory was mapped into 24 range units (i.e., vegetation types) which disclosed a variety of ecological potentials for multi-livestock species grazing during different seasons of the year. While the anthropologists investigated socio-economic factors that motivated varied decision-making in terms of livestock movements,[21] livestock scientists investigated constraints on livestock productivity, such as disease prevalence and feed variability.[22] Range ecologists monitored impacts of settlements on the woodlands,[23] and mapping and monitoring permanent vegetation transects across range units in terms of vegetation production dynamics.[24] Economists, meanwhile, worked on rates of livestock offtake that could be sustained under conditions of normal pastoral herd growth. Climatologists used instrumental data to reconstruct the features of past climates and climate variability. The interdisciplinary research results were used to develop management plans for the Rendille grazing lands.[25] Unfortunately, neither international donor agencies nor the Government of Kenya implemented the Western Marsabit grazing and development plans. This is just one example of how the vastly rich scientific research information goes to waste in African countries.

Whereas the UNESCO-MAB programs provided individual countries with opportunities to calibrate research methods to international standards, they also faced challenges.[26] First, despite the programs borrowing heavily from IBP, in reality they lacked an accepted scientific paradigm—forcing researchers to learn 'along the way,' or even relying on old paradigms such as the African environmental crisis (that has since been discredited, as shown in this work). Second, it emerged again that those responsible for research and management of natural resources produced information that, in fact, had limited practical value. By ignoring new emerging scientific directions (see below) and focusing on theories that had failed in the past, these ambitious research programs had limited impacts.[27] The value of ecosystem scale research is in terms of building LTER networks.

Long-term ecological research (LTER) networks

The idea of 'long-term ecological research' (LTER) emerged in the USA and the west from the 1970s. LTER requires careful management of research data in order to monitor trends and outcomes.[28] Where monitoring data are unavailable, interdisciplinary teams of researchers collect historical information on ecological dynamics from a variety of sources, in order to reconstruct historical insights into selected ecosystems.[29]

The success of LTER programs and their networks may be attributed to three major factors. First, the LTER approach developed conceptual frameworks that help in understanding both ecological and social perspectives of ecosystems (see later section). Integrating human actions with ecosystem dynamics and biogeographical drivers provide predictive tools on the behavior of human-managed environments. Second, through comprehensively managed documentation practices, LTER creates data banks that are ideal for testing ecological and social theories related to the exploitation of natural ecosystems. Third, in real world cases, LTER enables interdisciplinary research collaboration across political borders.[30]

In East Africa, although many of the colonial research sites and many research stations were abandoned and the data series from these earlier periods lost to posterity, the colonial archives represent a valuable scientific resource and could serve as a base on which to build LTER. In terms of continuity, an LTER program that has involved collaboration by international interdisciplinary scientists since the 1950s is the Serengeti-Mara ecosystem.[31] Others include work of scientists who used meta-analysis of environmental and social data to reconstruct long-term environmental and social history of the region of southern and eastern Africa.[32] In her recent book *Savannas of our birth*, Robin Reid[33] provides a thorough analysis of the relationship between pastoralists' use of natural habitats and the needs of wildlife. Other examples of long-term research programs include the Maasai ecosystems,[34] the southern Turkana ecosystem project,[35] the Borana rangelands project in Ethiopia,[36] and the UNESCO-IPAL project in northern Kenya that produced valuable data necessary for building the historical and socio-ecological background that will contribute to ongoing LTER.[37] The availability of such long-term data series allows for better prediction of future events, being able to separate natural from human-induced environmental changes.[38] Further analysis of LTER data series will allow scientific researchers and development agents to track emerging problems that influence decision-making in the management of natural resources.[39]

Systems analysis for decision-making

The idea of systems analysis is motivated by the industrial production model, and later computer systems and other technologies that were implemented in agricultural and range production studies to enhance decision-making. Systems ecology involves the quantitative enumeration of components and their interactions with subsystems, to capture and describe ecosystem dynamics.[40] During the decade 1980–1990, rangeland and pastoral research involved multi-disciplinary teams working on research of global significance.[41]

In Africa, researchers at the International Livestock Centre for Africa (ILCA) in 1970s and 1980s have used systems analysis for decision-making, working with their networks on pastoral and agro-pastoral production in various agro-ecological systems.[42] In the ILCA systems studies, interdisciplinary teams of scientists combined a multiplicity of methods for data collection and analysis, to assist decision-making in managing group ranches and pastoral herd production under traditional management systems. Three lessons have emerged from these studies. First, short-term studies are of little value for making effective management decisions. Second, production systems are dependent on climate variability. This finding confirms the perspective that has been promoted throughout this book. Third, awareness has emerged within the teams of scientists that any new development approaches would radically alter traditional pastoral production practices.[43] Examples presented from the systems studies have also confirmed that altering pastoral production is not necessarily as efficient as the systems of indigenous production. It was, therefore, this evidence that raised much interest in new ecology during the 1990s.

New ecology

The imperial science, as we have severally shown, had accepted the African environmental crisis hypothesis as the truth, even when there is an alternative explanation for ecological outcomes.[44] There are two contrasting research viewpoints on the matter, which highlight shifts in environmental management paradigms. On the one hand, there are those researchers who continue to subscribe to the old theory by concentrating on the immediate (proximate) impacts of land use, while on the other hand, there are those researchers who argue that such opinions are misleading. The latter argue for a new ecological thinking. In their opinion, it is preferable to investigate the ultimate causes of the problem of land degradation and the general ecological dynamics of the arid and semi-arid rangelands. While the adherents of proximate causes would link processes such as desertification with land uses, the opposing view associates the problem with much broader and overarching climate variability as the primary driver and land use as a secondary cause.[45] This then is the context of the 'disequilibrium hypothesis.'[46] We will explain this briefly.

Disequilibrium rangeland ecology and development

The old equilibrium theory (i.e., environmental crisis) had persisted until the decade 1980.[47] The shift that occurred thereafter was based on evidence that emerged from pastoralists' own adaptations and new interpolations of rangeland production dynamics in arid and semi-arid areas. Whereas in the past, researchers and development agencies blamed indigenous land use for environmental degradation, ecologists and social science researchers started to ask new questions, prompted by the need to understand why and how pastoral societies maintained their production in the absence of development interventions. Various studies have demonstrated that the western scientific knowledge systems alone is unsatisfactory in explaining their long-term survival in harsh environments.[48] The questions are motivated by emerging and better understanding of indigenous land-use practices—the rationale behind certain land-use practices, local solutions to problems, knowledge of indigenous peoples, their adaptive methods of resource use and their future worldviews. These included increasing evidence that the dynamics of the arid and semi-arid rangelands of Africa were in response to climate variability and the adaptive strategies to environmental variability were by mobility of the pastoral herds. These two factors motivated applications of the new ecology.

How is the indigenous system of resource exploitation explained by the new ecology? How would knowledge of the new ecology support management of variable environments? We consider brief responses to these two questions as follows. First, range ecologists and anthropologists conducting long-term research among pastoral communities in East Africa have gained insights into patterns of resource exploitation, use of mobility, practices of herd splitting to reduce risks to vulnerabilities and exploitation of variable resources across space and time.[49] Using their indigenous ecological knowledge, pastoralists have classified and appropriately allocated grazing areas during different seasons.[50] Their systems of range evaluation and monitoring—when combined with ecological knowledge—provide a new understanding of rangeland ecology.[51] Thus, contrary to earlier perceptions, indigenous knowledge and practices are robust and, in the majority of cases, offer better management insights than any alternative models. We will elaborate on this in the next section.

Second, the knowledge of new ecology proposes indigenous methods of managing variable environments.[52] In the new way of thinking, environmental degradation is explained as dynamic processes as opposed to progressive ones.[53] The resilience of the African grazing lands has disclosed that the perceived long-term view of environmental degradation should be abandoned and replaced with one of possibilities and opportunities.[54]

The disequilibrium model functions at spatial and temporal scales, as opposed to the equilibrium model, which works at fine scales. That is to say, evidence of land degradation might be observed at the scale of plots, as opposed to entire grazing territories of pastoralists.[55] While the equilibrium model predicts that vegetation indicators would decline with increasing grazing pressure, the disequilibrium model predicts variable responses in space and time.[56] The persistent African crisis hypothesis had, however, ignored these important ecological factors and therefore failed to address actual causal factors of land degradation. To sum up this work, we will identify some key emerging issues focusing on use of knowledge systems using a conceptual model.

Emerging issues

In this final part of the book, we will reflect, albeit briefly, on the use of combined indigenous and ecological knowledge systems for scientific research development in Africa for future development planning for five reasons. First, problems of scientific research and development of the past will be different during the twenty-first century—in terms of multiplicities of challenges, the changing scales of research as well as uncertainties associated with global drivers of environmental change, such as the much-debated climate change. Second, under the transformed indigenous systems of production, expanding populations, increasing conflicts over access to resources, limitations of knowledge as well as shifting development priorities of the African societies under uncertainties will demand new approaches. Third, one needs to identify barriers to progress in terms of changes in social institutions and decision-making processes.[57]

Fourth, resource managers would be confronted by fast moving events, in which knowledge of the past might be discredited and new ideas proposed which also need testing under changing land use and political conditions. Thus, the importance of science is to identify the types of knowledge that remain relevant. Fifth, twenty-first-century research should be able to evaluate extraneous factors that might influence changes in the indigenous knowledge.[58]

The challenge remains how to integrate ecological and indigenous knowledge for evaluations of impacts of management on the natural resources. For example, linkages between local land-use factors and global environmental changes associated with human actions (Anthropocene) and climate drivers are rarely tested conceptually and practically. The twenty-first-century changes would demand greater integration of ecological and socio-economic knowledge systems for decision making and for developing ecological and anthropogenic web-based LTER data systems for decision-making.[59]

Considering that both scientific and indigenous knowledge are changing, the context needs to be carefully defined and the scales at which the knowledge operates (i.e., global, regional, national or local scales) identified. Then the meta-data generated would be fed into the ongoing LTER and disseminated through web-based services.[60]

When using such an approach, new local terminologies and concepts about environmental conditions in relation to the anthropogenic indicators may described.[61] Relations between the anthropogenic and ecological proxy indicators may then be gaged for decision-making.[62] Further, the future should take advantage of technological advances such as remotely sensed platforms for rapid environmental assessments operating at regional and global scales. Meanwhile, we should acknowledge varieties of challenges that require more sophisticated methods of analysis, and communication skills to deal with varieties of technical and non-technical issues.[63] We will illustrate this with a conceptual model on how interdisciplinary research applying ecological and indigenous knowledge might be applied.

Social-economic and ecological conceptual model

Integration of indigenous knowledge into scientific knowledge for development needs to capture both the ecological and socio-economic dimensions of socio-anthropogenic environmental indicators, ecological indicators, research assessments and decision making (Figure 10.1). The ecological indicators are of two types: diagnostic and those describing ecosystem functioning. Diagnostic indicators measure responses to land-use impacts. They vary in relation to grazing pressure with overall responses influenced by the overarching climate variability.[64]

The socio-economic and ecological conceptual model (SEEM) consists of three components. The first submodel comprises ecological and anthropogenic indicators that serve as proxy for rangeland production dynamics and for assessing human perceptions of environmental changes and livestock management. The model has tools for assessing indigenous knowledge-based environmental assessments and for decision-making. The indigenous knowledge submodel uses societal behavior, historical knowledge and general world views. The information is used to determine the suitability of the resource for specific uses related to, for example grazing, vulnerability to the system to disturbance (that cause environmental degradation) and the

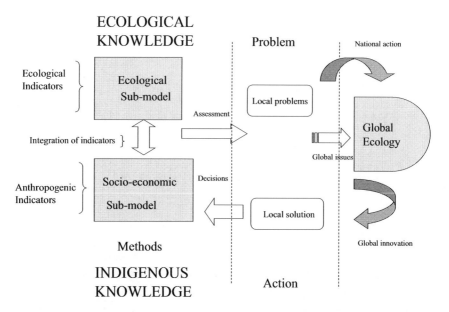

Figure 10.1 Conceptual model for the socio-economic and ecological model (SEEM) for integration of ecological and anthropogenic indicators for land-use assessments.

capacity to maintain resilience. In the socio-economic submodel, the indicators are livestock production performances and land-use potential. The second part of the model represents the problems assessed and solutions reached at local levels. The actions from the first two model components can be fed into the third component of the model that reflect national and global actions. At the national level, the information from the indigenous knowledge, combined with ecological knowledge are fed into action plans that reflect national obligations related to the global level concerns (such as global convections). At the global level, information from the grassroots through national action plans serve as lessons for improving policy guidelines.

Most anthropogenic indicators are composites of ecological and management indicators that influence the perceptions of local herders regarding how they value a given landscape for grazing. The three types of indicators (including the anthropogenic ones) play important roles in decision making. Thus, anthropogenic indicators, representing human perceptions about the environmental change along with exogenous factors (e.g., needs and capabilities) feed into decision making about management of the grazing lands. This means that while the ecological indicators are value neutral, the anthropogenic indicators are value loaded. Using these varieties of indicators, local communities in collaboration with ecologists may link assessments of the impacts of global problems such as climate change and environmental changes at the local levels.[65]

In rangeland assessments, all herding societies have terminologies that describe the relationships between livestock grazing, landscape potential and what they call 'grazing suitability.' For any landscape, grazing suitability varies with livestock types and the seasons of the year. Landscapes with high grazing suitability for cattle (grazers) are likely to have low suitability for camels (browsers). Furthermore, the capacity of individual landscapes to support a given stocking density of livestock for a given period is influenced by its soils more than its vegetation, and this is called 'landscape grazing potential.' Thus, grazing suitability is a vegetation-based indicator (which varies highly between seasons), while landscape grazing potential is based on the physical environment and is thus a more stable indicator.[66]

The value (positive or negative) of suitability varies according to the type of landscape, and season for grazing, as well as types of livestock. Herders rated the suitability based on production indices of livestock (i.e., milk yield, weight changes and other physical changes such as conditions of body hair). The other indicators are those that reflect the capacity of the landscape to resist grazing pressure and remain resilient after use (called grazing capacity), which reflects stocking that individual landscapes support. The potential is inferred from a variety of variables, including soils, vegetation and experience. For example, the Maasai pastoralists distinguish between 'degradation risky' (*engob orpora*) and 'less vulnerable landscapes' (*engob warkojete*)—the terms that always refer to soils.

Finally, future research should be built on the resourcefulness of local knowledge that demonstrates greater potential for developing more sustainable pastoral and rangeland development than has hitherto been appreciated.[67] The vision is what the pastoralists are themselves doing—which is a greater integration and diversification of pastoral livelihoods. Future research should focus on better understanding of peoples' adaptive strategies that have helped them to cope better with socio-economic changes—including pastoralists' participation in market economies, environmental management, education and greater integration into national and global economies, utilization of modern communication systems among many other initiatives. Addressing these broader issues would require a better integration of indigenous knowledge and socio-ecological knowledge systems to promote sustainable development in Africa, thereby avoiding being guided by false scientific theories such as the African environmental crisis.

Notes

1 Kiago, L.M., 'Perspectives on the assumed causes of land degradation in the rangelands of sub-Saharan Africa,' *Progress in Physical Geography* 37.5 (2013): 664–684.
2 Van Dyne, G.M., *The ecosystem concept in natural resource management* (New York: Academic Press. 1969).

3 Behnke R.H., Scoones, I. and Kerven, C., *Range ecology at disequilibrium* (London: ODI, 1993); Scoones, I., *Living with uncertainty: New directions in pastoral development in Africa* (London: IT, 1994).
4 Ishwaran, N., 'Science in intergovernmental environmental relations: 40 years of UNESCO's Man and the Biosphere (MAB) Programme and its future,' *Environmental Development* 1.1 (2012): 91–101.
5 Dickie, A., Wilson, Y. and Wilson K.A., 'Viewpoint: A management perspective on development assistance,' *Rangelands* 6.6 (1984): 271–273.
6 Bonneuil, C., 'Development as experiment: Science and state building in late and post-colonial Africa, 1930–1970,' *Osiris* 15 (2000): 258–281.
7 Galaty, J.G., Aronson, D., Salzman, P.C. and Chouinard, A. (eds.), *The future of pastoral peoples: Proceedings of a conference held in Nairobi, Kenya, 4–8 August* (Ottawa: IDRC, 1981), 7, 8.
8 Gragson, T.L. and Grove, M., 'Social science in the context of the long-term ecological research program,' *Society and Natural Resources* 19 (2006): 93–100.
9 Sinclair, A.R.E. and Fryxell, J.M., 'The Sahel of Africa: Ecology of a disaster,' *Canadian Journal of Zoology* 63 (1985): 987–994.
10 Sanford, S., *Management of pastoral development in the Third World* (London: John Wiley and Sons, 1983).
11 Bremeye, A.I. and Van Dyne, G.M., *Grasslands, systems analysis and man*, International Biological Programme 19 (Cambridge: Cambridge University Press, 1980).
12 Ishwaran, 'Science in intergovernmental environmental relations.'
13 Breymeyer and Van Dyne, *Grasslands, systems analysis and man*.
14 Di Castri, F., Hadley, M. and Damlamian, E., 'MAB: The Man and the Biosphere program as an evolving system,' *Ambio* (Special Issue) 10.2.3 (1981): 52–57.
15 Golley, F.B., *A history of ecosystem concept in ecology: More than the sum of the parts* (New Haven: Yale University Press, 1993), 163.
16 Ibid., 163.
17 Dyer, M. and Holland, M.M., 'UNESCO's Man and the Biosphere Program,' *BioScience* 38.9 (1988): 635–641.
18 Di Castri, F., 'International, interdisciplinary research in ecology: Some problems of organization and execution. The case of the Man and the Biosphere (MAB) programme,' *Human Ecology* 4.3 (1976): 235–246.
19 Ibid.
20 Le Houerou, Henry N., *The grazing land ecosystems of the African Sahel. Vol. 75* (Springer Science & Business Media, 2012).
21 O'Leary, Michael F., *The economics of pastoralism in northern Kenya: The Rendille and the Gabra* (Nairobi: UNESCO, 1985).
22 Lusigi, W.J., O'Leary, M., Crees, J., Bake, G., Muiruri, K., Oba, G. and Ndombi, J.M., *Integrated Project in Arid Lands (IPAL) Technical Report Number A-6 Part I. Integrated Resource Assessment* (Nairobi: UNESCO, 1984); Migongo-Bake, Wangoi, and Hansen, Richard M., 'Seasonal diets of camels, cattle, sheep, and goats in a common range in eastern Africa,' *Journal of Range Management* (1987): 76–79.
23 Lamprey, H.F. and Yussuf, H., 'Pastoralism and desert encroachment in northern Kenya,' *Ambio* (1981): 131–134.
24 Lusigi, W.J, Nkurunziza, E.R, Awere-Gyekye, K. and Masheti, S., *Range resource assessment and management strategies for South-Western Marsabit, Northern Kenya IPAL Technical Report No. D-5.* (Nairobi: UNESCO, 1986); Roba, H.G. and Oba, G., 'Efficacy of integrating herder knowledge and ecological methods for monitoring rangeland degradation in northern Kenya, *Human Ecology*, 37.5 (2009): 589–612.
25 Lusigi, W.J., *Integrated resource assessment and management plan for Western Marsabit District, Northern Kenya. Integrated Project in Arid Lands (IPAL)* Technical Report No A-6 (Nairobi: UNESCO, 1984).

26 Dyer and Holland, 'UNESCO's Man and the Biosphere Program.'
27 Ibid.
28 Hampton, S.E., Straser, C.A., Tewksbury, J.J., Wendy, W.K., Budden, A.E., Bacheller, A.L., Duke, C.S. and Porker, J.H., 'Big data and the future of ecology,' *Frontier in Ecology and the Environment* 11.3 (2013): 156–162.
29 Anderson, C.B., Likens, G.E., Rozzi, R., Gutierrrez, J.R., Armesto, J.J. and Poole, A., 'Integrating science and society through long-term socio-ecological research,' *Environmental Ethics* 30.3 (2008): 295–312.
30 Redman, C.L., Grove, J.M. and Kuby, L.H., 'Integrating social science into the long-term ecological research (LTER) network: Social dimensions of ecological change and ecological dimensions of change,' *Ecosystems* 7 (2004): 161–171.
31 Sinclair, A.R.E. and Norton-Griffiths, M. (eds.), *Serengeti: Dynamics of an ecosystem* (Chicago: University of Chicago Press, 1995), vii; Sinclair, A.R.E. and Arcese, P., *Serengeti II: Dynamics, management, and conservation of an ecosystem* (Chicago: University of Chicago Press, 1995).
32 Beinart, W. and McGregor, J. (ed.)., *Social history and African environments* (Oxford: James Currey, 2003).
33 Reid, R.S., *Savannas of our birth: People, wildlife and change in East Africa* (Berkeley: University of California Press, 2012).
34 Homewood, K., Kristjanson, P. and Trench, P.C. (eds.), *Staying Maasai? Livelihood conservation and development in East African rangelands* (New York: Spinger, 2009); Galvin, K.A., Reid, R.S., Behnke, R.H. and Hobbs, N.T., *Fragmentation in semi-arid and arid landscape: Consequences for human and natural systems* (Dordrecht: Springer, 2008).
35 Little, M.A. and Leslie, P.W. (eds.), *Turkana herders of the dry savanna: Ecology and biobehavioural response of nomads to an uncertain environment* (Oxford: Oxford University Press, 1999).
36 Coppock, D.L, *The Borana plateau of southern Ethiopia: Synthesis of pastoral research, development and change, 1980–91*, International Livestock Centre for Africa (ILCA) (Addis Ababa: ILCA, 1994).
37 Fratkin, E. and Roth, E.A., *As pastoralists settle: Social, health, and economic consequences of pastoral sedentarization in Marsabit District, Kenya* (New York: Kluwer Academic Publishers, 2005); Witsenburg, K.M. and Roba, A.W., *Surviving pastoral decline: Pastoral sedentarisation, natural resource management and livelihood diversification in Marsabit District, Northern Kenya Deel: Vol. I*. Doctoral dissertation, PhD dissertation, University of Amsterdam, 2004.
38 Fukumi, T. and Wardle, D.A., 'Long-term ecological dynamics: Reciprocal insights from natural and anthropogenic gradients,' *Proceedings of Royal Society B*, 272 (2005): 2105–2115.
39 Lindernmayer, D.B., Likens, G.E., Andersen, A., Bowman, D., Bull, C.M., Burns, E., Dickman, C.R., Hoffmann, A.A., Keth D.A., et al., 'Value of long-term ecological studies,' *Austral Ecology* 37 (2012): 745–757.
40 Simmonds, N.W., *Farming systems research: A review*, World Bank Technical Paper No. 45, 1985.
41 Stuth, J.W. and Lyons, B.G., *Decision support systems for the management of grazing lands: Emerging issues, Volume 11*, Man and the Biosphere Series (Paris: UNESCO & Parthenon Publishing Group, 1993).
42 Wilson, R.T., *Livestock production in central Mali: Long-term studies on cattle and small ruminants in the agropastoral systems*, ILCA Research Report No. 14, 1986.
43 Bekure, S., de Leeuw, P.N., Grandin, B.E. and Neate, P.J.H., *Maasai herding: An analysis of the livestock production system of Maasai pastoralists in eastern Kajiado District, Kenya*, ILCA Systems study, International Livestock Centre for Africa (Addis Ababa: ILCA, 1991).

44 Benjaminsen, T.A., and Hiernaux, P., 'From desiccation to global climate change: A history of the desertification narrative in the West African Sahel, 1900–2018,' *Global Environment*, 12.1 (2019): 206–236.
45 Kiage, L.M., 'Perspectives on the assumed causes of land degradation in the rangelands of sub-Saharan Africa,' *Progress in Physical Geography* 37.5 (2013): 664–684.
46 Behnke, Scoones and Kerven, *Range ecology at disequilibrium*; Scoones, I., 'Climate change and the challenge of non-equilibrium thinking,' *IDS* 35.5 (2004): 114–119.
47 Scoones, *Living with uncertainty*.
48 Behnke, Scoones and Kerven, *Range ecology at disequilibrium*.
49 Leslie, P., McCabe, J.T., Bollig, M., Greiner, C., Fratkin, E., Galaty, J.G., ... and Nelson, F., 'Response diversity and resilience in social-ecological systems,' *Current Anthropology*, 54.2 (2013): 114–144.
50 Roba, H.G. and Oba, G., 'Community participatory landscape classification and biodiversity assessment and monitoring of grazing lands in northern Kenya,' *Journal of Environmental Management*, 90.2 (2009): 673–682; Mapinduzi, A.L., Oba, G., Weladji, R.B. and Colman, J.E., 'Use of indigenous ecological knowledge of the Maasai pastoralists for assessing rangeland biodiversity in Tanzania,' *African Journal of Ecology*, 41.4 (2003): 329–336.
51 Wario, H.T., Roba, H.G. and Kaufmann, B., 'Shaping the herders' "mental maps": Participatory mapping with pastoralists' to understand their grazing area differentiation and characterization,' *Environmental management*, 56.3 (2015): 721–737.
52 Ellis, Jim, and Galvin, Kathleen A., 'Climate patterns and land-use practices in the dry zones of Africa,' *BioScience* 44.5 (1994): 340–349.
53 Olsson, L., Eklundh, L. and Ardö, J., 'A recent greening of the Sahel: Trends, patterns and potential causes,' *Journal of Arid Environments*, 63.3 (2005): 556–566.
54 Retzer, V., 'Impacts of grazing and rainfall variability on the dynamics of a sahelian rangeland revisited (Hein, 2006): New insights from old data'; Silcock, Jenny L. and Fensham, Rod J., 'Arid vegetation in disequilibrium with livestock grazing: Evidence from long-term exclosures,' *Austral Ecology* 38.1 (2013): 57–65.
55 Roe, E.M., 'Viewpoint on rangeland carrying capacity,' *Journal of Rangeland Management* 50.5 (1997): 467–471.
56 Oba, G., Weladji, R.B., Lusigi, W.J. and Stenseth, N.C., 'Scale-dependent effects of grazing on rangeland degradation in northern Kenya: A test of equilibrium and non-equilibrium hypotheses,' *Land Degradation and Development* 14 (2003): 83–94.
57 Bestlmeyer, B.T., Estell, R.E. and Havstad, K.M., 'Big questions emerging from a century of range science and management,' *Rangeland Ecology and Management* 65 (2012): 543–544.
58 Karl, J.W., Herrick, J.E. and Broning, D.M., 'A strategy for rangeland management based on best available knowledge and information,' *Rangeland Ecology and Management* 65 (2012): 638–646.
59 Oba, G., Sjaastad, E. and Roba, H.G., 'Framework for participatory assessments and implementation of global environmental conventions at the community level,' *Land Degradation and Development* 19.1 (2008): 65–76.
60 Ibid.
61 Peters, D.P.C., Belnap, J., Ludwig, J.A., Collins, S.L., Paruelo, J., Hoffman, M.T. and Havstad, K.M., 'How can science be general, yet specific? The conundrum of rangeland science in the 21st century,' *Rangeland Ecology and Management* 66 (2012): 613–622.
62 Roba and Oba, 'Efficacy of integrating herder knowledge and ecological methods for monitoring rangeland degradation.'

63 Peters, Belnap, Ludwig, Collins, Paruelo, Hoffman and Havstad, 'How can science be general, yet specific?'
64 Oba, Sjaastad and Roba, 'Framework for participatory assessments and implementation of global environmental conventions at the community level.'
65 Oba, Weladji, Lusigi and Stenseth, 'Scale-dependent effects of grazing on rangeland degradation in northern Kenya.'
66 Oba, G., 'Harnessing pastoralists' indigenous knowledge for rangeland management: Three African case studies,' *Pastoralism: Research, Policy and Practice* 2.1 (2012): 1–21.
67 Catley, A., Lind, J. and Scoones, I., *Pastoralism and development in Africa: Dynamic change at the margins* (London: Routledge, 2013).

Index

Page numbers in **bold** denote tables, those in *italics* denote figures.

acacia trees 32–3, 34, 38
Acholi (Uganda) 176
Aden Protectorate 190, 199, 204
administrative science 2, 14, 140–56, 218
African Association 47
African Exploration Fund 47
African Survey Report 52
agricultural production 47, 51, 81–4; increasing 52, 53, 54, 71, 77–8, 82; locust damage to 191, 193, 195, 196, 219; methods of 27, 51, 70, 81, 83; plantations 51, 77, 81, 143, 144; research on 48, 51, 55–6, 82; *see also* commercial production; crop cultivation
Agricultural Research Council 55–6
agriculture, mechanized 55, 59, 82, 83, 84, 150
agriculture, subsistence 5, 27, 71, 82, 123, 130, 132, 134, 220
agronomic research 11, 13, 99, 102–8, **103**, *104*, *105*, *107*, *108*, 109
agro-pastoralism 26, 27, 39, 49, 88, 122, 123–4, 129–30, 131, 132, 134–5, 217, 224
Akamba people (Kenya) 80, 133, 174
Albert, Lake *28*, 38
alcohol 48
ALDEV (African Land Development Organization) 54–5, 82, 87
Allan, W. 26
Alvares, C. 9
Amani Research Institute (Tanganyika) 47, 48, 49–50, *50*, 56–7, 58
Anderson, D. 73
Ankole (Uganda) 38, *164*, 167, 174, 179

anthropogenic indicators 227, **228**, *228*
anthropology 14, 26, 51, 55, 123–5, 126–7, 132–5, 217, 220, 222, 225
Anti-Locust Research Centre 194, 196, 201, 204
Arabian Peninsula 15, 190, 191, 200–1
Archer, S. 76
Arusha Declaration 62
Arusha (Tanganyika) 88
Asad, T. 26
Austin, Major H. 32

bananas 135
Banks, J. 46
Baringo (Kenya) **111**, **112**, 114, 115
beans 36, 106, *107*
beef 48, 53
Bender Shetler, J. 38
Bernacca, J.P. 176
Berry, L. 79
Bewg, W.P. 116
'big science' 4, 213, 221–4
biological research 47, 52, 56
birds 169, 202, 218–19
Blanchard, K. 124
Bogdan, A.V. 115, 116
botanical specimens 29, 30, 46, 49
Bougall, H.W. 116
bovine pleuropneumonia 39
Bradley, K. 56
British Empire 9, 47, 48–9, 51–4, 55–6, 57, 140, 165; justice system 141, 149–50, 218
British Overseas Food Cooperation 83, 84
British Trust Territory of Tanganyika 2, 49–50

Buchuma (Kenya) **103**
buffalo 174, 176
Bullen, F.T. 194
Bunyoro-Kitara (Uganda) 166, 176–7
Burton, R. 32
Burundi 163
bush clearing 83, 84, 148; for rangeland rehabilitation 100, 108–9, **111**, 113, 115–16, 118, 153–6, 172; for tsetse fly eradication 15, 88, 163, 167–9, 170–1, 172–3, 174, 176, 177, 179, 219
bush encroachment 39, 40, 47, **111**, 115–16, 166, 172
Busoga Island 167
Busoga (Uganda) 84, 166, 179
Buxton, P.A. 171

Caldwell, L.K. 9
Cambridge School of Agriculture 48
camels 87, 200, 229
Cameron, D. 49
Carruthers, J. 5
cash crops *see* commercial production
Castri, F. di 222
cattle 33, 37, 38, 39, 48, 87, 115–16, 133, 134, 170, *180*, 229; beef 48, 53; 'cattle complex' 11–12, 128; milk supplied to local creameries 133, 134; trypanosome-tolerant 163; weights of 110, **111**, **112**, 113, *114*, 118, 229; *see also* livestock
Chaga people (Tanganyika) 135
Chamberlain, J. 47
Champion, A.M. 78
Chanler, W.A. 187
Chepalungu highland (Kenya) *142*, 156, *164*
Chertow, M.R. 12
cholera 39
Christiansson, C. 80
Christie, J. 39
Church, A. 49, 127–8
Clarke, R.T. 107
Clements, F.E. 11
climate change 31, 80, 226, 228–9
climate variability 12, 13, 81, **86**, 87, 222, 224, 227
coffee 49–51, 135
Cohen, A. 4, 57
Colonial Agricultural Service 52
Colonial Development Act (1929) 51
Colonial Development and Welfare Act 1940 53, 54, 173–4, 1945 54, 56, 82

Colonial Development and Welfare Scheme 197–8
Colonial Development Corporation 56
Colonial Office 48, 53, 54, 56
commercial production 29, 30, 31, 51, 71, 74, 76, 80, 81, 82, 130, 132–3, 134; *see also individual crops*
Commission for Social Science 55
Committee of Civil Research 51, 58
Commoner, B. 71
communal lands 12, 27, 125, 130–1, 133, 153, 155
Conant, F.P. 124
Congo Basin 166
cooperatives 133, 134
Coryndon, R. 48–9
cotton 30, 81, 82, 132, 133
crop cultivation 27, 36, 38–9, 77, 151, 170; blamed for environmental degradation 4, 74, 77, 100, 102; combined with keeping livestock 26, 80, **86**, 88, 107, 126, 129, 131, 132, 150, 151–2; for commercial production 29, 30, 31, 51, 71, 74, 76, 80, 81, 82, 130, 132–3, 134; and locust swarms 192–4, 196, 198–9, 219; rotational 37, 84, 107, 152; *see also individual crops*
'Crown land' 76, 140, 143, 144, 145, 148, 149–50
Csanedy, A. 124
CSSRC (Colonial Social Science Research Council) 123
cultural ecology 124, 126–7

declinist hypothesis 71
deforestation 4, 73–4, 170–1, 176
demography *see* population
Department of African Affairs 154–5
Department of Tsetse Research 169
depression of 1930s 4, 51–3, 73, 169–71, 215
desertification 12, 74, 220, 222, 225
Desert Locust Survey Organization 56, 190, 197, 198, 199, 204
desiccation 59, 78, 99; European travelers on 4, 25–6, 31–2, 33, 34, 70, 214–15
development 5; administrative science for 1, 14, 140–56; African participation in 1, 14, 54, 88, 131, 133, 135, 140–56, 218; African responses to 2, 6, 9, 13, 58–9, 79, 118,

236 Index

development *continued*
122–35, 175, 200, 215, 217–18;
ALDEV 54–5, 82, 87; experimental 5,
8, 9, 14, 46, 53, 54–5, 58–9, 70, **85**, 87,
99–118, **111**, **112**, 135, 216–17; impact
of 1, 60, 71, 77, 84, 87–8, **111**, **112**,
129, 130–2; and imperial science 1, 4,
8–10, 45–62, 70, 141, 214; large-scale
programs 12, 49, 53, 54, 58, 59, 70–1,
77–89, **85**, **86**; and pastoralism 9, 10,
59, 76–7, 87, 88, 123–5, 126, 127–31,
132, 134–5, 143, 217, 221, 224, 229;
and peasant agriculture 9, 14, 58–9,
71, 74, 76–7, 79, 123–4, 127, 129, 130,
131–3, 135, 141, 143, 150–3, 170, 214,
215–16

disease 2, 8, 14, 29, 39, 47, 48–9, 57–8,
85, **86**, 87, 134, 135, 214, 222; *see also*
ticks; tsetse flies

disequilibrium model 11, 13, 99, 100,
101, 102, 109, 117, 216–17, 225–6

DLCOEA (Desert Locust Control
Organization of East Africa)
202, 204

Dodoth people (Uganda) 167

droughts 8, 31, 51–2, 70, 73, 76, 78–9,
82, 85, **85**, **86**, 87, 102, 106, 214–15;
USA 10, 72

'dust bowl' phenomenon 10, 12, 51, 70,
72–3

EAAFRO (East African Agricultural
and Forestry Organization) 56,
107–8, **112**

East Africa Commission 198–9

*East African Agricultural and Forestry
Journal* 53, 57, 83, 99, 103

East African High Commission 56, 59

East African Loan Scheme 169

EAVRO (East African Veterinary
Organization) 56

ecological collapse in late nineteenth
century 26, 39–40

ecological research 14, 97–156, 168, 169,
171, 213, 216–18, 220, 221, 222,
223–4, 227

ecology 5, 6, 11, 12, 27, 73–4, 75;
cultural 124, 126–7; indigenous
knowledge of 225–6, 228, 228; of
locust swarms 188–92, 196–7; new
ecology 213, 224–6

ecosystems 213, 221–2, 223, 224, 227

elephants 168

Elgeyo people (Kenya) 133–4

emergency programs 47, 169, 195,
197, 220

Endfield, G.H. 32, 166

Engledow, F.L. 48

environmental change 1, 5–6, 13, 14–16,
51–2, 71–2, 78, 214, 224, 226, 227,
228–9; European travelers on 25, 27,
31–2, 33, 35–9

environmental crisis hypothesis 1–16,
59, 213–20, 226; fires blamed for 4,
73–4; and imperial science 1, 4, 7, 62,
70, 214, 215, 224; indigenous land use
systems blamed for 1, 3, 13, 16, 72,
73–4, 77, 78–9, 99, 100, 107–8, 131–2,
187, 215, 216, 217, 218; origins of
3–4, 10–12, 62, 72–89, 220; and
peasant agriculture 2, 6, 8, 72, 73, 79,
132, 218; re-evaluation of 99–118; and
soil erosion 4, 13

equilibrium model (succession model)
11, 13, 99, 100–1, *101*, 108, 109, 116,
117, 216–17, 225–6

Eritrea 190, 191, 194, 197, 198

Esty, D. 12

Ethiopia 50, 187, 188, 190, 191, 194,
198, 200, 224

European Board 141, 144, 147

European missionaries 4, 25, 28, 31–2,
38, 215

European settlers 27, 30–1, 47, 51, 74,
76, 77, 81, 140–1, 144, 149, 164–5;
and local communities 59, 123,
132–3, 135, 143, 146

European travelers 2, 8, 25–44, 214–15;
on desiccation 4, 25–6, 31–2, 33, 34,
70, 214–15; on environmental change
25, 27, 31–2, 33, 35–9; on locusts 187,
193; on tsetse flies 163; on vegetation
7, 32–5, 38, 114

Evans, A.C. 106

experimental development 5, 8, 9, 14,
46, 53, 54–5, 58–9, 70, **85**, 87, 99–118,
111, **112**, 135, 216–17

experimental science 13, 54–5, 58–9,
61–2, 99–118, **103**, *105*, 187, 221, 222;
for locust control 199, 200–4, 219–20;
for tsetse fly eradication 165, 168,
169, 170–1, 173, 174, 177, 219

exports 46, 51, 70–1, 81, 82, 127, 130

famine 8, 11, 39, 40, 48, 51–2, 53, 79,
86, 88, 193, 214–15, 220

FAO (Food and Agricultural
Organization) 58, 60, 197, 198, 199, 202

Farva, T. 61
fertilizers 102, **103**, 106, 107, *107*, *108*, 117–18, 151–2, 217; phosphates **103**, 106, 107, *107*
fires 36, 39, 88–9, **111**, 195; banned 88–9, 115, 179; blamed for environmental crisis 4, 73–4; to control bush encroachment 115, 116, 179; for tsetse fly control 165, 170, 171, 174, 179–80
First World War 46, 48–9, 215
Fitzgerald, W.W.A. 35
food sufficiency 8, 46, 62, 81
forced labor 57, 59
Ford, J. 165, 170
Fort Victoria (Kenya) 177
Foster, M. 166
funding 47, 48, 49, 52, 53, 54–5, 57, 60, 61, 62, 79–80, 82, 84, 173–4, 197–8, 199, 202, 219, 220

game 15, 134, 154, 172, 173, 174, 176–7, 179–80, 219
Gem farmers (Kenya) 151–2
geodesic locations 31, 36, 47
German East Africa 2, 46–8, 49, 167, 168, 193
Gillman of Tanganyika 49
Glover, P.E. 115
goats 37, 116, 118, 163, 170
Goldschmidt, W. 123, 127, 132
Goldstone, B. 1–2
Goodenough, W. 170, 171
Grant, J.A. 36
grazing 9, 12, 70, 75–6, 81, 99, **103**, 117, 134, 135, 222–3, 227–8, 229; communal systems 12, 27; continuous 100, 108, 110–13, **112**, *114*, 118; and locusts 48, 187, 194, 200, 219; overgrazing 3, 4, 12, 72, 73–4, 75–6, 77, 79, 80, 88, 100, **111**, 113, 115, 116; perceived cause of land degradation 11–12, 74–6, 77, 79, 80, 100, 115, 135, 226; and rainfall variability 102, 108, 109–10, *109*, 118, 217; and rangeland productivity 102, 108, 110, 118; rotational 88, 100, 108, 110–13, **111**, **112**, *114*, 118, 217; schemes 2, 56, 71, 77, 84–9, **85**, **86**, 123, 131, 172, 174, 216, 219; seasonal patterns of 88, **111**, 113, 131, 134, 163, 222, 225, 229; USA 10, 11, 72–3; *see also* cattle; livestock; pastoralism/pastoralists
Greenbaum, L. 124

Grimes, R.C. 107
groundnuts 59, 82–4, 106, *107*, 216
Grove, R.H. 4
gullies 11, 73–4, 80, 103–4
Gunn, D.L. 201, 203

Hailsham, Lord 61
Hardin, G. 12
Harrison, M. 7
Haubi (Tanzania) 80
Häusler, S. 79
Havinden, M. 83–4
Henn, S. 52
Herskovits, M.J. 11–12, 128
Hill, M. 194
Hodgson, D. 88
Holocene period 80
Horn of Africa 15, 32, 39, 187, 190, 199, 204
Hoste, C.H. 75
Hughes, J.D. 5
Huxley, E. 12, 73, 74

IBP (International Biological Program) 213, 221, 222, 223
Ijomah, B.I.C. 70
ILCA (International Livestock Centre for Africa) 224
Ilkisongo (Kenya) **85**, 87
Imbulu (Tanganyika) **86**
Imperial Agricultural Research conference (1927) 51
Imperial Institute of London 196
imperial science 1–2, 4, 6, 10; and development 1, 4, 8–10, 45–62, 70, 141, 214; and environmental crisis hypothesis 1, 4, 7, 62, 70, 214, 215, 224; false assumptions of 10, 12, 114, 115, 168; and indigenous knowledge 7; infrastructure 2, 8–10, 45–62, 215; and land degradation 1, 100, 102; and tsetse flies 14, 164–5, 167–9, 180, 219
inclinist hypothesis 71, 72
indigenous knowledge 1, 7, 10, 25, 26, 27, 29–30, 31, 46, 72, 82, 125, 140, 225–6, 227, 228, *228*, 229
Indo-Pakistan 15, *189*, 190, 197, 200–1
International African Institute 122–3
International Institute of Agriculture 48
IPAL (Integrated Project in Arid Lands) 222, 224
Iraqwi people (Tanganyika) **86**, 135
Iringa (Tanganyika) **111**
Israel 61

238   Index

Isuria highlands (Kenya) 173
Italy 197
IUSES (International Union of Anthropological and Ethnological Sciences) 220

Jibe, Lake 28, 32
Johnson, W.P. 38
Jones, G.H. 106
justice system, British 141, 149–50, 218

Kabete research station (Kenya) 48, 56, 58, 59
Kalo rehabilitation scheme 88
Kamba reserves (Kenya) 79–80, 113, 135
Kaputei (Kenya) **85**, 87
Karamojong (Uganda) **86**, 88–9, **111**, 113, 134
Kavirondo District (Kenya) 154, 172–3
Kawanda Research Station (Uganda) 56–7
Keay, R. 58
Kedong (Kenya) **112**
Keen, B. 107–8
Kenya 2, *3*, 47, 62, 131, 140–56, 175; crop cultivation in 106, 132–3, 143, *145*, 148, 151, 155, 193; European settlers in 51, 81, 123, 132–3, 140–1, 143–50, *145*; European travelers on 32, 34, 187; grazing/pastoralism 79–80, **85**, 86–7, *109*, **111**, **112**, 115, 128, 134, 155, 222–3; IPAL project 222–3, 224; Kimalot land case *142*, 143–50, *145*; land rights in 140–1, 143–50, 153–6; land use in 77, 78, 113, 133–4, *142*, 143, 153, 155; locusts 187, 190–1, 193, 194, 197, 199, 202, 204; research in 48–9, *50*, 51, 54–5, 56, 58, 59, 78, 194; soil conservation 54–5, 59, 78, 79–80, **103**, 135, 151–3; tsetse flies and *trypanosomiasis*/sleeping sickness 15, 56, 58, 154, 165, 166, 167, 172, 174–5, 176, 177, 178, *179*; *see also individual places and peoples*
Kenya Land Commission 77, 128
Kenya, Mount 28, 34
Kericho District (Kenya) 143–50, 154
Kew Gardens 27, 49
Kigezi (Uganda) 133
Kikuyu land (Kenya) 34, 133
Kilimanjaro, Mount 28, 32
Kimalot land case *142*, 143–50, *145*
Kipsigis community (Kenya) 132, 133, 141, 143–50, *145*, 152, 154, 156

Kipsoi Arap Chemorore 149–50
Kisii District (Kenya) 154, *164*, 172
Kisongo (Tanganyika) **86**, 88
Kitale (Kenya) **112**
Kitui District (Kenya) 78, 79–80, **111**
Kondoa District (Tanganyika) 59, 80, 88, 135
Kongwa scheme 84
Koponen, J. 36–7
Kottak, C. 127
Kreike, E. 45, 71, 72
Kwai research station (Tanganyika) 47–8

Laikipia reserve (Kenya) 77
land alienation 59, 76, 77, 143–50, *145*, 216
Land and Water Preservation Ordinance (1943) 151
land degradation 11–12, 52, 71, 73, 74–6, 77, 79, 80, 100, 102, **111**, 115, 132, 135, 153, 225, 226
land reclamation 168, 169, 171, 172, 173, 174, 178
land rehabilitation 59, 72, **86**, **111**, **112**, 113–15, *114*, 118
land rights 140–1, 145
land tenure 27, 82, 85, 123, 218
land use: colonial policies of 58–9, 71, 76–7, 81, 86, **86**, 99, 130–1, 133–5, 143; indigenous systems blamed for environmental degradation 1, 3, 13, 16, 72, 73–4, 77, 78–9, 99, 100, 107–8, 131–2, 187, 215, 216, 217, 218; intensification 80, 100–2, *101*, 105, 106, 117, 216, 217; seasonal patterns of 26, 76; and soil fertility 106–8, *107*, *108*; *see also* crop cultivation; pastoralism/pastoralists
Lane, P. 11, 80
Lawi, Y.Q. 38
Laws, Rev. Dr. 37
Leach, M. 71, 72
Le Houérou, H.N. 75–6
Lesotho, Kingdom of 11
Lettowvortek, P. von 48
Lister, Lord 166
livestock 11–12, 14, 48–9, 55, 70, 78, 88, 100, 114–15, 116, 134, 135, 163, 224, 227, 228, 229; collapse in numbers of 39, 47, 220; combined with crop cultivation 26, 80, **86**, 88, 107, 126, 129, 131, 132, 150, 151–2; counting 76, 86, 89; destocking 12, 73, 80, **86**, 87, 88, **111**, 126, 127, 128, 131, 134–5;

and locusts 200; marketing **85, 86**, 134; multi-species 37, 87, 102, 222, 229; overstocking 12, 73, 74, 77, 79, 84–5, 135; pastoralists' connection to 11–12, 124–5, 127–9; perceived cause of land degradation 12, 73, 74, 75, 76, 79, 80, 102; removal of 15, 77, 79, 80, **85, 86**, 87, 115, 129, 130, 133, 151, 155, 167; *see also* cattle; grazing; pastoralism/pastoralists; rangelands
Livingstone, D. 27–9, 30–1, 33, 36
LNCs (Local Native Councils) 140, 143, 145, 147–8
locusts 2, 8, 15–16, 40, 48, 59, 115, 180, 187–204, *189*, *192*, 219–20; control programs 194–203, 219; desert locusts (*Schistocerca gregaria* Forsk) 15, 48, 56, 59, 187, 188, *189*, 190–1, 193, 196, 197, 199–200, 204; monitoring 195, 203–4; red locusts (*Nomacris septerfasciata* Serville) 15, 187, 188, 191–2, *192*, 193, 203, 204
London Missionary Society 32
LTER (long-term ecological research) 213, 223–4, 227

Maasai lands/people 28, 32, 34, 39, 49, 77, **85, 86**, 87, 88, 135, 156, 187, 191, 194, 224, 229
MAB (Man and the Biosphere) ecosystem programs 213, 221–3
Machakos District (Kenya) 55, 79–80, **85**, 109–10, *109*, **111**, 133
Mackenzie, J.M. 13
MacQueen, J. 35
Magubane, B. 125
maize 36, 37, 81, 106, *107*, *108*, 151, 193
Makueni District (Kenya) 87, 174, 178
Malawi, Lake (Lake Nyasa) 28, 36, 37, 38, *192*
Matengo people (Tanganyika) 36–7
Mau Mau rebellion 59, **85**, 133, 176
Mbarara (Uganda) *164*, 170
Mbulu district (Tanganyika) 54, 88, 135
McCann, J.C. 70
Means, R. 71, 72
mechanized agriculture 55, 59, 82, 83, 84, 150
Mediterranean region 75
Meredith. D. 83–4
Milner, Lord 49
missionaries, European 4, 25, 28, 31–2, 38, 215

Mitchell, P. 54
Mitton, J. 61
mixed farming 26, 82, **86**, 88, 130, 131, 132, 133, 135; *see also* crop cultivation: combined with keeping livestock
'model farmers' 82
modernization 5, 47, 60, 71, 81
Mohamed, J. 200
Morocco 194
Morris Carter Land Commission 143
Moshi (Tanganyika) *164*, 172
Mpwapwa (Tanganyika) 49, 50, **103**, 104
Muguga research station (Kenya) 48, 56, 58, 59
Mumoni (Kenya) 78
Muranga (Kenya) 133
Mutara (Kenya) **103**
Mwenu, Lake *192*, *192*

Nairobi 61, 80, 190, 194
Namibia 45
Nandi people (Kenya) **85**, 87, 132, 133, 154
Narok (Kenya) 177
Nash, D. 32
Native Lands Trust Ordinance 148–9, 153–4
'nature-culture trap' 71
new ecology 213, 224–6
Ngoni people 38
Ngoni–Zulu wars 28
Nigeria 56
Nile 28, 29, 30, 176
Njems plains (Kenya) **112**
Nowell, Mr 52
Nurse, K. 9
Nyambole, Chief 165
Nyando (Kenya) 176
Nyando River 177–8
Nyanza province (Kenya) *142*, 144, 146, 147, 148, 153–4, 155, 165
Nyasa, Lake (Lake Malawi) 28, 36, 37, 38, *192*
Nyerere, J. 62

Obarrio, J. 1–2
Odhiambo, T. 61
Ogaden (Ethiopia) 190, 200
Ohanga, A. 148–9
overgrazing 3, 4, 12, 72, 73–4, 75–6, 77, 79, 80, 88, 100, **111**, 113, 115, 116
Overseas Food Corporation 82

pastoralism/pastoralists 26, 27, 53, 59, 87, 220, 223–4; blamed for environmental degradation 12, 51–2, 79, 84–5, 87–8, 102, 110, 222; collapse of 8, 12, 39–40; connection to livestock 11–12, 124–5, 127–9; and development programs 9, 10, 59, 76–7, 87, 88, 123–5, 126, 127–31, 132, 134–5, 143, 217, 221, 224, 229; indigenous systems 26, 76, 126, 224, 225, 229; and locusts 15, 187, 200; the Maasai 39, 49, 77, **85**, **86**, 87, 88, 135, 156, 229; and tsetse flies 14, 39, 40, 164, 178–80, *179*; *see also* agro-pastoralism; grazing; livestock

peasants/peasant agriculture 48, 52, 53, 62, 125, 127; and development 9, 14, 58–9, 71, 74, 76–7, 79, 123–4, 127, 129, 130, 131–3, 135, 141, 143, 150–3, 170, 214, 215–16; and the environmental crisis hypothesis 2, 6, 8, 72, 73, 79, 132, 218; and tsetse flies 12, 170–1, 218; *see also* agricultural production

Pereira, H.C. 114
Perevolotsky, A. 75
pesticides 15, 177–8, *178*, 195, 197, 199–202, 219–20
pests 39, 49–51, 82, 84; *see also* locusts; tsetse flies
phosphates **103**, 106, 107, *107*
pigs 176, 179–80
pioneer research (1848–1913) 4, 46–8, 215
plantations 51, 77, 81, 143, 144
Pokot community (Kenya) 134–5
population 26, 30, 38, 57; decline 8, 11, 31, 38, 39–40, 47, 78–9, 166–7, 220; growth 11, 74, 79, 129, 226; removal/displacement 26, 28, 47, 54, 74, 77, 79, 131, 132, 135, 141, 148, 166–7, 171, 174, 180, 208, 216
post-independence period 2, 3–4, 5, 7, 10, 13, 61, 72, 75, 99, 220–9
potatoes 134
Pratt, D. 114
pre-colonial period 2, 7, 8, 11, 25–40, 46, 71, 72, 214

rainfall 52, 75–6, 78, 84, 85, 88, **103**, 105, 106, **111**, 114, 144; European travelers on 31–2, 33, 36, 38; and locusts 188, 190, 192, 203, 219; storm discharge 101, 105, 216; storm intensity 102, 105–6, *105*, 117; variability 7, 12, 100, 102, 106, 108, 109–10, *109*, 116, 118, 215, 217

rangelands 4, 11, 12, 13, 15, 77, 86, 87, 88–9, 116–17, 225; carrying capacity of 12, 76, 84–5, 86, **86**, 89, 100, 108, 109–10, *109*, 116, 118; productivity 101, 102, 108; range science research 13, 59, 75–6, 99, 109–18, **111**, **112**, *114*; restoration 113–15, *114*, 118; USA 10, 73; *see also* grazing; livestock; pastoralism/pastoralists

Rawlinson, H. 47
Red Sea 32, 188, 190, 191, 194
Regional Centre for Science and Technology in Africa 61
Reid, R. 223–4
Rendille nomads 222
research 1, 2, 4, 6, 7, *7*, 8–10, 12, 13–14, 16, 29, 45–62; on agricultural production 48, 51, 82; agronomic 11, 13, 99, 102–8, *103*, *104*, *105*, *107*, 108, 109; biological 47, 52, 56; ecological 14, 97–156, 168, 169, 171, 213, 216–18, 220, 221, 222, 223–4, 227; future 226–9; international collaboration in 4, 48, 57–8, 60–1, 122–3, 196–9, 213, 216, 220, 221–3, 224; in Kenya 48–9, *50*, 51, 54–5, 56, 58, 59, 78, 194; on locusts 194–203, 204; LTER 213, 223–4, 227; pioneer 4, 46–8, 215; range science 13, 59, 75–6, 99, 109–18, **111**, **112**, *114*; social science 2, 13–14, 51, 52, 54, 56, 122–35, 171, 213, 215–16, 217, 220, 221; station-based 4, 47–8, 49–51, *50*, 56, 58, 60, 79, 100, 104, 105, 168, 172, 215; in Tanganyika 46–8, 49–51, *50*, 54–5, 56–7, 58, 59; on tsetse flies 56, 58, 163–5, 167–76, 180; in Uganda 48–9, *50*, 56–7, 59, 62; veterinary 49, 56

reseeding 100, 108–9, **111**, **112**, 113–15, 118, 217
reserves 49, 73, 74, 78, 79, 81, 131, 140, 143, 144, 149–50
RGS (Royal Geographical Society) 27, 29, 47
Rhodes-Livingstone Institute 123
Richards, P. 7–8, 165
Rift Valley 141, 173, 191
rinderpest virus 39, 115, 166
river discharge 102, 105–6, *105*, 117, 216
Robertson, A.G. 176

Rocheleau, D.E. 70
Rockefeller Foundation 57–8
Royal African conferences 52
Royal African Society 166
Royal Society 46, 166
Rugwe (Tanganyika) 47
Rukwa, Lake (Tanganyika) 15, 191, 192, 204
Ruvuma River 28, 36
Rwanda 163, 203

Sahara Desert 72
Sahelian region 48, 75, 197, 220
Samburu District (Kenya) **85**, 128
Sampson, A.W. 11
Saudi Arabia 190, 197, 199
Schneider, H. 124, 128
scientific geography 25–6, 27–31, 32, 47
Scott Agricultural Laboratory 48
Scott, G.D. 113
Second World War 53–5, 57, 81, 172–3, 195–6, 215–16
sediment production 99, 101, 102, **103**, 104, 105, 106
seeds 46–7, 52; reseeding 100, 108–9, **111**, **112**, 113–15, 118, 217
SEEM (socio-economic and ecological conceptual model) 227–8
Seligman, N.G. 75
Serengeti 38, 223
Sharpe, A. 31, 38
sheep 37, 102, 163, 170
Shinyanga (Tanganyika) **86**, 88, *164*, 168, 170, 177
Shire Highlands 28, 31
Showers, K.B. 1, 5–6, 11
sisal 80, 81
slavery 8, 28, 30, 39, 166
sleeping sickness 2, 15, 39, 47, 163, 165, 166–9, 170, 171, 172, 179; *see also* tsetse flies
smallpox 39
smelting 11, 36
Smith, A.D. 187
Smuts, J.C. 48
socialism 62
social science research 2, 13–14, 51, 52, 54, 56, 122–35, 171, 213, 215–16, 217, 220, 221; *see also* administrative science
social services 8–9, 53
Society for the Preservation of Wild Fauna 47

socio-ecological systems 14, 31, 122, 125–30, 132, 214, 217, 224, 228, 229
Socotra, island of 190
soil conservation 2, 49, 54, 56, 59, 74, 82, 84, 104, 130, 135, 148, 175, 215, 216, 217, 218; European travelers on 37, 215; indigenous methods of 37, 131–2, 133, 140, 146, 151–2, 218; schemes for 12, 14, 55, 77–81, 88, 133, 141, 150–3; and tsetse flies 171
soil erosion 11, 37, 48, 49, 52, 54, 56, 57, 74, 77, 78, 80–1, 102, 103–5, **103**, *104*, 117, 131, 151, 153, 169, 171; and environmental crisis hypothesis 4, 13; and locusts 194; perceived causes of 11, 79, 133, 171, 175, 218; from vegetation clearing 10, 11, 59, 117, 216
soil fertility 4, 12, 52, 77, 78, 80, 83, 101, 102, **103**, 106–8, *107*, 108, 117–18, 132, 151, 152, 217, 218; European travelers on 35, 36–7, 39, 215; *see also* fertilizers
soil mapping 48, 51
soil moisture 76, 101, 102, **103**, 105, 106, 117, 188, 217
Somaliland/British Somaliland/Somalia 15, *50*, 187, 188, 190–1, 194, 196, 197, 198, 199, 200–1
sorghum 106, *107*
South Sudan 167
soya 106, *107*
spatial analysis 32, 214
spatial geography 25–6, 27–31
Speke Gulf of Mwanza *164*, 168
Speke, J.H. 30, 36
Stanley, H.M. 36, 38
Stanley of Alderley, Lord 52
Stebbing, E. 72
Steel, R.W. 45–6
Stefanie, Lake 28, 33
storm discharge 101, 105, 216
storm intensity 102, 105–6, *105*, 117
Stuhlmann, F. 48
subsistence agriculture 5, 27, 71, 82, 123, 130, 132, 134, 220
succession model (equilibrium model) 11, 13, 99, 100–1, *101*, 108, 109, 116, 117, 216–17, 225–6
Sudan 188, 190
Sukumaland (Tanganyika) 82, **86**, 88, **112**, 113, 133, 167, 170
Swynnerton, C.J.M. 168–9

Swynnerton, R.J.M. 59
Symanski, R. 129
systems analysis 213, 224

Talbot, L.M. 87–8
Tanganyika (post-independence, Tanzania) 3, 54–5, 62, 80, 132, 135; crop cultivation in 81, 82, 83, 84, 106, 133, 135; European explorers in 36, 38; exports 81, 82, 127; in German East Africa 2, 46–8, 168; grazing/pastoralism in 85, **86**, 88, **111**, 127–8, 135, 167; groundnut schemes 82, 83, 84; land use in 36, 38, 88, **112**; locusts 15, 191–2, *192*, 193, 197, 203, 204; research in 46–8, 49–51, *50*, 54–5, 56–7, 58, 59; soil conservation in 49, 54, 55, 59, 79, 80, 103–4, **103**, 106, 107, 135; tsetse flies and *trypanosomiasis*/sleeping sickness 15, 59, 166, 168, 170, 172, 174, 176–7; *see also individual places and peoples*
Tanganyika Trust Territory 2, 49–50
tea 143, 144, *145*, 148
technology 37, 55, 70, 126, 127, 129, 130, 214; mechanized agriculture 55, 59, 82, 83, 84, 150; as solution to environmental problems 71, 79
Teleki, S. 30, 32–3, 34
terraces 57, 80, 131, 133, 152, 153
Teso community 132
Thomson, J. 30, 33, 35, 37, 39, 187
ticks 39, 77, **85**, 87
'tragedy of the commons' 12, 74
Trans-Mara District (Kenya) 146, 147, 156, *164*, 173
Troup, R.S. 78
trypanosomiasis 2, 15, 39, 47, 56, 58, 163, 165, 167, 168, 171, 173, 174, 175, 177, 178, *179*
tsetse flies (*Glossina* species) 2, 8, 40, 47, 48, 77, 88, 128, 144, 163–80; control 39, 54, 56, 141, 154, 156, 163–5, 167–71, 174–8, *178*, 180, 218–19; *G. morsitans* 176–7, 179; *G. pallidipes* 175, 179; *G. palpalis* 177; *G. swynnertoni* 168–9, 173; research on 56, 58, 163–5, 167–76, 180
Tugen lowlands (Kenya) 134
Turkana region (Kenya) 28, 32, 191, 199, 224
Turner, M. 78
Tyrrell, J.G. 34

Uganda 2, *3*; exports 47, 81, 83, 84; grazing in **86**, 88, **111**, *180*; land rehabilitation 113; locusts 15, 191, 193, 197, 199; research in 48–9, *50*, 56–7, 59, 62; and settler farming 59; soil conservation in 78, 79, 133; and tsetse flies 15, 166–7, 168, 170, 174, 176–7, 179; *see also individual places and peoples*
Ukiriguru (Kenya) **112**
UNESCO (United Nations Educational, Scientific and Cultural Organization) 60, 61; IPAL (Integrated Project in Arid Lands) 222, 224; MAB (Man and the Biosphere) ecosystem programs 213, 221–3
United African Company (Unilever Group) 82
UN (United Nations) 57–8, 61; Economic Commission for Africa 60; FAO (Food and Agricultural Organization) 58, 60, 197, 198, 199, 202
USA (United States of America) 4, 81, 116, 213, 221, 223; 'dust bowl' phenomenon 10–11, 12, 51, 70, 72–3, 74
Uvarov, B. 195, 196

Van Beusekom, M.M. 46, 71
Van Rensburg, H.J. 116
Vayda, A.P. 5
vegetable oils 82
vegetation: change 11, 33–4, 38, 40, 47, 75–6, 110; clearing 15, 54, 59, 71, 73–4, 83, 84, 87, 135, 151, 154, 174, 180, 216; European travelers on 7, 30, 32–5, 38, 114; mapping 30, 48, 222; and soil conservation 104, 117; *see also* bush clearing
veterinary research and services 48–9, 56, 57, 85, **86**, 87, 127–8, 140, 174, 178
Victoria, Lake 28, 38, 141, *142*, 151, 154, 163–5, *164*, 166–7, 168, 170, 172, 173, 176, 177
Vivian, H. 187
Von Höhnel, L. 30

WaGogo people (Tanganyika) 80
Wa Kamba people (Kenya) 80
Wakefield, J. 82, 83
Walker, B. 110–11, 113
Walters, B. 5

WaSukuma people (Tanganyika) 80
water 30, 33, 73, 78; conservation 37, 49; development of supplies 55, 85, **85, 86**, 87, 88; *see also* droughts; rainfall
Weizmann Institute of Science 61
West Africa 72, 188
White, L. 7
Wight, D. 9
winds 114; erosion 10, 72, 74, 194; spread of pests 154, 190, 200, 204

World Bank 60
Worster, D. 10, 73
Worthington, E.B. 4, 55, 57, 78, 165

Yala River 178

Zambezi expedition (1858–1864) 28, 29, 30–1, 36
Zambia (was Northern Rhodesia) 83, 123, 191, *192*
Zimmerman, A. 46